594 29 1

THE OFFICE #02022

GREG DANIELS

RANDALL EINHORN 3/7/06

The
Office
BFFs

Tales of The Office from
Two Best Friends Who Were There

Jenna Fischer and
Angela Kinsey

DEY ST.
An Imprint of WILLIAM MORROW

DEY ST.

HarperCollins books may be purchased for educational, business, or sales promotional use. For information, please email the Special Markets Department at SPsales@harpercollins.com.

FIRST EDITION

DESIGNED BY RENATA DE OLIVEIRA

Library of Congress Cataloging-in-Publication Data has been applied for.

ISBN 978-0-06-300759-8

22 23 24 25 26   LSC   10 9 8 7 6 5 4 3 2 1

For our families.
Lee, Weston, and Harper.
Josh, Isabel, Jack, and Cade.
We love you all so much.

contents

introduction

Jenna

I'm Jenna Fischer.

Angela

And I'm Angela Kinsey.

Jenna

We were on *The Office* together.

Angela

And we're best friends.

Jenna

We are also moms, business partners, podcasters, lovers of knickknacks, sometime-hikers, avid scrapbookers, and Wine & Canvas artists. And now, we are the coauthors of this book.

Angela

If you are reading this, that means you bought our book. Thank you! If we could hug you, we would. We are huggers.

Jenna

Here is a photo of us
pretending to hug you.

Angela

Between producing a weekly podcast, multiple Target runs, and getting snacks
for the kids—do your kids snack as much as ours do?—you might wonder, "Why
did these busy ladies add writing a book to their list?"
I'll tell you! In April 2018, Jenna and I both decided
to do a big spring cleaning of our garages, attics,
basements, and sheds—basically, all the places
where we stash random stuff. Both of us had been
putting off this task for years, so we decided to
do it together. While digging through our boxes,
we found tons of *Office* memorabilia: journals of
our time on set, piles of photos of everybody and
everything, and little mementos we had collected
along the way. (I also found out that I apparently
hoard baskets. I had thirty-two of them! Jenna
hoards old lamps that no longer work. But that's a
story for our next book, *Baskets and Old Lamps:
Tales of Two Ladies Who Hoard*.) Finding our

Office treasures sparked lots of memories and gave us the idea to start our weekly podcast, *Office Ladies*, which we launched in October 2019. We've had a great time rewatching the show and breaking down episodes each week. But what about all our amazing photos? And our other best friend stories? Rather than keep these wonderful items to ourselves, we've decided to use them to create the book you are holding right now.

Jenna

This book is several things—a scrapbook, a BFF journal, and a love letter to fans of our show. We like to think that if something happened back then, one of us documented the moment. We couldn't be more excited to share our memories, photos, stories from life on the set of *The Office*, and details of our friendship of more than eighteen years.

Angela

Our first challenge was figuring out how to write this book together. Well, folks, we love a good chat. During our writing sessions, I would start a story, and then Jenna would jump in with her memories, and vice versa. So get a cozy chair and curl up with us, because we are going to share our memories with you the best way we know how: by chatting back and forth as BFFs do.

Jenna

And, thanks to this book, our garages are now clean and ready to fill with more stuff. Angela has already started collecting new baskets. I'm telling you, the woman can't pass a basket without buying it. If you really want to make her heart sing, send her a gift that comes in a beautiful basket. It is like you are giving her TWO gifts. We really hope you like our book. We worked hard on it. That's what she said.

1

job opening:
office work

In 2003, a group of strangers had
one very big thing in common:
We had all just been cast on a new
TV comedy pilot called *The Office*.
After years of living as struggling
artists, we were all very happy
to be employed and doing
what we loved. We could never have
predicted the impact it would
have on the rest of our lives.

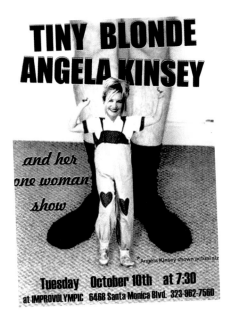

At this point, I was working two jobs and auditioning constantly. I had had a string of national commercials—most notably for Buick, Chrysler, and Lay's WOW Chips with Olestra. Yes, the chips that gave everyone abdominal cramping, diarrhea, and anal leakage. (They were eventually discontinued.) Between auditions, I was an operator at 1-800-DENTIST and ran the intern program at the iO West comedy club. I had been performing improv three nights a week for a decade. You know that annoying friend who was constantly handing you a flyer for their show . . . that was me.

During this time, I was married to Warren Lieberstein, and related by marriage to Greg Daniels. Greg and his wife, Susanne (Warren's sister), were always very supportive and came to several of my shows. In the summer of 2003, Susanne invited us over for a swim. I coveted these afternoon swims because our tiny apartment had only one AC window unit, and summers were rough. I had wedged myself into one of their daughter's brightly colored floaties and was trying to paddle to the steps of the pool when Greg sat down to chat. He told us he was going to be remaking the BBC version of *The Office*. I remember trying to suppress an "uh-oh" look on my face. A few other major networks tried to bring BBC shows to the United States and failed. The sensibility and tone of a show for a British audience had not transferred well to an American audience. I loved the BBC version of *The Office* and was worried that making it for an American audience would be a disaster. But I also felt that if anyone could pull it off, it would be Greg. He had been writing and producing on hit television shows for years and had won several awards for *Saturday Night Live*, *The Simpsons*, and a show he cocreated, *King of the Hill*. Greg is one of the most brilliantly funny people you will ever meet, on a set or off. He suggested I come in and audition, because he thought that my improv background would lend itself to the mockumentary style of the show. Plus, he wanted to use as many unknown actors as he could. Greg felt that the world of a small paper company in Scranton, Pennsylvania, would feel more organic if there were no big Hollywood names in the mix. I was definitely not a big Hollywood name, unless "Lay's WOW potato chip lady" counted. I was very excited for the opportunity—but also incredibly nervous.

Greg told me he would put me on the list to audition but with one caveat: No one could know that we were related. Greg felt strongly that letting this information get out to the network would only hurt my chances. We decided that we would not acknowledge each other at the audition. He could get me in the room, but I had to win the room over on my own. (I later learned that this ruse was Allison Jones's idea. She was a big champion of mine and had told Greg this was the best plan. Thank you, Allison!)

On November 17, 2003, I auditioned for the role of . . . Pam! Yep, fact! I signed in to the audition at 2:40 P.M. and was the sixteenth person that day to read for the role of our favorite receptionist. I know this not because I have an amazing memory, but because the incredible Allison Jones saved my audition sign-in sheet! When the series wrapped NINE years later, she gave it to me as a farewell gift. I ugly-cried, of course. I treasure owning this piece of my life history. Look at all the people who were there on the same day! Every female comedian I know went in for the role of Pam.

I remember my audition very clearly. It's weird how the brain captures the biggest moments of your life and slows them down. Every single detail is stuck in my brain. I wore a pink sweater and a black pencil skirt. I had worked really hard to prepare my scenes. I waited in a very small room before my audition. Kathryn Hahn was sitting on a sofa in the corner. We smiled at each other and said hello. She is a doll and so talented. I tried my best not to get anxious. I am not sweaty by nature—I usually run cold no matter the temperature—but as it got closer to my turn, I really began to sweat. I actually went into the bathroom and dabbed toilet paper in my armpits. (Sorry for the overshare, but that's how nervous I was.) When it was finally my time, I walked into a room full of producers. There was a camera on a tripod, and sitting beside the camera was the casting associate, Phyllis, my future Party Planning Committee rival. I was to read with her.

Greg was sitting in the very back of the room and neither of us made eye contact. My agent told me they were having everyone read two scenes, but if they liked you, they'd ask you to do a third. Phyllis and I did my first two scenes, and everyone was laughing. It felt great! Then I was asked to do a third. I worked hard to contain my excitement! Phyllis and I began the final scene, the one where Michael fake-fires Pam in front of Ryan, the temp. To jog your memory, in the scene, Michael wants to "prank" Pam by pretending to fire her for stealing Post-it notes. The fake firing goes terribly wrong, and Pam is very upset. She starts to cry and calls Michael a jerk. The scene was going well. Phyllis was killing it as "Michael." Imagine someone with Phyllis's sweet face smugly telling you that you've been PUNKED. When we got to the part where I was supposed to tear up and call Michael a jerk, I really let Michael/Phyllis have it!

Now, there are three times you can tell I am from Texas: when I am tired, tipsy, or pissed off. So I definitely slipped into a Southern drawl as I growled, "*Jerk!*" The room of producers burst out laughing, and I remember thinking, *Hmm, not so sure I am supposed to get a laugh at this point . . . but okay.* And that was it. Allison thanked me for coming in, Greg discreetly smiled from the back row and gave me a thumbs-up, and I walked out of there on cloud nine. I just knew I had that part.

The next day I got a call from Allison. I did not get that part. She told me they really liked me, but thought I was a little "too feisty" for Pam. I was disappointed, of course, but I felt good about my audition, and I was thankful for the opportunity. So I let it go and I moved on. That's just what you have to do as an actor. Plus I had another audition that week for an improv pilot that I was really excited about. It was about a group of people working at a hair salon in New York City for the Oxygen network. The working title was *Salon Royale.* I auditioned for the role of the promiscuous receptionist (feisty was no problem here), and I was cast.

The producers of that show flew me out to New York City first-class. I had never flown first-class for work, and it felt so fancy. The cast was full of amazing improvisers—Ian Roberts, Beth Cahill, Dave Razowsky—and the show was written and directed by Emmy Laybourne. Emmy's mom, Geraldine, was the president of Oxygen at the time, so I thought we had a good shot of making it to series . . . but alas. We didn't get picked up. So back to Los Angeles I went.

After back-to-back rejections, I was feeling pretty discouraged about acting. I decided to concentrate my energy on writing and put acting on hold for a while. Several weeks went by and I was feeling good about my decision to lean into writing, and then I got a call that changed everything.

I was working the box office at iO West when I got a call on my flip phone (remember those?). It was a number I didn't recognize, and I let it go to voicemail. As it turns out, it was from Allison Jones's office. The producers of *The Office* wanted to see me again for a new role, the "prickly lady in accounting." Allison told me the creative team thought I was right for the world of Dunder Mifflin, just not quite right for Pam. This time there was no big room full of producers; it was just the director, Ken Kwapis; Phyllis; and the tripod. I was told to come in wearing something drab, my hair plain, and with little to no makeup. Apparently, the prickly lady in accounting was no fashion plate. I wore a light blue turtleneck sweater with a gray cardigan and black pants, pulled my hair back in a low ponytail, and left my face bare. I channeled all my sass, and I got the part! And I was pretty sure that the "prickly accountant" would be an easier role for my mom to talk about at her ladies' Bible study than the "lustful salon receptionist," so everything worked out. I am so grateful to Greg for getting me in that room on November 17. That moment changed my life forever. And little did I know, the gal that was cast in the role of Pam would become my best friend forever!

Jenna

Before we started taping the first episode, Ken Kwapis suggested we all personalize our desks. I loved this idea. Because of my real-life office experience, I had *very* strong feelings about the types of supplies a receptionist should have on their desk. The invitation to personalize my workspace made me very excited.

Ken also suggested John Krasinski and I spend some time getting to know each other outside of work. "Have lunch, have coffee, create a rapport," was the suggestion, as "it will translate onscreen." This is common for actors who are cast in a new project together. It's key to try and get to know the people you are going to be pretending to be in a relationship with so you don't seem like total strangers onscreen. For example, during rehearsals for my job on ABC's *Splitting Up Together*, Oliver Hudson and I spent two days hanging out with the three children who would play our kids on the show. Like real parents, we sat reading each other bits of news articles off our phones while the kids wrestled. When I did the movie *Hall Pass*, I had drinks with Owen Wilson, who was playing my husband. Incidentally, I did not meet up with Scott Wolf before *Rubbing Charlie* and, well, you already know how that worked out. (Note: Scott Wolf is a delightful human being and I adore him. It's not our fault the show didn't go. We were fantastic.) And I couldn't forget what Stephen Merchant had said—that John and I, virtual strangers, were to be the heart of the show. So one night after rehearsals, we decided to kill two birds with one stone. John Krasinski and I went to a nearby office supply store and shopped for things to decorate our desks. I got a label maker, message pad, message sorter, daily calendar, file folders, multicolored sticky notes . . . the list goes on and on. I left with two bags of supplies. I think John got a tape dispenser and maybe some Post-it notes. The whole time we were shopping, we just kept talking about how excited we were to start shooting. We

wanted to do everything we could to go from pilot to series. John also shared about moving from New York and the adjustment to living in Los Angeles. I was happy to learn that we were both pretty boring people. In a good way. He felt stable. He had a good work ethic. And he was funny. We laughed a lot. I could tell he was going to be a good acting partner.

Angela

Greg had encouraged us to think about our characters and their backstories, so when it came to my desk area, I tried to imagine what a stuffy lady in accounting might bring to the office. I brought in a photo of my grandmother Lena and me. In the picture, my eyes are closed but I am smiling. It makes me laugh that Angela Martin would choose to frame a photo where her eyes are closed. Like,

perhaps that was just the best one of the bunch? I also brought in a day planner. I felt like Angela Martin would have an appointment book and it would be very comprehensive. The set dressers put a blue ceramic cat paper clip holder on my desk. The cat's left ear was slightly chipped, and I loved that little detail. It looked like a knickknack you would get from a garage sale in a small town. That cat paper clip holder did a lot to inform who Angela Martin was. It was clear to me that she must love cats, and that she didn't need fancy new things to make her happy. She was too humble for fancy. (In a judgmental way, of course.) People ask us all the time what we took from the set the day we wrapped the series, and I took that cat paper clip holder. It sits on my desk at home to this day.

Jenna

Walking onto the set for our first day of shooting, I was so nervous. I'd left my house at 5 A.M. for what was a forty-five-minute commute. I made myself a song mix I affectionately titled "Songs of Scranton." I drank coffee and bounced along the freeway. I tried to imagine I was driving to my real job at a real paper company in Scranton, Pennsylvania. When I arrived, I was taken to wardrobe. There were a lot of very quick introductions to various other cast members who were coming and going between wardrobe, hair, and makeup. It was then that I first met Leslie David Baker, who would soon be known to many as Stanley Hudson. He was so warm, friendly, and open that watching him switch over to Stanley, the checked-out grump, was hilarious. Our director had requested that everyone be on set and at our desks at 7:30 A.M. sharp. He asked us to all pretend to work while the film crew recorded us. He wanted to capture us like real documentarians would. Because this was the convention of the show—we were real office workers being filmed by a documentary film crew. When we were all in place, the set was cleared of all crew members except for the camera operator, boom operator, and director. They started rolling, and it all felt so *real*. It was very quiet at first. Then Phyllis and Leslie started improvising fake sales calls. I started to answer the phone and transfer calls. A lot of the shots you see in the opening credits of the show are from that very first morning.

Angela

I was also a bundle of nerves that first day. My call time to set was 4:30 A.M., so I didn't get much sleep the night before. We were filming in an empty office building in Culver City, California. The building was only two stories, and we filmed on the second floor. There was an empty soundstage next to the main building where the hair and makeup team was set up. It was cold and dark when I arrived, with only one small space heater in that big drafty room. We huddled around it and waited our turn. Our director had instructed the hair and makeup departments to keep our looks very simple. I was given a loose French braid and some powder and lip balm. That's all. The wardrobe department asked me to bring the clothes and shoes I had worn to my audition for Angela Martin, so I actually wore my own clothes in the pilot. With barely any hair and makeup and no wardrobe fitting, it didn't take much time for me to get ready. I walked onto the set early and realized I wasn't sure where I was supposed to sit. Ken Kwapis must have seen me looking around sort of lost. He came over to me and told me I'd be sitting in the corner in what would become the accounting department. He walked me over to introduce me to my deskmates. There I found seated at the desk right next to me—Oscar

Nuñez! I had known Oscar for years. We first met at the Groundlings and then went on to perform together in a sketch comedy show called *Hot Towel*. I played a horny Boy Scout and Oscar a crazy professor.

I was so thrilled to see my old friend that I yelled out, "Holy crap, Oscar!" Neither of us knew that the other had been cast. This was in the antiquated times before everything everyone is doing and saying was posted online. You could still be surprised by things. Imagine that?!

One of the very first photos I took on the *Office* set was of the accounting department. We took the photo in character, and it cracks me up that even in the first week, Oscar, Kevin, and Angela were clearly formed people. We already knew who we were in the world of the show. I think it speaks to how amazing the writing was on *The Office* and also to Allison Jones and her gift for assembling acting ensembles. (Note my chunky shoes. I bought them at Payless. This was prime early-2000s fashion.)

Jenna

I'll never forget seeing Angela pop her head up over the partition between our desks to introduce herself. Her face barely made it over the edge as she said, "Hello!" in her bubbly Texas twang. She was instantly funny, upbeat, and kind. I

liked her immediately. She was clearly nothing like her character, Angela Martin, which shows what a great actress she is. In addition to our chats over the partition, Angela would talk my ear off in the hair and makeup room, and she would keep talking as we walked to the snack table and then to set. I often joke that I had no choice but to become friends with Angela because she wouldn't stop talking to me! I was so grateful for her. I was nervous and she was an instant comfort.

Angela

My first memory of Jenna is hearing a little dainty sneeze come from behind the partition next to my desk. It reminded me of my neighbor's Peekapoo sneezing. It was adorable. She sat directly behind me and was physically the closest gal to me on set. Jenna seemed shy, but then again I am super chatty, and I probably scared her. (I can do that to people.) Every day that first week, I'd get up on my tippy-toes and pop my head over and chat. Those desk partition chats became our daily habit for the next nine years.

Jenna

The whole week seemed to speed by so fast. Before we knew it, the pilot was done, and we all went home to wait the almost three months it took to learn if our show would make it to series. Shortly after we'd filmed the pilot, I went to London for a friend's wedding. While I was there, I reached out to Ricky and Stephen to see if they were able to meet. I don't know where I got the courage to call, but since I'd basically been unemployed since shooting the pilot for *The Office*, this was the one potentially exciting thing I had in my life. I wanted to milk it for all it was worth. They agreed to host me for lunch at the exclusive Groucho Club. The Groucho is a famed private club for comedians, and I couldn't believe I was there. I don't like to think too much about that lunch because I'm certain I sounded like a raving idiot, going on and on and praising their genius nonstop. They must have taken pity on me, because they even agreed to pose for a photo afterward.

After the lunch, I was sitting on the tube reading a discarded UK *TV Guide*. Inside was an article about the casting of the American version of *The Office*. How crazy is that?! The article was not positive. It said, "The chances of NBC actually matching wits with the original are about as good as finding a designated driver at a Wembley football match." It included photos of the original cast members alongside photos of each of us from the American version. The article basically went on to break down how we were ill-suited for the roles and would ruin the show. It ended by predicting our show would be as palatable as "a plate of mushy peas." Huh. How did I feel about this? I'll tell you. MY PHOTO WAS IN A MAGAZINE! I was blown away. It was the first time I'd ever been in a magazine. I tore out the article and tucked it into my purse. For years I saved every press clipping about our show, even if I wasn't mentioned at all. I can't explain it exactly, but from the very beginning, this show felt special. It felt different from the rest. I wanted to keep a record of every moment. Even the ones where we were compared to mushy peas.

About two months later, Greg called and said he'd finished editing the pilot episode and sent it off to the network. He wanted to share it with the cast. If the folks at UK *TV Guide* were right, it would be the only episode of the American version of *The Office* ever produced, so we wanted to celebrate. I offered to host a viewing party. (It's something that would become an ongoing tradition when the show was on the air. We'd switch houses each week, watching together, but this was the first!) Everyone gathered at my house. I moved the furniture around in an effort to accommodate everyone, but there were so many people that folks were sitting on the floor—including Steve Carell. We ordered pizza and got set to watch.

Angela

At first, you couldn't get your DVD player to work.

Jenna

Yes, I was mortified. Everyone was in my house, sitting on my floor, waiting to see this show that we'd worked so hard on. It was so much pressure.

Angela

After some colorful language and trying a few different plugs, you changed the batteries in your remote and got it working. Night saved!

Jenna

And, if I remember correctly, we watched it twice. We all told Greg how much we loved it. And we did. We felt good about what we had created. Greg told us he had no idea which way the network was leaning and that we'd have to wait another month to find out. A month! How in the world was I going to fill the next thirty days without going out of my mind? I decided to stalk more original *Office* cast members. My manager, Naomi Odenkirk, had a client who was shooting a pilot with Lucy Davis. I went to the taping and met her afterward. She was bubbly and smiley. She told me how *The Office* had changed her life and wished me all the same success. I asked for a photo. Of course. Then I went home and waited. And waited. And waited.

Angela

During our month wait, I went home to visit my family's farm in Texas. It's about three hundred acres in the middle of nowhere. My dad would wake me up early in the morning to feed the cows. When I wasn't helping my dad, I was helping my mom and grandmother shell pecans. Hollywood felt very far away, and I was thankful for the distraction. While I was there, I got the news that NBC had picked up five more episodes of *The Office*. We were officially a series! My whole family was so excited. They knew what a long journey this had been for me. Mom said we should celebrate, so she put on a pot roast. A pot roast *and* homemade rolls. Bertie Jo (that's my mom's name) was going all out. Some meals you remember for your whole life, and that was one of them for me. Good news and a good pot roast, a celebration indeed!

Jenna

When I got the call that the show was getting picked up, I screamed. My very pragmatic agents congratulated me and then, I guess to temper my expectations, told me that five episodes was a very small order and it indicated very little confidence in the show. They were basically saying, "Have fun, but don't spend all your money in one place." In fact, my agents continued to send me other pilot scripts while we were shooting Season 1 of *The Office*. A recurring theme of our early years was people explaining to us how our show would never really make it. I told them I was simply excited to be employed for now. I couldn't wait to get back to work with everyone again.

Our pilot had been a direct adaptation of the British pilot script, but the network wanted the next five episodes to be original. Greg assembled a staff of writers to start breaking down stories for the first all-original episodes. That group was: Mindy Kaling, Mike Schur, and B. J. Novak, plus three consultants, Paul

Lieberstein, Larry Wilmore, and Lester Lewis. One of the first stories they came up with was based on a real-life experience of their writers' assistant, Tom Huang. When Tom was in college, he took a class in which they did an exercise where they had to put notecards on their heads with different ethnicities, and then they had to go around and regard one another as that ethnicity using stereotypes. This turned into "Diversity Day." B. J. Novak, who was only twenty-five years old at the time, was tasked with writing the episode, which the writing staff nicknamed "The Pilot After the Pilot." It would establish what the audience could expect from the American version of *The Office* moving forward. Good thing for us, B. J. nailed it.

Angela

The morning we filmed Michael Scott's Diversity Day seminar, the props department handed us our notecards and showed us how to place them on our foreheads. They were taped to our heads at 7:30 A.M., and we wore those cards for twelve hours. We only took them off at lunchtime. Hours went by, and we forgot all about them. Mine said JAMAICA. I wish I had taken a picture of us on our snack break. Imagine seeing the cast eating nachos with these ridiculous cards on their foreheads. Standing by the salsa bar was Jenna with JEWISH taped to her forehead talking to Brian with ITALIAN taped to his. By the end of the day, the double-stick tape had left skinny, rectangular bald spots on our foreheads. But it was worth it. The cast was completely in sync. All our reactions, every moment, felt perfect. I remember looking around that conference room and thinking, *Oh my God, if we can just get people to watch this show, we're gonna be a hit.* From the very beginning, it felt like the cast of *The Office* had a "group mind." (Bear with me, but this group mind idea is from the improv world, and I always relate back to that.) By group mind I mean we had this shared comedic collective consciousness. When you are performing improv as a group, no single person leads . . . the goal is to find your way together—listening, reacting, and being in the moment. I felt like our cast had this kind of comedic mind meld. The magic came from a combination of great writing and smart casting, but I think it was also due to the fact that the original cast shared a lot of history with one another. You already know that I knew Greg by marriage (and as a result Paul as well), and that I had performed with Oscar in sketch comedy shows. But I also knew Kate Flannery, our saucy Meredith. For years Kate and I performed improv together at iO West. But wait—there's more. Jenna and I had been living a few blocks apart as struggling artists, using the same grocery store, but never met. Jenna, Phyllis, and director Ken Kwapis are all from St. Louis. Brian Baumgartner and Rainn Wilson had done regional theater together. Then there's the fact that B. J. Novak and John Krasinski were childhood friends in Newton, Massachusetts, and even played in the same Little League baseball division. Do you see what I mean here?! For the most part we were a group of strangers, yet somehow it felt like destiny that we would all come together on this show. You take these people whose lives have been crisscrossing for years, you put them in a tiny little office, write them amazing scripts, and it was comedic lightning in a bottle!

Jenna

It's impossible to predict if a television show or movie project will be a success. And with *The Office*, we spent the first two seasons believing we could be canceled at any moment. No one looked at this group of people and said, "Bingo! We've got a hit television show on our hands!" But what you did feel, standing on that set all together, was magic. You could feel the chemistry of these people that Greg had so masterfully gathered together. And that includes our writers, directors, and crew. Every person on set was essential. It's just as Angela said: It was as if we'd been crisscrossing one another our whole lives up until that point just for this purpose. Every role we hadn't gotten, every show before that didn't go, made it so we were now together for this one. We had no idea if fans would like the show. Or how long the magic would last. We were all just grateful to be there, creating something together.

2

world's best job

Between the two of us, we've worked on a lot of film and television projects over the years. We can say with authority that *The Office* was a truly special place to work. One of the unique features of the *Office* set was the ease of collaboration between the different departments. This was no accident. Showrunner Greg Daniels had a vision for an innovative method of making television that centered around giving everyone a voice in the process. The magic that was created from his system was, as Michael Scott might say, "incalcalacable."

Jenna

"Find a job you love, and you'll never work another day in your life." I remember hearing this phrase when I was a kid, and it pretty much describes my time working on *The Office*. A typical episode of *The Office* took one week to shoot. An average day of shooting was about twelve hours long. So . . . quick math . . . that's about sixty hours on set each week. But it never felt like work.

Angela

Generally, when you're shooting a movie or television show, you do a scene with one or two other actors, and then you go home or back to your trailer to wait to shoot another. But on *The Office*, our set was just one big room. Even if you weren't speaking in a scene, you were still part of the background. Here is a photo I took of the "bullpen," as we called it. With two cameras running at all times, you were always going to be on camera.

There was no heading off to your trailer for a break—we were all in it together, all the time. The reality was that many of our work hours were spent in the background of our castmates' scenes.

Jenna

And that was true for everyone, even the star of our show, Steve Carell. I remember once, after spending a particularly long time in the background, Steve came out of Michael's office and said to me, "Oh my gosh, I understand why Michael is always coming out of his office to chat with people—it's so lonely in there." I understood. Pam's desk was lonely too.

I would look across the room and wish I had a deskmate. I spent a lot of my background time playing FreeCell. (Not really that different from what I did at my countless day jobs as a real receptionist.) At that time, none of the computers on our desks had internet, but they were equipped with games. This led to some pretty fierce FreeCell competitions between the cast and crew. For those not familiar, FreeCell is basically solitaire, but all the cards are dealt face-up. The goal is to solve the deal in as few moves as possible. Playing this game became an obsession. The crew played during breaks, and the cast played while in the background of scenes. I think Kate Flannery holds the record for all-time best score with the fewest moves. But Phyllis was also pretty darn good.

Angela

I could only play solitaire for so long before I'd get antsy. I spent the majority of my background time writing in my journal or doodling. I kept a set of colored pencils in my desk drawer, and there was never a shortage of paper (of course), so I would draw. Here's a doodle I did during one of those long background scenes. I guess I was dreaming of an island vacation??

Oscar would also draw, and he is really good. He would often pass me notes with elaborate drawings during a scene to try to make me laugh. They were usually of the accounting department or an illustration of a story I had told him. I saved many of them. Here are a few of my favorites.

Oscar's Accounting Department doodle:

Apparently, I told him a few stories about my cats:

And I guess on this day, I really wanted a Coca-Cola:

Jenna

Angela and I are both big journal gals. When the gang took a break from fighting it out on FreeCell, I also spent my background time writing in my journal or making shopping lists. Steve read film scripts in his office. Or sometimes, the newspaper. (But he'd have to hide them inside of something Michael would actually read, like *Cracked* or *American Way*.) Rainn was one of the first in the cast to upgrade from a flip phone to a Blackberry. He was instantly addicted. We were jealous that he could read and answer emails on set. Phyllis sometimes paid her bills and balanced her checkbook in the background of scenes. If you look closely at episodes during Season 1, you can see her writing checks. I used to worry someone would pause their TV, zoom in, and steal her account and routing numbers. (This probably isn't possible, but that's how my brain works. I have a little Dwight in me. *That's what she said*.)

Angela

Being in the background also meant we had to be in character all day, every day. In our little accounting corner, we would come up with ridiculous improvised "office work" to try to make one another laugh. For instance, Oscar would play with his giant adding machine. Imagine an adding machine from the 1970s, much like the phone E.T. built to call home. The keys were so enormous that the machine was nearly the size of his computer keyboard. I don't know where the props department got that thing, but I imagine it had lived in an NBC storage vault for decades. I would look over at Oscar and he would be very judiciously adding numbers from a spreadsheet, hitting the buttons with only his knuckles. Brian pretended to work using a giant red pencil that was actually a piggy bank. I liked to take fake phone calls, get annoyed at the fake caller, roll my eyes, and then hang up in a huff.

27

Jenna

Kate and I had a long-running background improvisation about how corporate had recently converted to a confusing new computer program for logging sales orders. It was all based on some prop sales sheets we found in a folder. We decided the new program was faulty because the printed sales sheets categorized items using an all-numeric sales code, while the new computer program used an *alpha*-numeric code. Different codes for different systems—such a typical corporate snafu, and totally something officemates would complain about. We did this improvisation for *years* when our characters were paired together in the background of scenes, quietly lamenting the idiocy of the new system. I really wish I still had one of those sales sheets. If I did, I'd frame it and give it to Kate as a gift.

Angela

In the pilot episode, everyone in the office is worried about rumored downsizing. I had two scripted lines: "I bet it's gonna be me. Probably gonna be me." In response, Kevin said, "Yeah, it'll be you." That was it. The rest of the week, I was only in the background. That meant I had *a lot* of time to kill. All that downtime gave birth to Sprinkles. As any fan of *The Office* knows, Sprinkles is my character Angela Martin's beloved fluffy white cat. But what you might not know is that the entire Sprinkles story line was birthed on a single green Post-it note during the pilot episode.

Ken Kwapis, our director, asked some of the supporting cast to help fill out the background of scenes by doing busywork in various parts of the bullpen. If you rewatch the pilot, you'll see a few of these moments. Kevin is going through packages at the mail cart, I make copies at the photocopier, and then there were people crossing behind the interviews in the conference room. The writers called the interviews between Dunder Mifflin employees and the documentarians "talking heads." Ken was establishing the world of the mockumentary, and in those early days they wanted people crossing behind the talking heads to show the hustle and bustle of an office. He asked me if I would make a big loop through the bullpen passing out papers. I was so thrilled to have something to do. I asked him what he wanted me to give out. He told me it didn't matter. Clearly, this was not a plot-propelling moment. Earlier, while at my desk, I had doodled a little cat on a Post-it note. This gave me an idea. I made a bunch more and wrote on each one, "It's Sprinkles's 3rd Birthday! Come celebrate! Tuesday in the parking lot." I had the idea that Angela found a cat in the parking lot and adopted it. Its third birthday was coming up, and she was going to make sure everyone acknowledged it properly. While filming my pivotal background walk behind the talking heads, I handed out the invitations. Everyone in the office received one . . . except Jim. I decided that Jim would probably say something sarcastic about the cat party, and Angela Martin was not having it. Sprinkles's birthday was very important to her, and she wasn't going to invite just anyone. Especially not a smart aleck. So Jim was out.

Jenna

When Angela gave me my invitation, I thought it was hilarious. I stuck it to my computer screen, as folks in offices do with random sticky notes. A few days later, I had to shoot a flirty scene between Jim and Pam at the reception desk. After a few takes, Ken came over and said the scene felt a little stiff, and he wanted us to improvise. He reminded us of an improvisation we'd done during the audition process, when they had me stand at the copier and directed John to walk over and start a conversation. John came up to me and said, "What are you copying right now? What is that?" And I responded with a flirty sass, "I'm working. I don't know if you're working, but I have work to do." The dialogue we came up with wasn't very clever, but underneath those boring words we played out a subtext of two people who were delighted to be standing close and saying anything to each other. Ken suggested we try improvising in a similar way, telling us to talk about any mundane thing while the cameras rolled. And so, when the scene started, I saw the Post-it note on my computer. It gave me the idea to say the line "Are you going to Angela's cat party on Sunday?" (I'm not sure why I said Sunday when the Post-it clearly says the party is on Tuesday.) As Angela predicted, John as Jim shot back, "Yeah, stop, that's ridiculous." And we giggled together. It was a great moment. And it made the cut. But not only that, the exchange planted the seed that Angela was a crazy cat lady. The writers went on to flesh out the story of Sprinkles for many seasons thereafter.

Angela

This is just one example of why our show was so creatively fulfilling. We were constantly given permission to participate in the creation of our characters' backstories, personalities, and lives outside of work. I love that the writers and producers then took those little seeds and grew them into huge, wonderful story lines.

Jenna

While preparing for the role of Pam, I wrote out a long character history. It was something I had been trained to do in theater school. I am, if anything, a good student. It was important for me to create a detailed personal history for Pam as I believed it would ground my performance. I spent most of my time thinking about why Pam and Roy had been engaged for so long and not gotten married. There had to be a reason. I made up a backstory that Pam and Roy didn't have enough money for their wedding because Roy spent their

wedding money on a pair of Jet Skis with his brother. I imagined their arguments when Pam found out what Roy had done: Roy's justification that he'd spent "separate money," his insistence that she could use one of the Jet Skis whenever she wanted, and Pam's resignation and resentment over the whole thing. One day, out of the blue, Greg asked me, "Why do you think Pam and Roy haven't gotten married yet?" My homework was about to pay off. I told Greg the Jet Ski story, and he lit up. He said, "Oh! We must add this to the show!" A week later, it appeared in one of Pam's talking heads. It stayed alive all the way to the "Cocktails" episode in Season 3 when Roy and his brother finally sold the Jet Skis (at a loss).

This is one of many reasons why I think Greg Daniels was so amazing. He listened to us. He believed we were the experts on our characters. He wanted our input. And, let me tell you, that is a rare thing. In my jobs following *The Office*, I was surprised to learn how little the writers and producers wanted to hear my thoughts about my character. In those cases, the message that came through was "The creator has a vision; the writers write it, the actors perform it. Everyone stay in your lane."

Angela

Greg is a very curious person and loves to hear people's stories. He would often ask us questions about our jobs before *The Office*. Many of us, including Jenna and me, had worked in actual offices. As a temp, I had worked in mail rooms and at reception, been an assistant and an operator, and sat through many human resources meetings. I had a lot of stories to share. I remember rambling on and on about a thermostat war between the call center and the IT department at 1-800-DENTIST, and the time we had a flasher in the women's restroom that resulted in an upgrade to the security system. One year, for extra money, I even volunteered to help with the holiday party. True story. Back then, 1-800-DENTIST had an elaborate company Christmas party, and if you stayed after work to help with the decorating you could earn extra money. Our office manager was in charge of the party and would get very stressed out about this event. (I might have channeled some of her energy for Angela Martin.) Greg would jot down notes, and every now and then I'd see something from one of my actual life experiences pop up in a script. It was so exciting to feel like I'd inspired even a small part of the show.

Jenna

Greg deliberately wanted to change the structure of how a traditional sitcom operated. In addition to everything we've already mentioned, he also had the idea to give some of the writers acting roles on the show. On most sets, the writers and actors are kept separate. In some cases, they barely interact or even know each other. In fact, I know of one television show that is shot in New York while the writers are back in Los Angeles. You can't get more separate

than that. Greg was interested in seeing what would happen if he made the two groups more fluid, so he cast writers B. J. Novak (Ryan), Mindy Kaling (Kelly), Paul Lieberstein (Toby), and Mike Schur (Mose) in recurring roles on the show.

Angela

The writers were on set with us, making observations about how we interacted in real life and how our own personalities might influence the backstories and personalities of our characters. For example, after a long day of filming conference room scenes, the cast became punchy and started goofing around during camera setups. John was entertaining everyone by doing impressions of the cast and crew members. We were all cracking up. Mindy, B. J., and Paul were there too. Next thing you know, there's a story line where Jim does impressions of his coworkers, first in Season 2's "Drug Testing" and then again in "Product Recall" in Season 3. His "bears, beets, *Battlestar Galactica*" impression of Dwight would become a fan favorite.

In another example, Steve Carell played in an actual hockey league and would tell us stories about his team during breaks. Clearly the writers were listening, because Steve's real-life love of hockey became the inspiration behind both "Michael's Birthday" and "Threat Level Midnight." And from our

experience as real office workers, Jenna and I often had ideas. Once, when Greg was on set, we pulled him aside to pitch him a plot about Jan hosting a Women in the Workplace seminar for all the women in the office. Greg said, "I love it, what happens next?" And we answered, "We don't know, that's all we got." Greg grabbed B. J. and asked us to pitch the idea again. They started jotting down notes and building out our simple idea into a full show. It was so cool to see them work right there in the moment. A few weeks later, we filmed the episode "Boys and Girls" based on our premise!

Jenna

We were encouraged to mingle with all the writers, including the ones who weren't performing on the show. The writers' offices were on the second floor of the building, next door to where we filmed. We used the exterior of their building to shoot parking lot scenes, and the bottom floor of their building was our lobby and

warehouse set. So when you see photos of the exterior of "Dunder Mifflin," it was actually the writers who were inside, not the actors. We used a few other parts of their building as well. Remember the stairwell where Dwight pumps himself up with air guitar before his performance review? That stairwell led to the writers' floor. And any time Michael had to look out of his window to the parking

lot below, those scenes were filmed up in one of the writers' offices that had been dressed to look like Michael's office. Since we were frequently in and out of that building shooting, the actors would often stop by the writers' room for a visit.

Angela

I loved visiting the writers' room. In the center of the room was a big conference table where the writers could gather on computers to work. Next to the conference table was a set of sofas. The actors would all pile into that little living room area to hang out. Over the years, that space morphed from a living room to a jam space with a drum kit and keyboard. Then later it was filled with games. Our writers would spend long hours in that room, and they needed creative outlets to keep them going. In the early seasons, there was a very competitive game of *Call of Duty* between the writers and editors at *The Office*. They would play off and on throughout the day, but on their lunch breaks, it got heated. It came as no surprise when we sat down to read "E-Mail Surveillance" that the Stamford branch had a competitive *Call of Duty* game as a story line.

Jenna

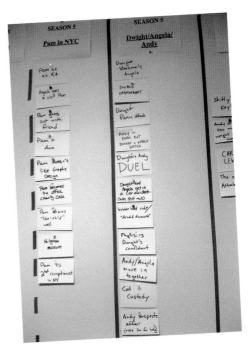

My favorite thing about the writers' room was the hundreds of notecards taped to the walls. Every evening, the writers would be assigned homework to prepare for the next day. The homework might be something like "Come up with five story lines for Dwight," "Office pranks," or "Obstacles for Jim and Pam." Then the writing team would pitch their ideas to one another. The best ones would be written on index cards and taped to the wall. Each character on the show had a column with index cards underneath with possible story lines.

There were also columns for A-plots, B-plots, cold opens (the standalone scenes that started many episodes, like Michael running past the speed radar in "The Duel," which was based on writer Aaron Shure's real life), and random jokes. For example, B. J. Novak once simply said, "Booze cruise," and that became a card. My imagination would churn, thinking of all the ways these cards might turn into an episode. Of course, I was always most interested in the Pam column, and I'll never forget seeing the card during Season 3 that said "Dueling Christmas parties" and another years later that read "Pam slaps Michael." I remember there was a card that never came to fruition that read "Double date: Jim/Pam, Angela/Dwight." I still wonder what that could have been!

Angela

If we weren't crashing the writers' room, we were crashing the edit bays. Our editors' offices were downstairs from the writers', down a long hallway that led to the lobby of the Dunder Mifflin building. Remember where everyone was lined up on Pretzel Day? That was the editors' hallway. Our editors—Dave Rogers, Dean Holland, and Claire Scanlon—would often play us clips as they were editing scenes. Dave brought his dog, Bryce, to set, and after my daughter, Isabel, was born, we would always walk over to say hello. Sometimes there would be a debate about which jokes to keep or cut, and Greg would pull cast and crew members into the bays to watch and offer our opinions. For example, they shot two different options for the end of Season 3, where Jim drives back from New York to ask Pam on a date. In one, he interrupts her during a talking head. In the other, he finds her as she's getting off the elevator for the day. Everyone voted for the scene with the talking head, and that's what ended up in the episode.

Jenna

As you've probably noticed, authenticity was important to Greg. It's why he liked to draw on our real-life office stories. So when he was looking to hire a cinematographer, he looked for one with experience as a documentarian. That's how he found Randall Einhorn. Randall was an extreme sports documentary camera operator. He once skied down a mountain in Jackson Hole with a camera on his shoulder while filming Olympian Shaun White. To say this man would do anything for a shot is an incredible understatement. I've seen Randall crawl, roll, sprint, stuff himself into the backseat of a car, and even stand as still as a statue (which might be the hardest of all to pull off) to capture the perfect shot. In their first meeting, Randall told Greg his vision for how to shoot our show. He described it this way: "It's kind of like a tofu hot dog. It's good food that's made to look like bad food." He went on to say, "You can't shoot it like normal TV." In standard film and television shows, the instinct is to push in for a close-up when scenes get emotional. Randall said we should back away. In his experience shooting reality television and documentaries, when a conversation was intimate, he would back away from it. The subjects were more likely to share openly if they couldn't feel the camera nearby. Or in some cases, if they didn't even know it was there at all. As a result, the moment feels almost stolen, and the scene feels more intimate. Greg loved this approach. We did this type of shooting all the time for *The Office*. We called it the "spy shot." In later seasons, Randall also directed many of our episodes. Like Greg, he was one of the original creative minds behind the series.

Angela

It took two cameras to capture all the action on *The Office*. While Randall was capturing the main scene with our A camera, Matt Sohn, our B camera operator, was grabbing the reactions from the supporting cast. These guys were the perfect pair. They had met while both working as camera operators for the reality competition show *Survivor*, and they seemed to share a secret language. They could communicate with each other with the glance of an eye. Between the two of them, every line and reaction got covered. Watching them work looked very much like watching a dance.

Matt spent a lot of time with us in the accounting corner. I feel like Matt is the reason all the "Angela eye rolls" made it into the show. He had this amazing way of finding little moments that filled out a character's personality. A perfect example of this is from the "Health Care" episode in Season 1. At the nine-minute mark, the accountants are walking back to their desks after the team confronts Michael about Dwight's horrible health care plan. Oscar, Brian, and I improvised some dialogue as we walked back to the accounting nook (because remember, we were always in character). Matt caught it out of the corner of his eye and said, "If you guys tighten it up, I'll get it on camera." We took his advice, and this improvisation made it in the episode!

ANGELA: Did you talk to him?
OSCAR: What was that?
ANGELA: You let him walk all over you. It's just pathetic.
KEVIN: What are you guys talking about?
ANGELA: Nothing, Kevin.

The exchange showed the odd dysfunctional family that is the accounting department: close, but full of disdain for one another. Thanks to Matt Sohn, I learned a valuable lesson. He taught me that if I kept my improv moments short, they had a better chance of making it into the episode. I would keep this in mind throughout the run of the show.

Another reason why our show looked so authentic was due to our production designer, Michael Gallenberg, and the set dressing, props, and art departments. Michael worked out of a trailer on the far side of our parking lot. One of my favorite things to do when I had time was to pop over and look at all the photos on the walls when Michael was charged with creating a new set. You know how in crime shows the detectives cover their walls with photos, documents, and drawings, and then connect them all with string? That's what it was like in Michael Gallenberg's trailer, except they were photos of office buildings, apartments, New York City, and Scranton. When his department had to re-create real Scranton businesses like Poor Richard's or Cooper's Seafood, they would get photos of the real locations and study them meticulously. Along with our locations manager, Kyle Alexander, Michael's team would drive around Los Angeles looking for restaurants with similar interior and exterior architecture, and then go in and redecorate them to look like the real thing. Sometimes we needed two locations—one for the exterior and one for the interior. No matter where they chose, their work was always flawless.

Once a new world was built, the set dressing team, headed by Steve Rostine, chose the desks, the wall hangings, the plants, the lamps. They filled the shelves with random clutter. They were in charge of every detail, including making sure we had lit EXIT signs over our fake doors. If you look back at Season 1, you will notice that in the first few episodes Pam's office chair didn't have arms. I would look across the bullpen and watch in envy as people casually rested their elbows on their armed chairs. I so longed for a place to put my elbows. One day, I asked Steve Rostine if there was any way to swap my chair for a new one with arms. He gave me a wink and the following week I had a new chair with arms! My elbows were delighted! It's not lost on me that we eventually had a running story line that Pam was obsessed with getting a new chair. But by that time, thanks to Steve Rostine, I had a fantastic chair, and I was not giving it up!

Angela

Phil Shea was the head of the props department for the entire run of our show. He is a brilliant prop master. The props department works closely with actors, since they are responsible for anything we might hold in our hands or use in a scene. Angela's Babies Playing Jazz poster, Pam's teapot, Dwight's bobblehead, Meredith's Big Gulp cup, and Phyllis's flowers from Bob Vance are all examples of props. Phil Shea is responsible for all of them.

When I think of Phil, I always think of him smiling and running. Most of my conversations with him took place as he fast-walked/jogged across our set parking lot. The list of things he would have to make or buy for episodes was long, and with only one week to prepare, he was always in a time crunch. Here's an example of some of the props he had to assemble for the "Moroccan Christmas" episode: dozens of custom-made Princess Unicorn dolls, Kevin's fez hat, the fancy scroll invite to the party, new eyeglasses for Phyllis, Angela's nativity set, sunglasses made out of paper clips and a brown plastic folder (for a deleted-scene gift from Pam to Jim), Michael's intervention printout from the Mormon Church website, and fake bags of trash for Michael and Meredith to fall into, not to mention he had to fill the conference room with party food, cookies, and multiple bottles of fake booze. I'm sure I missed a few, but you get the idea. He was a very busy guy. One of my favorite tidbits about Phil was his penchant for presenting prop options

on a silver serving tray for review. For example, when he had to make a fake dead bird for the "Grief Counseling" episode, he brought several to set and showed Greg and our director their options on a silver tray. Imagine them poring over the carcasses, earnestly discussing the pros and cons of each. After that, Phil brought out a tray with different homemade bird coffins. You never knew what was going to be on Phil's silver tray, but it was always fun to find out.

Jenna

Without our trusty grip and electric departments, you wouldn't have seen any of the hard work of the actors or crew. Led by Dale Alexander and Brad Lipson, respectively, these guys literally kept the lights on at Dunder Mifflin. You would routinely see them standing on desks, removing ceiling tiles, and setting lights. They would swoop in after rehearsal and swoop out by the time we started filming. Most impressively, these guys could light a scene in under fifteen minutes, which kept our days shorter than average. They were very fast and very stealth.

Angela

You know those fancy director's chairs you see actors sitting in with their names on them? They make those chairs so they can send the actors off the set and out of the way when the crew needs to make a lighting or set adjustment. Well,

we didn't have those fancy chairs. We didn't have the budget for them. If we wanted a chair, we sat at our desks between scenes. (Which might be why Jenna wanted that chair with arms so badly.) As a result, we often mingled with our crew while they worked. Usually, when Dale was perched above accounting, I'd brainstorm with him about home projects. Back when I was still living in a small apartment, I had a litter box problem. No matter where I put the litter box, it seemed to stink up the whole place. But then I had an idea. I lived on the first floor of the building with a tiny patio. I thought that if the litter box was attached to the side of the patio, then my cat could go through an opening in a window and use the litter box outside, and thus my apartment would be less stinky. I drew out my idea and showed it to Dale. He was intrigued. Then he offered to make it. He even brought it over to my apartment and attached it to my window. We called it the Catty Shack. And it worked! Seriously, it was kinda brilliant. Dale, why didn't we ever try to sell these??

Jenna

While Angela was fixing her stinky litter box thanks to Dale, I was brainstorming about torn pantyhose with our boom operator Nick Carbone. Let me explain. Our sound department was led by sound mixer Ben Patrick. Ben sat at a sound cart hidden within the walls of our set. He kept track of the sound coming from everyone's personal microphones—the ones we had strapped to our bodies at all times—and the sound coming from our two on-set boom operators, Nick Carbone and Brian Wittle. These are the guys who held long microphones on sticks above our heads all day, capturing our dialogue. It's a feat of upper-body strength that never failed to impress me. These guys also hid microphones on our desks, in visors of cars—they were always finding creative ways to capture the sounds of the scene. They were amazing. In fact, Ben's department was Emmy-nominated for Outstanding Sound Mixing for a Comedy or Drama Series five times for their work on the show.

In addition to holding a boom microphone above my head, Nick Carbone put a personal microphone on my body every single day for nearly nine years. When I think of the people I miss most from this time of my life, he is definitely one of them. I don't love having to wear a microphone (who does?), but he was so kind and made me laugh constantly.

It's a very intimate thing to put a microphone on an actor. Most of the time the microphone got taped to my bra and then a wire went down my belly and around to the middle of my back, where a mic pack was tucked into my waistband. This worked great if I was sitting at my desk. But if I had a scene where I was standing or walking or you could see my back, the bulge of the pack was visible, and we had to find a different solution.

The men had it easy because they could put the wire down their pants and attach the pack to their ankle. But that didn't work for me because Pam's go-to look was a pencil skirt. So if I was standing up, the wire would have to go down my leg, and the microphone pack would be attached to my upper thigh with a leg wrap that closed with Velcro. (I don't have to explain how itchy and uncomfortable that was.) Now add in the pantyhose Pam always wore. Every time the Velcro rubbed against my leg, the pantyhose would run, and every time this happened, I'd have to change. I was going through four or five packs of hose every single day. Finally, in coordination with the wardrobe

department, Nick engineered a leg wrap that used hooks instead of Velcro. This was basically a bra closure attached to a leg wrap. No more itching. No more runs in the pantyhose. It was genius.

But wait. There's more! Nick knew that I like to really go for it at the holidays. Meaning I like to eat the pies and the turkeys and the mashed potatoes, and in short, I would often come back from the holidays a full size larger than when I left.

So he made sure each leg wrap had multiple size settings. The leg wrap always fit. Do you see why I love this man? My pantyhose didn't run AND I got my pie. We called this adjustable leg wrap "the Jenna," as in, "Next scene, Pam is standing up—grab the Jenna!"

After *The Office* was over, I was cast on the ABC series *Splitting Up Together*. When I walked on set the first day and was introduced to the sound team, it was the same team from *The Office*. Brian was there. Nick was there. I immediately burst into tears upon seeing them. And guess what? Nick went over to his sound cart and pulled out the Jenna. He had saved it. We used it on that series too.

You see, a groundbreaking television show wasn't the only thing that grew from Greg's innovative work environment. It also gave rise to the Catty Shack and the Jenna. And best of all, it bore close friendships that would last long after the cameras stopped rolling. Greg created a family.

The most impactful relationship to come out of the show for me was my best friendship with Angela, and I can't believe we've gotten this far into the book without telling you how that friendship started! It was the "Basketball" episode of Season 1, and the two of us were seated next to each other on a metal bench in the warehouse as the men shot their game scenes. We had a few moments when our characters were featured in the story, but for the most part, we were in the background. With no FreeCell, no journals, and no partition between us, we gabbed every chance we got. We told each other our life stories on that bench. We shared details of our childhoods and of our moves from our hometowns to Hollywood. We learned that we'd been going to the same grocery store in West Hollywood for years and never knew it. And we both liked the same Target! We also goofed around and made jokes. At one point Phyllis said, "You two are adorable. Give me your camera, I have to take a photo of this." I can say with absolute certainty, this was the birthplace of our best friendship.

Angela

At the end of "bench week," Jenna and I were leaving the set and walking to our trailers across the big parking lot between the two soundstages. We'd shot late into the evening, and we were pretty loopy. We were laughing and talking, and then we spontaneously linked arms and began to sing the *Laverne & Shirley* theme song: "Schlemiel! Schlimazel!" Unbeknownst to us, Steve Carell was quietly walking behind us. When we saw him, we were so embarrassed! This was peak dorkiness. But he just smiled at us and said, "No matter what happens with the show . . . you will have this. This friendship is what you will take with you." And he was right. When you watch *The Office*, you are watching a group of people who are having fun and becoming good friends. We formed a deep bond with our castmates and crew during those nine years, and I think we passed that feeling on to our audience. It reminds me of something my writing professor in college used to say: "What is a pleasure to write is a pleasure to read." It was a pleasure for us to make the show, and I think because of that, it is a pleasure to watch.

3

booze cruise

There were two big traveling episodes that bookended the series of *The Office*. One took place on a boat where we almost lost a few cast members at sea; the other took place on a bus where the entire cast was almost poisoned. We've always said if we ever wrote a book, we'd have to share these stories. Since we are discussing the early years of the show, we'll start with "Booze Cruise." It is certainly one of the funniest and most memorable episodes of *The Office* and a fan favorite. So let's pull up anchor and head out to sea!

Angela

Oh, the Dunder Mifflin booze cruise! This was an epic episode in the series for so many reasons. It was Season 2 and Michael decided to take the staff on a very special outing, one only he would choose. That special event? A booze cruise on Lake Wallenpaupack . . . in the middle of winter. Lake Wallenpaupack lies about thirty-four miles from Scranton, nestled in the Pocono Mountains. With fifty-two miles of beautiful uninterrupted shoreline, a *summer* evening booze cruise might have been fun, but in January, not so much. Nighttime temperatures average around 12 degrees, so we imagine there are no booze cruises happening. (Although we hear the ice fishing is fantastic.) If you ever wondered if our show was really filmed in Pennsylvania, this episode is a good indication that it was not. But supposing we could be on a boat on Lake Wallenpaupack in the winter, what would possess Michael to host a booze cruise for his employees? Well, corporate sent down an edict that there could be no more parties on the company dime. Michael, appalled by such a concept, found a loophole—as long as he calls the outing a "leadership training exercise," corporate will cover the cost. In brilliant Michael Scott fashion, he plans for the staff to get on the *LeaderSHIP*, where discussion of productivity and workflow can occur—alongside lots of partying, of course.

Jenna

"Booze Cruise" was significant because it was the first episode of the show to air on Thursday nights as part of NBC's coveted "Must See TV" comedy lineup. This promotion was a huge win for us. *The Office* originally aired at 9:30 P.M. on Tuesdays, and ratings were a struggle. Over time, our numbers improved, and with the move to Thursday, it felt like we were hitting the big time. *Cheers, Seinfeld, Friends, Will and Grace, Scrubs* . . . these are all successful comedies that aired on Thursday nights on NBC. The move indicated to all of us that NBC might just have confidence in our little show. But this isn't the only reason this episode is so pivotal. It is also when Angela and the other supporting cast members became series regulars. Up until that moment, the only cast members under regular contract were Steve Carell, John Krasinski, Rainn Wilson, B. J. Novak, and me. The rest of the group were considered "guest stars"—meaning NBC was under no obligation to include their characters in all the episodes, and they could be written out of the show at any time.

Angela

I remember the exact moment when I got the call from my agent that NBC was officially offering me, and the rest of the supporting cast, a series regular role on the show. I was standing on the dance floor of the boat with Kate and Brian, waiting to do a scene, when suddenly our phones started buzzing. Our agents were calling us all at the same time. I immediately wanted to find Jenna and tell her. She would know more than anyone what this meant to me. I saw her standing on the dock outside, and I ran down the gangway toward her hollering and waving my arms. I'm sure I looked ridiculous, but as soon as I got to her, and she could make out what I was yelling, she grabbed my hands, and we both started screaming and jumping up and down. The whole set was one big joyful celebration. I gave Oscar Nuñez my camera and asked him to capture the moment. Oscar said something along the lines of, "Oh, you two are so silly." But he gave us a big hug and snapped the picture. It's one of my favorites.

Jenna

I'll never forget it. This news meant job security for my BFF and for the whole show. We *must* have been doing well because NBC had moved us to Thursdays, and now they were going to pay everyone to be there all the time. Orders for future seasons seemed likely too. It felt like a turning point in all our lives.

Angela

This episode also felt like a big deal because it was our first time shooting on location in another city. And of course, there was also this enormous boat that we were filming on. A real boat! In the ocean! At night! We weren't on the soundstage anymore.

Jenna

We were just outside of the Long Beach harbor, about forty miles south of our home-base set in the San Fernando Valley. Because we had to spend three nights in Long Beach, the production put us all up at a hotel. It was the first time I had ever traveled for work. In my imagination, after shooting, the cast and crew would gather back at the hotel, all eating room service, drinking cocktails, laughing together, and living like rock stars. I brought my poker chips. I mean, this is what I thought happened when actors made movies—that every night was a big slumber party.

Angela

We barely even saw the hotel.

Jenna

I have no memory of the hotel. I don't even remember what it was called.

Angela

We'd report to the docks around 3 P.M., get on the boat, and shoot all through the night. Our shoot day ended as the sun was coming up, and then we would pile into a van and return to the hotel. The van ride was only five minutes, but I remember Oscar elbowing me because I was snoring. That's how quickly I fell asleep.

Jenna

We'd collapse in our rooms, try to sleep for a few hours, then head back in the afternoon and do it all over again. By the third night, we were all delirious. When I think back, those three days really feel like one long day.

Angela

You might think the move to Thursdays, the new series regular contracts, and the big location shoot also translated into a bigger budget for the show, but it didn't. Our line producer, Kent Zbornak, had to figure out how to make this episode using the same small budget as before. A line producer is responsible for all the practical decisions of the show. They keep everyone on a budget (which is set by the network), oversee the various noncreative departments, and organize the weekly schedule for cast and crew. If you like spreadsheets, this is the job for you. While Greg Daniels was responsible for the creative decisions of the show, Kent was responsible for the logistical ones. They were the perfect duo. And luckily, Kent

51

Angela

Oh, the boat was a total blast!

Jenna

There wasn't anywhere to go between scenes so we all just hung around in different booths on deck. We'd go from booth to booth, visiting one another.

Angela

The booth hangouts were one of my favorite memories from this episode. We were all together, a boat full of comedy performers confined in a small space. Everyone was doing bits, making jokes. We were loopy from lack of sleep and laughing so hard.

Jenna

We should mention that we had two amazing guest stars on this episode: Amy Adams and Rob Riggle. Amy had already appeared on two other episodes, so we knew her well. In her first appearance, her character of Katy came to Dunder Mifflin to sell purses. At the end of that episode, Jim asks her out on a date, making Pam jealous. For this episode, Jim brings Katy along on the booze cruise as his plus-one. I was seated next to Amy for most of the filming, and we had a blast. I think it's important to share that Amy Adams wasn't AMY ADAMS when she was cast as Katy the purse girl on Season 1 of *The Office*. She was a struggling actor just like the rest of us. We'd all share stories during our downtime about failed auditions, roles that went to someone else, and our anxiety over job security. She was sweet and funny and fit right into our little group.

Angela

There was a lot of buzz going around the industry that Amy was going to be an Oscar contender for her role in the movie *Junebug*. And sure enough, two weeks after we finished filming "Booze Cruise," she was nominated. (If you haven't seen it, check it out. She's amazing!) It was so wonderful getting to know her then. Like Jenna said, her journey was very relatable to us. She was a hardworking actor—some things had gone her way, some things hadn't. To see this electricity surround her over the Oscars as she maintained her humble, sweet personality . . . well, you just couldn't help but root for her. Our whole cast was so happy for her when the nominations were announced.

Jenna

And then there was Rob Riggle. He was cast as the boat captain, Captain Jack, with whom Michael forms a rivalry. Rob is a real Marine Corps veteran. He joined the Marines in 1990 with the intention of becoming a naval aviator but left after some years to pursue comedy. He has appeared on *SNL* and been in many movies, like *The Hangover* and *Step Brothers*. His breakout role was on *The Daily Show*, where he played their "military correspondent." And he was part of the Marine Corps Reserves for twenty-three years before he retired in 2013. Rob reminds me of my family back in Missouri. Sincere, ready to like and accept you, with a big hearty laugh. I loved being around him.

Angela

I've known Rob for years. We met during "Booze Cruise," but years later we did a pilot for Fox called *The Gabriels* where we played husband and wife. The show didn't make it to series, but we had a ball and remained close. Rob is always there for his friends. I recently called him with a fan question for our podcast. He

answered his phone right away, and we began chatting like no time had passed. I could hear lots of voices in the background and asked him where he was. He nonchalantly said, "Oh, I'm having dinner at a pub in Scotland." Scotland?! I talked his ear off for thirty minutes while he was trying to eat dinner in Scotland! If someone called me during dinner in Scotland, I would have said, "Can I call you back?" But not Rob. He sat there and let me prattle on.

Rob also has a big heart for service. Together with his Kansas City pals Eric Stonestreet, Jason Sudeikis, Paul Rudd, and Dave Koechner, he helps host a charity event every year for Children's Mercy Hospital. I've gone as Rob's guest a few times. I can tell you, he's the real deal.

At around two o'clock in the morning on our first night of shooting, while Steve and the crew were off rehearsing his famous dancing scene, we got antsy. It seemed like a good time to pull out our old-timey cameras and start taking photos.

I don't remember who came up with the idea that we should each make sexy faces, but that's what we did. We had a competition for who could look the most "smoldering." Then someone suggested we bite our fingers while sneering down at the camera. We went around the group and everyone gave their best sultry pose.

Jenna

In reality, we all just look nuts. And very, very tired. Except maybe Oscar. He actually nailed it.

Angela

Eventually our director Ken Kwapis gathered us on the dance floor for Steve's big dance scene. And of course, there had to be a big dance scene because, as Michael Scott would say, "Sometimes you just have to be the boss of dancing." Of all the scenes we shot for this episode, I'm not sure we laughed harder than we did during this one.

Jenna

One of the craziest parts of the whole thing was that there wasn't any music playing. The band started playing the song so Steve could hear the beat, but then stopped as soon as Ken called "Action." This is so they could edit the dance sequences without any weird jumps in the music, which would be added in post-production. Imagine watching Steve do all these crazy moves in total silence. Also, none of his dancing was choreographed. Steve improvised the whole thing.

It was amazing. We shot six takes or so, trying to hold it together. It wasn't easy, because Steve did something different every time. When Steve did the now-famous leg-slapping move followed by the very, very slow and sad worm on the floor, we all lost it. Everyone agreed it couldn't get better than that. We wrapped for the night. It's a good thing too. I don't think we could have ever recovered.

Angela

The next night, we shot the scenes where everyone on the boat is pounding drinks. Weeks prior at the table read for this episode, I told Greg about a spring break trip I had taken in college. I shared with him that I went on a sunset booze cruise in the Cayman Islands. The boat crew formed a dance line that ended with the captain pouring snorkel shots into everyone's mouth. People got pretty wasted. Greg thought the idea of snorkel shots was hilarious and told our prop master, Phil Shea, to make sure we had snorkels on the boat. (Of course, our prop snorkel shots were filled with iced tea and NOT with actual booze.) During the scene when Roy does a snorkel shot with Captain Jack, Greg called me over to do a tutorial with the fellas. See, Mom and Dad, that college degree came in very useful!

Jenna

On the last night of shooting, we finally pulled up anchor and set out to sea. We had to get all the scenes that take place on the bow and upper decks of the boat—like the one with Dwight and Angela when Dwight is fake-steering the boat, and when Meredith and Captain Jack sneak away to make out—when you'd be able to tell if the boat was moving. This was also the night I shot the now famous scene with John Krasinski where you think Jim might finally tell Pam how he really feels about her. Pam goes outside on the deck because she's frustrated with her boyfriend, Roy, who is busy doing snorkel shots and ignoring her. Jim comes out to find her, and Pam says, "Sometimes I just don't get Roy." This is the first time in the series that Pam complains about Roy to Jim. She creates an opening for Jim to tell her how he feels. Jim doesn't speak, just stands there silently for almost half a minute . . . twenty-seven seconds to be exact. There is no dialogue, but a lot goes on in those twenty-seven seconds. You see Jim thinking, but not saying, so many different things. You see Pam trying to signal to him that she wants to hear his feelings, but she doesn't say anything either. Eventually Pam breaks the silence and says, "Well, I'm cold." She walks back inside, leaving Jim to regret his missed opportunity. Now, there was nothing in the script that said we should pause that long. The script simply says, "They look at each other." But on the day of the shoot, Ken and Greg told us to take our time and let the moment "play out naturally." When they turned the episode in to the network, Greg fought to keep all twenty-seven seconds of silence. In comedy television, where the goal is to pack in a new joke every three to five seconds, Greg was willing to use a lot of real estate for this moment between Jim and Pam. After the episode aired, fan boards dubbed this moment "The 27 Seconds of Silence," and it was a big hit.

Angela

Should we talk about what else was going on while you were shooting this scene?

Jenna

Do you mean how half of the cast got lost at sea?

Angela

Yep! When they started shooting the Pam and Jim scene, I think they knew it was going to take a while. Their scenes always took a while, because they were usually the most nuanced as far as story. Every detail had to be perfectly crafted to have that relationship progress at just the right pace. It was the last scene of our shoot day, close to four in the morning, and they told the rest of us that we were wrapped. But we were still out to sea, and the boat would not be going back to shore until the Jim and Pam scene was done. We were given the option to either stay on the lower deck or leave on little dinghies that would take us to shore. Picture a small inflatable rubber boat with an outboard motor you steer with your hand. For reference, my uncle used to have one he used for fishing in the narrow bayous of Louisiana. It barely fit his fishing gear and one other person. After looking at the dinghy, several cast members chose to stay on the boat and sleep in the booths, but I guess Rainn, Brian, Phyllis, and I were feeling adventurous or we just REALLY wanted an actual bed, so we opted for the dinghy.

Getting into the tiny dinghy was tricky. We had to climb down a ladder that hung off the side of the big boat and jump into the tiny dinghy, while both the boat and the dinghy were bobbing up and down and back and forth. Luckily, we all made it onto the dinghy without falling into the ice-cold water. We took off for what was supposed to be a ten-minute boat ride to shore. It was pitch-dark, and the water around us looked like black glass. After a few minutes, our engine made a strange whirring sound, and then everything went quiet. The dinghy glided to a stop. Our driver tried a few times to start the engine again, and then we heard him say something to the effect of, "The engine's dead. Gonna radio for help."

Jenna

I was up on the deck shooting with John when Greg got a panicked call on the radio: "We've lost the boat with Phyllis!" And then we heard "But don't worry, we are sending a new boat now." What?! Lost the boat with Phyllis?? What was going on?! We stopped shooting as Greg got more details.

Angela

Jenna and Greg later shared with me that they didn't know anyone else was on the dinghy except for Phyllis. But in fact, there were four cast members and a boat driver floating out to sea. For about twenty minutes, we drifted in the darkness. It was oddly peaceful. A little cold, but peaceful. We huddled together for warmth and waited. Eventually, a new dinghy pulled up. Now we had to get from one dinghy to the other in pitch-darkness. Our two boat drivers were trying to hold the dinghies together, but they were bobbing up and down in the water, so this was rather difficult. We had to throw our legs over the side and do an awkward straddle from one rubber boat to the other. My legs are really short, so I did a very ungraceful flop/roll into the other dinghy. It wasn't pretty, but we all managed to get to safety.

So, guys, next time you watch "Booze Cruise" and you see Jim and Pam stare longingly into each other's eyes for twenty-seven seconds, think of Rainn, Phyllis, Brian, and me huddled together on that tiny dinghy, staring longingly at shore.

Jenna

The sun was coming up when we finally finished our shoot and heard "That's a wrap!" on "Booze Cruise." This episode was a huge turning point in so many ways . . . for the show, for my BFF, for my character, and for me personally. It had been almost ten years since I'd moved to Los Angeles to be an actor. As we sailed back to shore, the rising sun casting a warm glow over the water, I remembered all those evenings from my childhood, watching *Cheers* on Must See TV with my family, dreaming about one day moving to Los Angeles to take my shot. And now, in just a few weeks, I would be on Must See TV. I had to pinch myself. It wasn't until I saw Angela at breakfast the next morning that I got the full lowdown on the dinghy incident. But the whole shoot still felt like a big win. We celebrated by snapping a final picture and having brunch in the lobby before heading home, wondering where this adventure would take us next.

Angela

Tired but still happy from our successful shoot and our fun brunch, I started my drive home. Once I pulled out of the hotel, there were just three intersections, and then I would be on the freeway. It felt like a metaphor. Goodbye to my struggling actress days, goodbye to that little dinghy, and hello . . . to a huge new chapter of my life. The Cranberries song "Dreams" was playing on the radio of my twelve-year-old Chevy Blazer. I was singing at the top of my lungs with the windows down. "Oh, my life, it's changing every day . . ." And then my engine made a sputtering noise, and my car started jumping and came to an abrupt halt. My Blazer died in the middle of the intersection. A few nice strangers helped me push it to the side of the road, and I called AAA. The rest of my journey home was in the front of the AAA tow truck with my Blazer on a flatbed trailer behind us. Normally this would have completely stressed me out, but that day, I knew I'd be okay. A few weeks later I bought a Honda and started a new episode on *The Office* as a series regular!

4

behind the
scenes

We've shared stories of what life was like on set while filming *The Office*. But to fully understand the experience of working on Saticoy Drive in Panorama City, California, you've got to leave the bullpen and head to the parking lot, the home of our hair, makeup, wardrobe, and catering. Some of our most intimate and meaningful moments involved the incredible people who worked as our off-set crew. Join us as we take a deeper look at how the sausage was made (or the feet were grilled) at Dunder Mifflin.

HAIR TODAY, GONE TOMORROW

Angela

Our first stop in the morning every day was hair and makeup. Our hair and makeup teams were housed in one big trailer in our parking lot. Even though we usually started before the sun had come up, there was always music playing and smiles beaming as we entered that trailer. Some of my happiest times were in there, all of us singing at the top of our lungs and laughing. The hair and makeup trailer felt like a little family within our bigger set family. Maybe it had to do with seeing people that early in the morning. I used to love watching the guys in the cast roll in with their hair all messy—bedhead is the great equalizer. John would come in with coffee in hand, and our makeup artist Laverne Caracuzzi would offer him a hot towel and razor. Hairdresser Debbie Pierce would heat up her teeny-tiny flat iron to smooth out "Dwight's" bangs. Production assistants would come in and out with containers of hot breakfast for the actors to eat while they were in "the works." When my daughter was a toddler, she loved coming into the hair and makeup trailer. I think the festive music, fancy-looking brushes, and makeup bottles were magical to her. One time she was sitting in my lap as my makeup artist Kenneth Paul (or K.P. as we called him) said something about my

forehead being a little shiny as he powdered it. Well, that stuck in her mind. She thought "shine" was a makeup term. From then on whenever she came into the makeup trailer, she would ask the makeup artists if they could give her a little "shine." So they'd fake-powder her face and apply a little bit of lip balm, making her feel like she was the fanciest of fancies. The hair and makeup trailer was also a great spot to get a sneak peek at upcoming story lines. I remember walking in one day and seeing five red wigs on stands that had been cut to look exactly like Kate Flannery's hair. I had to know what was in store! "What's this all about?" The head of our hair department, Kim Ferry, told me very matter-of-factly, "Oh, in the next episode Meredith's hair catches on fire." There was also the time I looked over and found B. J. Novak had become blond.

Now, a lot of people assume that hair and makeup trailers are a hotbed of gossip. I'm here to tell you, they *are*. It's like everyone loses their edit button when they walk through the door. We heard about everyone's dating life, relationship squabbles, and odd bodily functions. One day the trailer conversation might sound like a dermatologist appointment. "I have a zit on the end of my nose, and it hurts! Help! And while you're at it, can you pluck that wiry hair in the middle of my forehead?!" The next day it might switch to a therapy session. But the beauty of the hair and makeup trailer is that it is also a vault. From a nasty toenail fungus to a recounting of an awkward date . . . what's discussed in hair and makeup stays in hair and makeup.

Jenna

Back then, I was not a morning person. I thought 9 A.M. was "waking up early." Having to be at work before six in the morning was a shock to my system. Steve Carell, on the other hand, requested early call times. He had two young kids and would say, "I'm up anyway. I'd rather get started early and get home for family dinner." Later, when I had kids of my own, this would make sense to me. But at this time in my life, I was child-free, eating dinner at 9 P.M. and watching movies until after midnight. Setting my alarm for 5 A.M. was brutal. But I loved the hair and makeup trailer. Being in that trailer first thing in the morning was joyous. I started in Kim Ferry's hair chair, her mirror always displaying the latest photos of her two boys. She kept my hair clips in a little dish labeled JENNA'S DISH, which always made me smile. I do love little dishes.

Kim didn't mind that I was a grumpy morning person. She'd spritz my hair and get to scrunching, transforming me into Pam while I sipped coffee trying to wake up. There wasn't a lot of wiggle room when it came to our characters' hair and makeup. It was designed to be rather unspectacular, as if we'd done it ourselves in about fifteen minutes at home. Kim and I loved whenever we got to do something

outside of Pam's normal hairstyle. "Valentine's Day": sparkly headband! "Casino Night": loose curls! Wedding hair! Updo! You've never seen two women so excited to warm up a flat iron. When I moved to Laverne's makeup chair, Angela would take my place in Kim's hair chair, and we'd be side by side, ready for a download. This was my favorite part of the morning. As Angela said, we shared a lot about our lives in that trailer. There was a special intimacy to the space.

When I came back to work after having my son, just five weeks after he had been born via C-section, I was not in a good place emotionally. I didn't want to leave him. I was nursing. I was swollen. I was in pain. But the show was not on hiatus, and in our business, there is no paid maternity leave. So every episode I missed was a missed paycheck. I needed to go back to work.

Luckily, my first week back was an easy one. I had only a few scenes to shoot. Still, I pulled into the parking lot nervous to put my postpartum self on display. I felt so vulnerable. I had shared my fears with Angela, of course, and she told me, "Don't worry, lady, I'll be there. We will get through it together." When I stepped into the hair and makeup trailer that first morning, the ladies and Kenneth Paul all cheered. They gave me hugs. They told me I looked beautiful. They surrounded me with a love and support I can't even properly put into words. Angela had told that group I needed them. When I left the trailer, I felt a new energy and confidence.

The value of a good hair and makeup team is so much more than the practical work they do. The tone set by these two departments is crucial to the vibe on a production. The feeling in that space informs the rest of the day. Our team was incredible. We started each day with love and singing and a little gossip—the best way to start any workday, if you ask me.

FIT ME BABY ONE MORE TIME

Angela

Imagine walking into a store that has racks of clothing, in only your size, chosen just for you. That's what it was like walking into the *Office* wardrobe trailer for a fitting. Except, in my case, they were racks of clothing for Angela Martin. Angela Martin's wardrobe consisted of a lot of gray, a lot of poufy blouses with multiple tiny buttons, and a lot of sweater vests. Our original costume designer, Carey Bennett, would add the most wonderful details to my wardrobe. For example, she replaced original sweater buttons with cat head buttons. We felt like this was something Angela Martin would do.

I am on the petite side, and I told Carey I bought a lot of my clothing in the kids' section at Target. (I mean, that "colonial doll clothes/ GapKids" talking head from the "Women's Appreciation" episode wasn't far off!) Carey began looking for clothes for me at children's stores but had a hard time finding anything resembling "office" attire. She decided to try vintage clothing stores because clothes from years ago ran smaller, and that is where many of my classic Angela looks were born. Normally every outfit they create for an actor has a "double," a second identical version of every costume in case of a mishap . . . spilled coffee down a blouse, ketchup stain at lunch. Because many of my outfits were one-of-a-kind vintage pieces, they did not have doubles, so Carey asked me if I could wear a bib at lunch. I would take four paper

73

towels and tuck them into every nook of my collar. I looked like a Pilgrim in an elementary school play as I ate. After a while I gave up on my paper towel bib and just completely changed clothes to eat. Of all the vintage pieces I got to wear as Angela Martin, my favorite was the blue suit with the pillbox hat I wore to Phyllis's wedding. I felt like Jackie O!

Jenna

I don't like shopping. I especially hate trying on clothes. (This is clearly the chapter where I reveal my inner grump. But if I can't be candid in my own book, where can I be?) Luckily, Angela and I have this in common. We can get lost in the gift wrap section of Target for hours, but we don't care much about the latest trends in clothing unless they are drawstring related. My mom and sister, on the other hand, love to shop. They've been known to spend seven hours at the Osage Beach outlets in Lake Ozark, Missouri, gathering bags of bargains. I'm done after two stores. I'd spend those summertime outlet runs as a kid people-watching or reading a book on a bench. Sometimes I'd practice my accents and see if I could convince people I was an exchange student visiting from Kent, England. I got pretty good at it. By high school, I was attending an all-girls Catholic school that required a daily uniform. This meant an end to the back-to-school trips to the mall! I was overjoyed! All I needed was the required plaid skirt and a button-down shirt in four colors.

While some actors may have been bored by Pam's drab wardrobe, I was absolutely fine with her uniform of interchangeable pencil skirts and cardigans. I basically did one big wardrobe fitting at the beginning of each season, and I was set for the year. All that said, I remember the first time I had a fitting for Pam to wear jeans. It was Season 2, for the episode "E-Mail Surveillance," when Jim has a barbeque at his house. I had just done a movie where I'd been fitted in designer jeans by 7 for All Mankind. My butt looked so good in them that I told our costume designer Carey we should get some for our fitting. Carey told me quite flatly, "Pam can't afford $150 jeans. I went to Old Navy. These are cute, try them." From the beginning, Carey insisted we all dress according to our

characters' paychecks. She was dedicated to shopping at the places our characters would actually shop. She bought most of Pam's office attire from Ann Taylor Factory stores, Meredith's wardrobe from Liz Claiborne, and Phyllis's matching sets came mostly from Dress Barn. Carey's go-to places for the men: Mervyn's and JCPenney.

While Pam's wardrobe was routine, Dwight's was anything but. In later seasons, our costume designer Alysia Raycraft would often be tasked with building elaborate costumes from scratch, including Belsnickel, the Hay King, and Recyclops, to name a few.

You could often find Alysia sketching in her design book, her walls filled with fabric swatches and a half-dressed mannequin next to her desk. Alysia is an amazing designer, and I remember discussing the idea of having her build Pam a wedding dress from scratch. Oh, we were so tempted!! (Angela and I are on the same page here as well—we don't love fussing with everyday fashion, but we do love a good gown!) In the end, Alysia found a beautiful A-line dress at David's Bridal, and we stayed with the show's original vision of having characters wear what they could realistically afford.

Alysia told me the producers and director had specifically requested Pam wear a veil. But when we tried it, I didn't love it. I thought I looked better with my hair down and without the veil. Alysia photographed me in the dress both with and without a veil. In hopes of influencing the decision, I only smiled in the photos without the veil. (It's a little trick I'd learned. Always smile in the photos of the outfits you really like. When they review all the photos, they are naturally drawn to the ones where you look happy!) Alysia even drew little hearts around the "no veil" photo. What we didn't know at the time was that the veil was an important plot point. It rips, Pam cries, Jim cuts his tie, and they run off to the falls to be married. In the end, I loved Pam's wedding look. And when we wrapped the episode there was a little surprise from Alysia in my trailer. No, it wasn't the veil. It was Pam's wedding necklace with a sweet note saying I should keep it. I still have it today. Thank you, Alysia!

6004/6005
♂ WOMEN ♡

Pam ♚

LET'S EAT

Jenna

I LOVE TO EAT! I have absolutely nothing grouchy to say about food. And even though Angela has the stomach size of a little bird and is notorious for only eating half of everything . . . half a banana, half a cheese stick, half a donut . . . she also loves food. If you love food as much as we do, the set of *The Office* was like heaven. On the set of *The Office*, the food was an art form in itself.

Just backstage was a snack shack run by Peter Evangelatos and Vartan Chakirian. Peter and Vartan reminded me of Jack Lemmon and Walter Matthau in *The Odd Couple*. They fought all the time, but you knew they loved each other. For years, Peter had been John Travolta's personal craft service man on all his films. We would beg him to tell us stories about John Travolta, but Peter would just smile and shake his head—we never got anything out of him but kindness. Vartan was just as much of a teddy bear as Peter. He had a deep scratchy voice and a big hearty laugh. Their snack shack was loaded down with everything: trail mix, cereals, granola bars, fruit, chips, nuts, plus a fridge filled with yogurt, veggies, stuff to make sandwiches, and every type of milk you could imagine (soy, almond, whole, skim, vanilla . . . like, just so many milks). They were always setting out new treats. In the mornings they put out pastries and donuts (just ask Angela), and in the afternoons you might find a home-baked muffin, bread, or cookies. They always had cakes for cast and crew birthdays and life milestones.

But the best part of the day was "hot snack." Every morning around 10:30 A.M., Peter and Vartan set out a special hot snack for the cast and crew. The production staff always tried to plan our days so that we could all take a break at

77

this time. Kelly Cantley or Rusty Mahmood, our assistant directors, would announce, "HOT SNACK is here! HOT SNACK!" We would pounce. Since we all got to the set so early, by 10:30 A.M. we had quite the appetite. A "hot snack" might be hot dogs, shrimp scampi, chicken fried rice, pork dumplings, pigs in a blanket with dipping sauce, turkey chili, or the cast favorite albondigas soup. This nourishing soup is made with meatballs and veggies, and it was an especially comforting meal as it warmed our hands and bellies on our very cold set. Even though the writers and editors had their own snacks over in their building, they always came over for hot snack and social time with us. I'm sure we were the main draw.

Angela

Sounds amazing, right? That's not all. We were also provided a full breakfast and lunch each day by Sergio Giacoman and his team from Big Time Catering. In the very early hours of the morning, at two A.M., Sergio, Alan Mork, and their crew would arrive to set up the food truck. Alan would joke that he was like Michael Scott. He would wake up and immediately start cooking bacon. Leslie and Phyllis were usually the first to arrive, and their orders would go in at 4:45 A.M. On average, between the cast and crew, Big Time Catering fed 150 people breakfast and lunch. If you had a particular favorite, Sergio would make it for you and then add it to the menu. For example, Rashida Jones made up a breakfast that really caught on: black beans, turkey bacon, avocado, egg whites, with two corn tortillas on the side and Sergio's special salsa. (Sergio used to make his own salsa, and it is the all-time best salsa I have ever eaten.) It was so popular it became a permanent option on the breakfast menu and was aptly named the Rashida. A few of the other specials that made the menu were the Creed (goat cheese, spinach, onions, and egg whites) and the Johnny K (tomatoes, broccoli, a little bit of cheese, and egg whites). I like portions half-sized, because I fill up fast. I would ask for only half of a breakfast burrito. I couldn't eat the whole thing, and I didn't want it to go to waste. Sergio loved this idea—you could order any item from him "Angela size" and receive a smaller portion. I once overheard a crew member order "the Rashida, Angela size," and it made my day!

Lunch was usually at 1 P.M., and it featured a Vegas casino–worthy buffet with every food category you can imagine. There were always meat, fish, and vegetable choices, a salad bar and dessert bar, plus a special of the day. Steve Carell couldn't stay away from the hot pan of chocolate chip cookie bars. They were kept in a chafing dish to keep them warm, and my goodness, they were delicious. On the last day of each season, Sergio and his crew would make surf and turf, treating us to lobster, steak, and a potato bar with all the fixings. After finishing twenty-plus episodes, that day always felt like a real celebration.

When my parents visited from Texas, they came to the set for a table read and lunch. I was so excited to have them there, and the whole cast popped by to say hello. After they had flown home, I asked my sister what my parents said about their time on set and meeting the actors. She said all Dad talked about was the food. "You would not believe how they eat!" was my father's exact quote. That was his takeaway from spending an afternoon on a hit television show: the lunch buffet.

Jenna

The cast and crew ate together at long cafeteria-style tables. We only got a thirty-minute break for lunch, so we would often scoop up a feast from the buffet, find a seat, and eat quickly. While I enjoyed eating with everyone, most days Angela and I would sneak away for a ladies' lunch in my trailer. I had two TV trays that I'd bought at Bed Bath & Beyond specifically for our lunches, which we set up in front of my couch. Sometimes we spent our thirty minutes discussing whether one of us should get bangs. Or "Does taking a walk count as a workout if you stop for a scone along the way?" Big discussion. Angela thinks it counts. I said no. My favorite were the conversations that started with one of us saying, "Lady, can I be snarky for a second?" You knew something good was coming!

Before meeting Angela, I didn't really have a close friend in Los Angeles. I had friends, but this was different. I felt so safe with Angela. We could be silly, *and* we could be serious. When I was cast on *The Office*, all my professional dreams started coming true. But other parts of my life were not where I'd hoped they would be. I started confiding in Angela during those lunches. She told me she could relate to how I felt. Her love and acceptance as I shared the parts of me that felt weak or insecure and her eagerness to help me process everything meant the world to me. Sometimes that's all you need to help you move forward: You need the right person to listen. Angela became, and still is, that person for me. When I share with her, I see things more clearly. And because she is so kind to me, I'm more kind to myself.

Now listen—I should say, these deep heart-to-hearts were not all we did at lunch. Sometimes we'd pop over to John Krasinski's trailer, where all the guys would congregate to play *Madden NFL*. Or we'd grab the basketball and shoot hoops. But more than anything, those lunches cemented our bond.

Angela

One of the things I miss the most about filming *The Office* is my standing lunch date with Jenna. You know how your iPhone will give you a weekly screen report of how many hours and minutes you have spent looking at your phone? I have always wondered what my BFF screen report would have been during our time on the show. How much time did we spend each week chatting, texting, and just staying in touch? We normally started talking at 5 A.M. in hair and makeup, then we would talk between scenes in the morning, then we would have lunch together and REALLY dive in, then we would talk in between scenes in the afternoon, then we would call each other on our car ride home and talk the whole way until we parked our cars and had to walk inside our houses. One time we were gabbing away on set, and Rainn looked up and exclaimed, "What *more* do you have to talk about?!" We both burst out laughing. Apparently, A LOT more.

But as Jenna said, our true heart-to-hearts started in her trailer at lunch. There on Jenna's brown velour couch, I poured my heart out. There were many tears and many laughs shared in that trailer. I have said before that Jenna is my life anchor. Nothing really makes sense to me until I can bounce it off her. Jenna is the type of person that has an endless patience for whatever is bugging you. I could talk to her for months about how I wanted to put a second fridge in my garage, and whether or not I would *really* use it. And most importantly, she accepts me where I am. Sometimes I am at my best, and other times I am just not where I want to be. But she is steadfast. She is my constant, an unwavering source of support no matter what. I had never had that kind of unconditional acceptance in a friendship before. And I guess, Rainn (if you are reading this), when you finally find a friend like that . . . you have a lot to talk about!

Jenna

Angela and I weren't the only ones creating true friendships on *The Office*. Looking back, so many close relationships were made. Forged in early hours in hair and makeup, over warm cups of soup on chilly days, and countless hours joking around on set. You can see why we liked to work there, because that pretty much sums up what life was like behind the scenes at Dunder Mifflin, food and talking. Oh, and donuts. Lots of donuts. Angela size.

5

holidays

Ain't no party like a Scranton party, 'cause a Scranton party don't stop! It's time to call the Party Planning Committee and celebrate Dunder Mifflin style. Buckle in for lots of costumes, lots of decorations, and lots of folks who love a holiday.

If you need proof that we are two gals who love a holiday, I'd like to present these photos from our first Halloween together as evidence.

It was Halloween 2006, *The Office* was in its second season, and Angela had just moved into her first home. She invited me over to celebrate. The real estate agent told her the neighborhood was great for trick-or-treaters, so she bought a GIANT orange tub and filled it to the top with candy. (I'm actually glad we have this photo, because otherwise I'm not sure you'd understand how large it really was.) When I arrived, I gave her some cupcakes I'd decorated to look like scary eyeballs, and she presented me an adorable Halloween headband featuring a tiny witch hat that she'd found in the seasonal aisle at Target, just like the one she was wearing. In addition, she had hung a Halloween wreath covered with flying bats on her front door. This woman was my kindred spirit. We cranked up some spooky music and prepared for a throng of trick-or-treaters. And then . . . no one came. I mean, *maybe* the doorbell rang six times. So we switched gears, put on a scary movie, and ate the candy and cupcakes ourselves.

Angela

Not convinced? Need more evidence that we love a holiday? This is how Jenna comes dressed for a Christmas party.

I mean look at her! This is my kinda gal! You name the holiday, and Jenna will show up with a T-shirt/earring combination to commemorate it. Her Fourth of July tank top with American flag earrings is a must-see. If Jenna's holiday superpower is her festive attire, mine is crappy crafting. I mean I am really *not* good at crafting, but I really love it, especially for holidays. I have told Jenna that I want to launch a television show called *Crappy Crafting with Kinsey* on which I drink rosé and create holiday decorations using my elementary-level skill set. A few years ago, I started making holiday wreaths with my kids. I also make custom birthday wreaths, because why not? Sometimes I do a collage of the things I know the birthday person loves. The birthday wreath I made Jenna included miniature trinkets of bread, books, her love of family, travel, and eating one egg a day. They are random, kitschy, and straight from my heart.

HALLOWEEN

Jenna

Luckily for us, *The Office* loved a holiday too! Both on set and off. Halloween was a very special, highly anticipated occasion on our set. When it was time to shoot the Halloween episode, there was a buzz across all departments—wardrobe, hair, makeup, set dressing. Halloween was everyone's chance to break out!

Angela

We *loved* the Halloween episodes. Our set dressers decorated every inch of the office bullpen. It was so fun to walk onto the set those weeks and see the place transformed. The props department put candy corn in the little dish on Pam's desk, and every year Jenna ate so much of it she got sick. Each year I would tell her, "Jenna, pace yourself." But it never helped. She would have a stomachache by 2 P.M. the first day of filming. And while the decorations were great, the costumes were my favorite. We had an accounting department tradition of taking a group photo every year while wearing our costumes, and they are some of my favorite photos of the three of us. However, these episodes brought on their own type of hardship. The giggles. It was really difficult not to laugh on a normal day of filming, but try delivering lines to Kevin dressed as Charlie Brown or to Oscar while he is pretending to type on a keyboard with dinosaur hands.

Getting through scenes without breaking in ridiculous costumes was tough, but probably the toughest part of filming Halloween episodes was the weather. We usually filmed them in August. That is triple-digit weather in Southern California. One afternoon during Halloween week, Jenna and Rainn were about to walk to set, and I snapped a photo of them. Rainn had only been outside for a few minutes and was already starting to sweat his makeup off.

Jenna

Each year we were so excited to see what our characters would be for Halloween. Fans will sometimes ask if we had any say in how our characters dressed for these episodes. The simple answer is no. Most of our costumes were plot-related, such as the year Kevin, Dwight, and Creed all dress as the Joker, or when Jim dresses up as Popeye with Cece as Swee'Pea and Pam as Olive Oyl, or when Dwight is Kerrigan from *StarCraft*.

Angela

There was one person in the cast who had some influence over her Halloween costume: Mindy Kaling. Since Mindy was also on the writing staff, she got to be part of pitching costume ideas. Mindy loved putting together her Halloween wardrobe. I personally feel like she had some of the best costumes each year. But let's be honest, Mindy is a style icon. She dresses better than any of us off-camera as well.

Jenna

One of my personal favorite episodes of *The Office* also happens to be our very first Halloween episode. It aired during Season 2 and was called, appropriately, "Halloween." It was written by Greg Daniels and directed by one of our favorite directors, Paul Feig. We loved Paul. He is a compassionate and approachable type of guy and quick to laugh. He also knows how to mix almost any cocktail. You might recognize his name, as he has directed some hugely popular films, like *Bridesmaids*, *Ghostbusters* (2016), and *Last Christmas*. During his time on *The*

Office, Paul directed fourteen episodes, including "Dinner Party" and Steve's final episode, "Goodbye, Michael," and also served as one of our executive producers for all of Season 5. Before working on *The Office*, Paul had created the critically acclaimed single-camera comedy series *Freaks and Geeks*, which relied heavily on the same cringey, grounded comedy we were doing on *The Office*. Paul was instrumental in helping us find our way in those early seasons of the show.

One of my favorite things about Paul is that he wears a suit and tie to work every day. This is unusual. Most directors and crew members dress in jeans or cargo pants. Maybe they wear a blazer, but never a tie! Paul told us his mom bought him his first three-piece suit when he was eight years old; he loved it so much he wore it constantly, and so began his passion for suits. He even wore a suit while performing stand-up comedy in his twenties. Now he wears them every single day. He has a variety of vintage suits with vests and pocket squares and the coolest tie collection in the world. As a tribute to Paul, when he was directing, our crew would all wear ties on Fridays. They called it Paul Feig Day. It was so fun!

Angela

The plot of our first Halloween episode is simple: Michael is told that he must fire someone during the month of October due to cutbacks at Dunder Mifflin. In true Michael fashion, he waits until the very last day of the month, i.e., Halloween. Greg Daniels told us that he'd always wanted to examine firing someone from the point of view of the boss, not the employee. He said you always see stories of the people being fired but rarely stories about the person having to do the firing. One of our writers, Larry Wilmore, pitched the idea that the firing should happen on Halloween when everyone is dressed in costumes and excited for an office party. It makes the whole thing all the more uncomfortable to watch.

Jenna

But there was one problem with this plot: To film this episode, Greg would have to fire a cast member. I can't imagine how this must have weighed on him, because Greg is such a kindhearted human being. He didn't want to fire any of the core cast, even though this was before "Booze Cruise" when most of the supporting characters were still only under weekly contracts. He also didn't want to hire someone new, throw them into the mix, and then cut them. He said it felt like cheating and wouldn't do justice to the plot. He had to fire someone we'd seen on the show already.

Angela

We had two regular background actors at that time: Creed Bratton and Devon Abner. Both had appeared in the mix of some conference room scenes or crossing behind someone as they did a talking head, but neither had spoken any lines. But since they'd been established in the world of *The Office*, they were employees of Dunder Mifflin. This meant they were up for firing.

So now Greg was faced with the dilemma . . . which one to fire. Greg and Michael had the same decision to make. Greg took both actors aside and found out that Devon was about to leave and do an off-Broadway play in New York. This made Greg's decision easier. Devon's character would be fired, and Creed would go from being a nonspeaking background actor on our show to having a five-page scene with Steve Carell! The scene was such a hit with fans, they lit up the internet message boards, and the writers began to write more for Creed. Creed eventually became a series regular. All because Greg needed someone to fire.

In addition to this being the episode that cemented Creed's place in the *Office* family, it was also the first time, since our pilot, that the creators of the original British version of *The Office*, Stephen Merchant and Ricky Gervais, visited our set. They spent almost a full day with us that week. We were all geeking out, and of course, I asked for a photo with them. I love this photo. I'm the only person dressed in a costume (you can only sort-of see John's three-hole punches in this shot). When I look at this photo, I like to imagine that I was doing a play about a cat, and this is a backstage pic taken when my close friends, including Ricky Gervais and Stephen Merchant, came to the theater to see me perform.

Angela

We were all nervous about this visit. I mean, Ricky and Stephen are the comedy geniuses who had created the BBC version of *The Office*. They were why we all had a job. I'll never forget meeting them for the first time. I was walking through the lunch area, and I saw Ricky and Stephen finishing their meals. Our producers introduced me to them and then said, "Ricky's actually going back to the video monitors now, because he's going to watch everything we are filming from lunch on to the end of the day. Angela, your talking head is first up." I think I vomited a little in my mouth before forcing a smile and saying, "Oh, fantastic!" Ricky smiled back and answered, "Don't worry, I don't *tsk* too loudly," and he waved his finger back and forth at me. I nervous laughed while he cackled and patted me on the shoulder. I felt like I had passed some type of comedy club initiation. Years later, I found out we share the same birthday, and we had a "Twitter moment." I am pretty sure this means we're best friends now.

Angela Kinsey ✔ @AngelaKinsey · Jun 25, 2013   ···
Happy Birthday to my @theofficenbc birthday twin @rickygervais!Hope you have a great day Ricky!Oh & thanks for giving me a job for 9 years!

💬 1   ↺ 23   ♡ 82   ↑

Ricky Gervais ✔ @rickygervais · Jun 25, 2013   ···
"@AngelaKinsey: Happy Birthday to my birthday twin @rickygervais! & thanks for giving me a job for 9 years!"

Happy Birthday to you too :)

💬 31   ↺ 16   ♡ 60   ↑

Jenna

For as much fun as we had shooting the Halloween episodes, we made sure that the actual holiday was just as much fun, if not more so. Every year, during the actual Halloween week, our crew would dress up, and we'd have a costume parade during lunch. One year, the crew got together and dressed as our characters from the show. That was hilarious. They got all the details just right.

When my son was one year old, I thought it would be cute to dress him as a Wimbledon tennis player for Halloween. My husband, Lee, is a huge tennis fan. We had gone to Wimbledon when we were engaged, and in a gift shop we found a tiny white Wimbledon shirt for toddlers. I snatched it up and saved it. Since the players wear all white, it was an easy costume to assemble. I bought white shorts, little white shoes, and a hat. When Phil Shea, the head of the props department, heard me talking with Angela about Weston's costume, he arranged for a tiny, perfectly proportioned tennis racket and bag to be made. I'm not talking a plastic toy racket—I mean an actual metal tennis racket, just miniature. It was literally the cutest thing on the planet. And it made the outfit. Even though Weston could not officially compete in the crew awards, we marched in the parade just to show off Phil's work.

Angela

Halloween was a particularly fun week for kids on set. Many of our crew members would bring their families by for visits during Halloween week. My daughter, Isabel, was always so excited to see everyone's costume. Although sometimes when she saw Mommy in costume it would take her a moment to adjust. She loved me as a penguin, but her least favorite Angela Martin costume was Nancy Reagan. She didn't understand why her mom suddenly had short brown hair. Isabel would point at the wig and say, "Mama, no!" I didn't mind the wig. I thought it was kind of fun. But I was not a fan of the very hot, very itchy suit. So at lunch I would walk around as half Nancy/half Angela to cool off.

Jenna

Our workdays were long on *The Office*. We averaged about twelve hours a day, usually something like 6 A.M. to 6 P.M. But that was nothing compared to most television shows. I know of productions that often work until "Fraturday" . . . a nickname for working until 2 or 3 A.M. every Friday night. Once in a while, we'd go as late as 7:30 P.M., or have a night shoot, but not often. And never on Halloween. On Halloween, we always finished early. Looking back I'm not sure if this was good luck or great planning. But I don't remember a single Halloween in nine years where we worked late. It was amazing because many members of the cast and crew had families with young children and they could be home in time to celebrate.

Angela

In fact, every year, our camera operator Matt Sohn and his wife, Melissa, would throw a party at their house after work for the entire *Office* group and our families. Unlike me, they lived in a great neighborhood for trick-or-treating. We'd show up at their place for food and crafts with our kids and then canvass the neighborhood for candy. Even cast members without kids were welcome. B. J. Novak made it part of his Halloween tradition every year to help hand out candy at Matt's house. It was that much fun.

Jenna

The Office was very unique. This reality hit me very hard the first year I was working on a new show after *The Office*, *Splitting Up Together*. Halloween was on a Tuesday that year. The Friday before, the producers came to me and said,

"Jenna, we've run late this week. We had to drop a couple of scenes, and the only day we can rent a crane in order to get that missed shot is Tuesday next week. We're going to have to tack it on to the end of the day. You'll probably be done around eight P.M." My kids were three and six at the time. They were in bed before eight o'clock. I had just been told that I would completely miss Halloween.

Missing things is part of being a working parent. I knew that when I started my career. Television hours can be long and unpredictable, and part of being a working actor means turning over your schedule to the needs of the production. But, if I'm being honest, missing moments with my kids was harder on me than I expected. The missed bedtimes and school concerts and leaving before my kids woke up in the mornings and FaceTiming them for dinner was taking a toll. And at that moment, finding out I'd be missing Halloween just crushed me. I called Angela crying. I knew my bestie would understand how my mom heart was breaking.

Angela

Missing any special occasion with your kids is very hard. As working parents, this is something we all have to deal with at some point, but it is never easy. I could hear the sadness in Jenna's voice, and it broke my heart. I shared with my kids that Jenna might have to miss Halloween with her family, and they felt just like I did. "Noooo! That can't happen!" they all exclaimed. I had an idea of how we could help, and they were eager to pitch in to make my plan happen.

Jenna

On Sunday morning, two days before Halloween, my phone rang. It was Angela. "What are you doing tonight at five o'clock?" "Nothing," I replied. "Well, I know what you're doing. Dress your kids up in their costumes, and get to my house. I've talked to a couple of neighbors on my street, and I bought Halloween candy for them to give to your kids. We're going trick-or-treating. You will not miss Halloween on my watch." I started sobbing, and then I did what I was told. Angela was not messing around. I dressed up my kids in their costumes and drove to her neighborhood at 5 P.M. Angela and her family were waiting for us. We walked around collecting candy from her sweet neighbors, and then we went back to

her house and roasted s'mores in the backyard. It was perfect. I know it all might sound silly in the grand scheme of things that are important in life. But Angela knew that Halloween with my three- and six-year-old was significant to me. That my mom heart needed it. Along with her community of neighbors, she created a special memory for us. One that we'll never forget. I've shared so many Halloweens with her, but that one . . . that one is the most special of all.

Angela

Looking at the pictures of that evening brings happy tears to my eyes. Tears for my best friend, who is such an amazing mom and values family over everything, tears because my children were so excited to help, and tears for the kindness of my neighbors who instantly said yes to make it all happen.

CHRISTMAS

Jenna

If you thought Halloween was big at Dunder Mifflin, wait until we tell you about Christmas. Every inch of our set would be covered with Christmas decorations, and I mean every inch—get ready for holiday garland around your computer screen and no less than two dozen poinsettia! Angela and I would joke about where Dunder Mifflin got its budget for holiday celebrations. Did Michael pay out of pocket? Because surely corporate would never allocate so much funding for decorations. And just like Halloween, we loved seeing everyone dressed up in holiday attire while shooting these episodes.

Angela

While all the *Office* Christmas episodes are incredible, the first one, "Christmas Party," inspired some amazing off-camera memories and traditions. This episode was directed by Charles McDougall. I'm certain I speak for all the actors when I say Charles will always hold a special place in our hearts. He directed eight episodes of *The Office*, and "Christmas Party" was his first. Imagine meeting a quiet British man in a gray sport coat, soft-spoken and serious about his work. Then imagine that same man screaming "ACTION!" at the top of his lungs as if he were rolling on the Roman chariot race in *Ben-Hur* rather than on a few people pretending to do office work. That was Charles. This duality was so charming, and it cracked us up.

Written by Mike Schur, this episode had it all. A tree that was too big, a Secret Santa gift exchange that turned into a cruel Yankee Swap, a teapot, a poster of Babies Playing Jazz, a sad oven mitt, and a very pissed-off Angela Martin. Mike Schur told me once that he loved seeing my character trying to keep it together, getting more and more stressed out until she finally unraveled. Well, this episode delivered that in spades for Angela. I actually got a headache from all of the frowning and glaring I had to do in that episode. Despite the throbbing head, this episode was some of the most fun I've ever had on set. We broke into laughter, A LOT, especially during the Yankee Swap gift exchange. Charles McDougall had to keep reminding me that I *had* to be angry. He would start off each take with, "Okay! Everyone happy, Angela pissed, and . . . ACTION!"

It is during this first Christmas episode that Michael famously turns the Secret Santa gift exchange into a Yankee Swap. All the gifts that were purchased (or made) with a certain person in mind are suddenly shuffled around, and everyone tries to get their hands on the iPod Michael bought for Ryan. Feelings get hurt; people get angry. Phyllis is especially gutted when Michael rejects, and then continues to insult, the oven mitt she knitted for him.

I remember it was a challenging shoot day for Phyllis. Most of the cast was cracking up and goofing around between takes. But, in order to stay in character, Phyllis had to go off to the side by herself. She basically spent the entire day crying, alone. (When the scene was finally over, I gave her a big hug.) But even Phyllis had to laugh when we first saw Angela Martin's gift from Toby— the poster of two babies playing brass instruments. We had read about this moment in the script, but none of

us were truly prepared for what it would look like in real life. It took us about ten minutes to pull ourselves together and continue shooting. One of my personal favorite moments was when we decided to see if Angela could fit inside one of the Yankee Swap gift bags. She could!

Angela

Another special aspect of this episode was the snow. The crew hired a company called . . . get this . . . Snow Business (lol) . . . to turn Dunder Mifflin's parking lot into a winter wonderland. We never get snow in Los Angeles, so even fake snow felt magical. Some fun facts about fake snow: First, the snow on the ground is basically real snow. Snow Business brought in a machine that looked like a combination of a wood chipper and something you might see Wile E. Coyote try to build to catch the Road Runner. That machine freezes water into little particles and blows it out a giant tube, in this case all over the Dunder Mifflin parking lot. The snow that falls from the "sky" (or in our case, from a man on the roof) is not real. You get three choices for the falling snow: cornstarch, plastic, or soap. Greg watched a demonstration of all three and picked soap, as he thought it looked the most realistic. As my character was having a screaming meltdown in the parking lot, some of it fell into my mouth, and I can confirm: They definitely used soap.

Jenna

The next night the entire cast had to shoot a very simple scene of us all walking to our cars through the snowy parking lot. It was footage without any dialogue that would play underneath a Michael talking head. It meant staying late, waiting for nightfall. We were punchy and wired, like a bunch of kids up past their bedtime. I remember walking into the parking lot that night, cars covered in "snow," the moon high in the sky. It was enchanted. After we shot the scene a couple of times, Charles said, "One more, and then I think we've got it. ACTION!" Near the end of that last take, one of the guys (probably John) picked up some snow and flung it at another one (probably Brian). And then it was on. We all started picking up snow and had a huge impromptu snowball fight. The cameras kept rolling and captured it all. I love when I watch that scene now, because it's one of the moments when our real selves blurred with our characters. We were coworkers, who loved one another, having a snowball fight after work. We just happened to also be making a television show in the process.

Angela

We had a lot of fun pretending to celebrate Christmas at Dunder Mifflin, but we also had a lot of fun *actually* celebrating the holiday. As with Halloween, we would shoot these holiday episodes long before Christmas, so when December finally came around, it was like we got a second celebration. From the moment you entered our soundstage, you were greeted with holiday cheer. I remember one year the hair and makeup department had a Christmas tree by their touch-up tables backstage, and right around the corner, our sound department had a tree as well. Peter and Vartan at craft services would decorate the snack table, and on our last week of filming before our winter break, the crew would all dress in holiday garb.

There was a lot of gift-giving too. The cast would give the crew gifts, and the producers gave out gifts in green Dunder Mifflin holiday bags. One of my favorites was a cozy blue robe that I still wear to this day, even though my dog gnawed a hole in the right sleeve. As a cast, we gave one another gifts as well. Jenna made us all Christmas ornaments—

mine still hang on my tree each year—and I made everyone T-shirts inspired by Dwight quoting Billy Zane from *Titanic*. Kate gave us candles, and there were bottles of wine, fruit baskets, sweet treats, and handwritten cards. Everyone was so thoughtful.

Jenna

I still exchange holiday cards with many of our cast and crew, and I look forward to decorating my home with their faces every year. As you can see, the cast and crew of *The Office* celebrated nearly a decade of milestones and holidays together.

Creating your own holiday traditions when you live far away from your family of origin is a mighty task. My mom was one of five siblings. My dad has one brother. During my childhood, everyone lived in St. Louis, including my grandparents and great-grandparents. Holidays were filled with a series of visits to great-aunts and grandparents and involved dozens of cousins and even more gifts. I haven't gone home for Christmas since my own children were born, but if I flew home to surprise everyone, I'd know exactly where to go, at what time, on what day, without even asking. Every year the plans were the same. And I loved it. But once I became a parent, my husband and I wanted to create our own holiday traditions, and we wanted our kids to wake up to Santa in their own house. So while we see lots of family throughout the year, we don't travel for the holidays. Now Christmas is filled with friends who have become our surrogate family. In my

version, Oscar is their crazy uncle and Angela is their loving aunt. Her kids—Isabel, Jack, and Cade—are their cousins. Angela always hosts some sort of holiday potluck, and anyone who needs a family to be with during that time is invited. Because that's how Angela is, you guys. If you need a family, she's there. Her husband, Josh, has usually baked up some delicious sweets, and Creed brings his guitar. Every year it's a little different depending on who attends, but it's always fantastic.

My husband, Lee, and I host an ice-skating party every Christmas Eve. We rent out the local ice rink for two hours. The rink is divided into two parts: one half for skating, the other for hockey. We bring hot chocolate, coffee, and donuts. We invite our kids' school friends and anyone else who needs a tradition at the holidays. Oscar and his family are always there. Angela is there too. It means so much to us that we've created these yearly traditions together. And finally, no Christmas season would be the same without Angela's adults-only Yankee Swap party.

Angela

That's right, our Yankee Swap on the show was so much fun to shoot that I decided to turn it into a real yearly holiday party! It started out small. I decorated my front door with a festive wreath, put out a cheese plate, and invited a handful of friends. But with each passing year, the party grew. Coworkers, friends, family, and my neighbors now all stop by. I keep adding decorations to the house, and folks, we are inching toward Clark Griswold territory. I put up tons of Christmas lights, and there's a huge inflatable polar bear with an igloo and spinning penguins to greet everyone as they come inside. My house can no longer hold the crowd, so I started opening the back doors and the party now spills out into the backyard. There's a taco truck, a huge dessert table (thanks to my husband), a makeshift bar, a fire pit, and we even hand out sparklers at the end of the night. I can't wait to see everyone and what gifts they will bring. On my invitation, I state that regifting tacky items is *encouraged*, and my guests do not disappoint. And if you plan on hosting a Yankee Swap, put Oscar Nuñez at the top of your guest list. He really gets the crowd going, making up chants and taunts. One of his most catchy was, "Give him the hose! Give him the hose!" in regard to a garden hose that was an aggressively traded item. Things have gotten physical. I have had my hand swatted at by my normally shy, soft-spoken neighbor as I stole a Superman apron from him, and then there was the time that Jenna elbowed our friend Amy as she nabbed a coveted fake ponytail that had been traded three times. And I still have the creepy porcelain clown I won the first year I hosted this party. It felt right to keep it.

Jenna

Angela's Yankee Swap parties are legendary. People come ready for fun. I find that practical gifts make the best offerings at the Yankee Swap: small ax, new garden hose, electric bug zapper shaped like a tennis racket . . . we've brought all of these, and people fought hard for them. Angela mentioned the fake ponytail extension was a prized gift one year—I'm proud to say I went home with that one, and then smugly wore it to the party the following year.

Back when we were shooting that first Christmas episode in 2005, I could never have imagined that this group of people would become my real-life holiday family and that I would still be celebrating the holidays with them fifteen years later. Or that I would battle Ed Helms for a miniature Egyptian sarcophagus that Zach Woods brought to Angela's Yankee Swap. But I did. And I won. As soon as the description on the box was read aloud, I knew I had to have it: "The sarcophagus coffin and the mummy are not fixed to each other and so if you remove the mummy, the sarcophagus can function as a keepsake or jewelry box." I have it on my dresser and inside are my snowman earrings—ready and waiting for the next holiday party.

6

the women of dunder mifflin

The women of Dunder Mifflin are an outstanding bunch. There is the talent you see onscreen, of course. But that's just the start. We want to give you a more intimate look at our fantastic group of gals. Because hot damn, they deserve it.

Jenna

Let's be honest. When *The Office* started it was a bit of a sausage fest. I was the only female cast member under regular contract. Mindy Kaling was the only female writer. Our casting director, Allison Jones, had been a huge influence on the shape of the show. But we had only one female executive producer, the incredible Teri Weinberg, and the only female department heads were in hair, makeup, and costumes. Angela, Phyllis, Kate, and Melora Hardin (who played Jan) rounded out the supporting cast. Sprinkle in a few women on the production staff, and there you have it. It's no wonder we became a tight-knit group. Since this is our book and we are in charge here, Angela and I would like to take up some space and talk a little bit about what made the women of Dunder Mifflin so awesome.

Angela

Let's start with our original costume designer, Carey Bennett, who was with us for Seasons 1–4 of *The Office*. Her role as one of the visionaries of our show is often left out of the narrative. This is a massive oversight, because so much of the look of our show has to do with Carey. And I don't just mean the costumes. When Carey was tasked with doing the costume design for our pilot episode, she launched into some detailed research. As she put it, "I'd never worked in an office. And I never assume that I know what I'm talking about. I always try to go to the source and see something in real life." So she opened a phone book and found a small local paper company located in Glendale, California, called them up, and asked if she could visit.

Jenna

Carey told us that when she took her tour of the little paper company, she realized that every character from *The Office* was working there. For example, there was an employee wearing a shirt with a photo of a howling wolf. She made a note—"Dwight . . . wolf shirt"—because this felt like something he would wear outside of work. In addition to taking detailed wardrobe notes, she also took hundreds of photos of the space itself, little gems like the inspiration posters on the walls, funny clippings posted on people's desks, a deer head in the warehouse. She assembled these photos into a slideshow, put it to music, and played it for Greg Daniels, director Ken Kwapis, and our original production designer, Donald Lee Harris. Not surprisingly, they flipped out and asked Carey if she could arrange another tour. They took even more photos on the second visit and then used them to inform their design of the *Office* bullpen and warehouse sets.

Angela

During "The Fire" in Season 2, Carey's attention to detail paid off again. In that episode, she needed to create wardrobe for the Scranton Fire Department. Every fire department in the country has a unique patch, and she wanted to get Scranton's right. She could have just done a general patch, but that wasn't good enough for Carey. At that time (2005), you couldn't find images on the internet as easily as you can today. So Carey called the chamber of commerce in Scranton and connected with a woman named Mari, who offered to walk down to the fire station, take a photo of the patch, and send it to Carey.

Jenna

This started a relationship between our show and Mari at the Scranton chamber of commerce that really enhanced the look of *The Office*. Mari organized a huge meet and greet for our prop master, Phil Shea, and local Scranton business owners. Phil went to Scranton, where they set him up with a booth in the Steamtown Mall. Hundreds of Scrantonites lined up to meet Phil and offer their special items in hopes that they'd be featured on the show: magnets, stuffed animals, pizza boxes, flyers . . . it's why the set is covered in local treasures. And it was all set in motion by Carey.

Angela

The pedigree of the women on our show was incredible. Take Kate Flannery, for example. Kate was a member of Second City's national touring company and an original member of the Annoyance Theatre in Chicago. For over twenty years, Kate has been one of the stars of a hit comedy lounge act called the Lampshades with fellow improviser Scot Robinson. This woman has chops. She can sing, dance, act, and is an amazing improviser. Anyone who's seen her do a high kick into a deep lunging squat while belting out a song during a Lampshades show knew she'd be fantastic on *Dancing with the Stars*. She can do it all. If you get a chance, go see one of Kate's shows with Jane Lynch and the Tony Guerrero Quintet: *Two Lost Souls* and *A Swingin' Little Christmas!* Both are fantastic!

Of all the women on the show, I have known Kate the longest. She is a tried-and-true friend, there for you no matter what. We were on the phone the other day trying to figure out how long we've known each other. We think we are at twenty-four years as friends. Our timeline starts in our twenties, as struggling actresses balancing odd jobs and auditioning. We were both trying to make rent and get onstage any time we could. We spent countless hours together both onstage in various shows and backstage at the iO West theater in West Hollywood. I have helped her zip into a red bedazzled jumpsuit for the Lampshades, and she has helped me put on wigs for sketch comedy shows. We have both bombed onstage and had nights where we felt like queens of comedy. Imagine my delight when we got to live out our acting dreams together on *The Office*.

Jenna

I don't think anyone was asked to do more stunts on our show than Kate. During her time on *The Office*, her character of Meredith was attacked by a bat and hit by a car; she set her hair on fire, flashed her coworkers (several times), drank hand sanitizer, was forcibly dragged to rehab, and shaved her head . . . just to name a few. There were also several gags that ended up on the cutting-room floor. Like a scene in "Back from Vacation" (Season 3), when a series of shelves falls on Meredith as she's doing inventory in the warehouse. With only a few exceptions, Kate did all her own stunt work. The thing I admire most about Kate is her old-school approach to performing. She and Creed are similar in this way . . . they will do anything to entertain an audience. She gives 110 percent to every performance. It doesn't matter if it's a stunt or eight hours of background work. She's all in.

We used a stunt woman, Marie Fink, to double for Kate when her hair was on fire. But it was Kate who took several blasts of fire extinguisher foam to the face. And that's really Kate under a trash bag in the kitchen as Dwight tries to trap a bat on her head. That's really Kate on the hood of Michael's car, and yes, Pam really hits her in the face with a football. And while she didn't actually shave her head, the four hours Kate spent in makeup to achieve that look counts as a stunt in my book.

Kate and I were often paired together for background work, but we didn't share a major story line until the "Lice" episode in Season 9. In this one, Pam unknowingly infects the office with lice. Meredith freaks out and ends up shaving her head to keep from getting them. But in the end, Pam and Meredith go out for beer and karaoke and bond over the difficulty of raising kids without help, as this happened while Jim was away in Philadelphia launching his business. Kate and I were excited when we got this script, because we finally had a Pam/Meredith plotline. We had one whole shoot day all to ourselves, something that had never happened. We got to go on location and sing. It was one of my favorite days of shooting ever.

Angela

The other woman in the bullpen was none other than Phyllis Lapin Vance, winner of the 8th Annual Dundie Award for Busiest (Bushiest) Beaver and my Party Planning Committee nemesis. Even though our characters were frenemies, in real life we were thrilled when we had scenes together. Our biggest challenge was getting through them without dissolving into laughter. Case in point: the scene in "Launch Party" (Season 4) where Phyllis nails me in the face with a pile of Post-it notes. When we had scenes with a lot of dialogue together, we would meet in her trailer and rehearse our lines before we filmed. It was during this time that we became friends. I came to adore this woman. We both grew up going to church, and in those early days of the show we would get together and pray. We would pray about whatever was weighing on our hearts, for our show, and for the cast and crew. I remember those moments so fondly.

Jenna

I felt an instant connection with Phyllis because we are both from St. Louis. We bonded over our love of toasted raviolis and gooey butter cake (both St. Louis inventions) and, of course, the St. Louis Cardinals. During our first season the Cardinals were in the World Series against the Boston Red Sox. There were a ton of men in the cast and crew who had lived in Boston—John, B. J., Steve, Greg Daniels, Mike Schur—and several of them would gather in John Krasinski's trailer to watch the games. Meanwhile, Phyllis and I watched in my trailer. The Boston Red Sox swept the Cardinals 4–0 that year. It was brutal on set for us St. Louis gals.

HOWEVER, in 2011, the Cardinals WON the World Series in an epic battle against the Texas Rangers. (By this time, we'd added another St. Louis native, Ellie Kemper, to the cast.) You can only imagine how excited we were when World Series MVP David Freese and Matt Holliday visited the set. The three of us were seriously giddy with excitement. As far as I know, no one from the Boston Red Sox ever visited. Take that, boys!

While I wanted to do victory laps around the bullpen and really rub it in the boys' faces, Phyllis was happy to gloat quietly from her chair. In general, Phyllis is one of those people who listens more than she speaks. (Which is *very* different from how I operate.) One day while we were getting snacks during a break, I told her I really admired this quality. Phyllis smiled and said, "Sometimes I can be standing close to people, and they don't notice I'm there." Then she leaned in and whispered, "I've heard A LOT of stuff, Jenna. A LOT." I laughed so hard at that. What does Phyllis know??!!

Angela

In our early days, it was mostly just the four of us gals on set. We bonded quickly and effortlessly. We laughed a lot. When we found out we'd been picked up for a second season, we decided to celebrate with a fancy brunch at the Ivy on Robertson Boulevard. This is the famous restaurant where all the Hollywood stars go to be seen. The paparazzi have a permanent spot on the sidewalk, and they snap photos of celebrities dining on that patio. (By the way, if anyone tells you they didn't want to be photographed having lunch at the Ivy, they are lying. It's literally why you go.) We had Jenna's agent make a reservation for a patio table. The agency even told the restaurant we were celebrating the pickup of *The Office* for a second season and that Jenna would be dining with her costars. We were so tickled thinking this would get us some kind of fancy-schmancy star treatment. When we arrived, the maître d' took us to an inside table, all the way in the back of the restaurant by the doors to the kitchen. Jenna piped up with, "I'm sorry, we requested a table on the patio." The maître d' coldly replied, "That's reserved for VIPs." Our choice was clear. The table by the kitchen or goodbye. We couldn't help but laugh. This wasn't exactly the schmancy treatment we had envisioned. We toasted with our mimosas to the tune of clanking dishes, busboys arguing, and a lovely breeze from the staff rushing past our table in and out of the kitchen.

Jenna

The waitstaff was over-the-top snooty and dismissive of us that day. We wondered if this was part of their training, like the famous Chicago diner Ed Debevic's, where the servers are purposely rude to you as part of the charm of the restaurant. My order came out wrong, and Angela was never served her iced tea. The whole experience was so incredibly cartoonish we still laugh about it today. We were definitely reminded of our place in the Hollywood ecosystem.

As we were leaving, we saw a gang of paparazzi rush past us down the sidewalk. They chased someone into a store and were taking photos through the window. Angela bravely pulled one of the photographers aside and asked who they were following. "Jason Alexander." What happened next is perhaps one of my favorite Angela stories ever. Still a little stung by our Ivy experience, Angela was determined to salvage a "star" moment

for us. She coyly said to the photographer, "Do you know who she is? She's Pam from *The Office*." (Obviously, if you have to ask, they don't know.) He looked at us blankly. Angela then motioned to the group. "We are the ladies of *The Office*." Still nothing. Angela pushed harder. "On NBC. *The Office*. On NBC." Finally, the guy's face lit up. "Are you serious?!" But he didn't raise his camera. Instead, he reached into his pocket and produced a business card. He said, "Here's my card. If you ever want to tip me off on when celebrities will be out and about, I'll give you a finder's fee." And then he pushed us aside because Jason Alexander was getting into his car. It took us a minute until we all collectively realized that he thought we worked IN AN OFFICE at NBC. OMG. We *died*. It was so funny I thought we were going to pee our pants. We asked the hostess to take our photo instead.

Angela

It's hard to believe, but the following year we went back. Again, to celebrate the pickup for the new season. (I know, we are gluttons for punishment.) Again, Jenna had her agent make the reservation. This time, I brought along a little cake that said OFFICE LADIES SEASON 3 on it to celebrate. Unfortunately, Kate couldn't join us, as she got hired for a gig at the last minute. The Ivy nearly denied our reservation because our "entire party" didn't show up. I thought telling them we were on a television show might help save our spot. So once again, I proudly told the maître d' we were on *The Office*, to which he replied, "Which office??" He wasn't having it. He told us we had fifteen minutes for our party to be "complete" or they would give our table away. There was a Coffee Bean on the corner and I thought maybe we should just go there instead, but Jenna was determined. By this time, she had graduated to one of the big-time agencies in town, WME. We knew the Ivy wouldn't want to piss off WME, so Jenna mentioned maybe she should call her agent who had made the reservation. (She had seen this trick in a movie.) Well, it worked! They seated our incomplete party, and this time we did indeed get a table on the patio.

We shared a lovely lunch on the patio. Angela got her iced tea. Things were going good. When it came time for dessert, Angela took out the cake she had brought. Within seconds, Snooty Waiter (who had clearly been trained on the same day as Snooty Maître d') was next to our table telling us that NO outside food was allowed in the restaurant. We had to put our cake back in the box. Fair enough. (But we took a photo first and put up with the stink eye.)

After lunch, as we stood in line for the valet, a man and his date brushed right past us and took a spot at the front of the line. The paparazzi surrounded him,

clicking away. They did not take our photo, of course. We didn't care. We had given up on ever getting our photo taken. But that's when I realized the person who had just butted in line was a big-deal singer. I was a little starstruck. I tapped his shoulder and mumbled, "Ummm . . . hello. I literally love your voice. Excited to see what you do next." I am not exaggerating when I say that he looked at me like I was a turd. Well, by then, Angela had had enough. I mean, she was willing to forgive Big-Deal Singer for butting in line, sort of, but *no one* is allowed to be a douchebag to her best friend.

Guys, this fella is tall. Over six foot. Angela is five foot one. But I tell you what, that gal stepped right up to that man and took him down with a look I can only describe as chilling. I think I saw him shudder. His whole posture changed when my girl stepped in, and he meekly shook my hand.

The next year, we skipped the Ivy. We had learned our lesson by then. But I'm not going to lie, I'm a little tempted to go back now just to see what happens. At least us gals got some good stories out of the experiences.

Angela

While the main actresses on set every day were Jenna, Kate, Phyllis, and me, we also had Melora Hardin and Mindy Kaling join us from time to time. Melora Hardin played the role of Jan Levinson for forty-two episodes of *The Office*. Jan is introduced in the pilot episode as the vice president of Dunder Mifflin. She works in the corporate offices in New York City and is often tasked with giving Michael bad news. In later seasons, Jan becomes Michael's love interest. Melora played her role beautifully. I used to love to watch her in a scene. She and Steve made a terrific acting team. If you want to see some of the best comedic acting ever, watch Melora Hardin in "Dinner Party" (Season 4). In twenty-two minutes, she plays out awkward moments full of jealousy, disdain, pride, absolute rage, and a deep sadness. It's not easy to slowly and comedically unravel while staying believable. Kids, study this performance. It really doesn't get much better.

Jenna

Of all the women in our cast, Melora had the most professional acting experience when we started the show. She'd been acting since she was six years old. I fully geeked out when I found out she had been in two episodes of one of my favorite shows growing up, *Little House on the Prairie*. And she was originally cast as one of the lead actors in *Back to the Future*. The original Marty McFly was Eric Stoltz, and Melora was cast as Marty McFly's girlfriend, Jennifer. But when the studio decided to recast Eric Stoltz with Michael J. Fox, they said Melora was too tall to play Michael J. Fox's girlfriend, and they recast her too. Can you imagine!! A two-movie deal, just gone! Melora was only seventeen years old when this happened. That probably would have made me quit acting completely, but Melora soldiered on. She's a pro.

On a personal note, she always felt like a big sister to me. She gave me advice about how to navigate many of the non-acting aspects of the business. By this, I'm referring to the information your agent might tell you but that you really trust when it comes from a colleague. My favorite tip from Melora: During ten-hour press junkets, which are most often done in hotels, ask the studio to book you a room so you can get a full hour to yourself (and maybe a nap) during lunch. It's one of those things you can have, but only if you know to ask. As a new actor, I was usually too shy to ask for anything when I started on *The Office*. All too often women who self-advocate get labeled as "difficult" or "divas." But the truth is that asking for a room is self-care, and it made me better equipped to make it through on junket days. It took some practice, but I slowly got used to asking for what I need. Melora set a good example in that regard. She was not afraid to advocate for herself or others. At the 2005 Emmy Awards, the press asked Steve, Rainn, John, B. J., and me to pose for photos with the Emmy backstage. Melora piped in: "Hold up. We are all part of the cast." And then she added herself and the rest of the actors to the photo.

Angela

Melora was the first working mom/actress I ever met. She was also a very confident hands-on mother. She would routinely come to set for wardrobe fittings with her baby strapped to her chest. So when I became pregnant, I asked her many questions about how she navigated set life as a new parent. Her tips were so helpful and included many things I hadn't even thought of. For example, she told me if I planned to breastfeed that I would need a mini fridge at work to store my milk during the day, and also a way to transport it home safely. It sounds obvious, but I hadn't thought about where I would store my milk at work, let alone how to get it home. I had a mini fridge in my trailer, but it didn't work. I'd never needed it before, so I hadn't cared. I asked the transportation guys if they could fix it, and I bought a little cooler for my car ride. Because of Melora, I was breastfeeding-ready for my return to work.

She also told me that since my daughter was going to be a Taurus and I was a Cancer, we would be very compatible. I didn't know much about astrology then, and still don't, but she explained that Taurus is an earth sign and Cancer is a water sign, and so the two will always need each other. I was about eight months pregnant at the time of this conversation, so I burst into tears. I just loved the sound of that, and also . . . hormones.

Jenna

And then there was the amazing Mindy Kaling. Mindy split her time between the set and the writers' room at *The Office*. For a long time, Mindy was the only female writer on our show. The lone female voice. After her play *Matt & Ben* was acclaimed at the New York International Fringe Festival in 2002, she was granted two interviews for writing jobs in Hollywood. One of the shows was canceled while she sat in the waiting room. The other was with Greg Daniels for *The Office*. He hired her for what would be her first job writing for television. Mindy wrote many of my favorite episodes: "The Dundies," "The Injury," "Niagara," and she made history writing "Diwali"—the first American television comedy series to depict that Hindu festival.

Angela

My first memory of Mindy is her smile. We were gathered for one of our first script readings, and Greg went around the room, asking everyone to say their names as we were all still getting to know one another. Mindy was wearing a brightly colored sweater and sitting with the male writers. I was instantly drawn to her. She was chatty, and I like chatty. She seemed to know a lot about the most random aspects of pop culture. It was so entertaining. I just loved talking to her.

Jenna

As far as *The Office*, I don't think any character went through a bigger change than Mindy's character of Kelly Kapoor. Kelly Kapoor starts off as a rather quiet and stiff customer service representative seated in the corner of the back annex. Her hair is up in a tight French twist, and she wears paisley blouses that button up to the neck. She is very serious and rarely smiles or laughs. But as you track her character over the course of the first two seasons, you'll notice a transformation: The hair starts to come down, the blouses change, and eventually she is seen smiling and jabbering away to Jim about her crush on Ryan, her love of Beyoncé, and the color pink (and also the singer Pink). From there she gets full hair extensions and starts a hilarious on-again/off-again romance with Ryan the temp. We asked Greg Daniels about the transformation of Kelly Kapoor. He told us it was due to a subtle but relentless campaign waged by Mindy in the

writers' room, behind the
scenes. He said they finally
just gave in and let Mindy
write her own personality
into the role of Kelly.

Hanging out with Mindy
is kind of like attending a
twenty-four-hour slumber
party. Like Kelly, she loves
fashion and she loves to
talk, but unlike Kelly, she also loves to
hear your stories. She loves your birthday as much as her own—well, maybe not
exactly as much, but close! She loves to send gifts. She chose the most expensive
item on my baby registry—my breast pump. (I had questioned if I should even
include it on the registry, to be honest, and I was so touched that she sent it.) But
the most impactful thing about working with Mindy, for me, was her unapologetic
ambition. I'd met a lot of ambitious women in my life, but Mindy was different,
because she was not afraid to speak openly about her desire to be successful.
Mindy and I had many conversations about what we hoped to accomplish in our
careers. We have even asked each other questions like, "What net worth is your
ultimate goal?" It was incredibly empowering to encounter another woman on the
rise who would speak so frankly and strategically about what she wanted to achieve
in her life. It empowered me. I am not at all surprised by all of Mindy's success
after leaving *The Office*. She's one of the smartest people I know.

Angela

While on *The Office*, Mindy and I shared some heart-to-hearts in the stairwell
outside of the writers' room. We would sit on that staircase and talk about
our relationships and our love of family. In the last few years, we both shared
a tragedy. Mindy's mother and my father died a few years apart, both from
pancreatic cancer. I knew how much Mindy loved her mom and she knew how

me and we both started screaming with joy. It was amazing. When we all got way too drunk at my bachelorette party, Ellie held my sister's hair as she vomited. Also, Ellie dressed up in a cocktail dress and pretended to be a cat on the red carpet to help support my animal rescue charity. She's just a ton of fun, and reliable too.

Angela

As you can tell, the women of *The Office* are good at building one another up. And I would definitely add Rashida Jones to that list. I met Rashida when she played Jim's new love interest Karen Filippelli on Season 3 of *The Office*. She had the unfortunate task of playing a character meant to keep Jim from Pam. This whole story line made Rashida nervous. She was afraid people would hate her, that fans would yell at her on the street. On the show, Pam and Karen are at odds, and Angela full-on hates her when Karen creates the Committee to Plan Parties. But in real life, nothing could be further from the truth.

Jenna

I don't think it's an exaggeration to say we were a little enamored of Rashida at first. We hung on her every word. Rashida's parents are Quincy Jones and Peggy Lipton. She knows fancy people and told us fancy stories. But she is also remarkably grounded. Rashida was popular with everyone on set. She may have gotten a few of the cast and crew hooked on Sudoku. We loved her. During her run on the show, the audience couldn't help but fall in love with her too. Some fans became quite torn on who exactly they felt Jim should end up with. Karen was supportive, witty, centered, and confident. She encouraged Jim to follow his dreams. Eventually, message boards for Team Pam and Team Karen popped up, with people arguing their position. Jim eventually picks Pam, and Karen leaves. We were sad to see Rashida go. Of course, she went on to star in a new show from Greg Daniels and Mike Schur, *Parks and Recreation*. But she has done so much more. She's the ultimate multihyphenate: actor-writer-producer-director-podcaster-brand representative-activist-philanthropist, and for me, role model.

Angela

When I was growing up in Indonesia, I had a group of friends from Europe. They always looked amazing, spoke multiple languages, had eclectic taste in clothes and music, traveled extensively, and were so cultured. Of course, I wanted to be just like them. Rashida reminded me of those girls. I was and still am charmed by her. We've stayed in touch since she left the show; she is definitely one of the women I turn to when I need encouragement. She always has the best advice with the most memorable catchphrases. During one of our talks, she told me that a toxic person in my life was too "emotionally expensive," and she was right. But come on, how great is the phrase "emotionally expensive"? As I navigated coparenting and joint custody, Rashida emailed me and said, "You have such a great ability to neutralize and harmonize, it's fantastic. You're a survivor!" That meant a lot to me but again, "neutralize and harmonize" . . . classic. Classic.

In November 2013, Rashida and I went to Belize together as ambassadors for an ocean preservation group I work with. We were going there to see their barrier reef—it is second in size only to the Great Barrier Reef in Australia. Our goal was to bring awareness to this reef and the fragile ecosystem that depends on it for survival. I asked Rashida to partner with me, and that trip is one of my favorite travel memories. First of all, she is a world-class traveler. Like a super pro. I will never forget how many little bags of self-care items she had in her carry-on. Several types of vitamins, hydrating sprays, and so many lotions. I couldn't help but stare as she applied her lotions and sprayed her face pre-takeoff. She clearly had a system and a routine. I asked her what she was doing, and she told me she has so many "lotions and potions" when she travels that her friends gave her that nickname. In that moment, I was very aware of how much cooler Rashida Jones is than me. My friends called me *Hambone* because once in high school I stood in my friend's kitchen during a party and ate ham straight out of the refrigerator. I didn't even bother to turn on the light, get a plate, or get utensils. I just stood there in the dark, eating ham with my bare hands. Rashida is *Lotions and Potions* because she is well traveled and knows how to take care of herself. I am Hambone.

That trip was pretty incredible. We swam with sharks, sea turtles, and thousands of fish; rode on a boat at sunset with calm waters around us; ate the best ceviche in the world; and even found a beachside bar named the Office. Rashida is truly the coolest, and I would travel with her again in a second. Rashida, hear me out: *Celebrity Amazing Race?*

Jenna

As time went on, we added more amazing women to the mix. Amy Ryan had a recurring role. Jen Celotta joined Mindy in the writers' room and also served as coexecutive producer and showrunner alongside Paul Lieberstein starting in Season 5. I definitely felt a shift in the way we told women's stories when Jen was a showrunner. Pam's art school story line was under her guidance. Angela had a love triangle with Dwight and Andy. Kate was front and center in "Moroccan Christmas" when Michael drags Meredith to rehab, and the same for Phyllis in "Crime Aid" when Phyllis tries to help Dwight win back Angela.

Most exciting was watching some of our female crew members step in to direct. Jen Celotta and Mindy Kaling both directed episodes, as well as editor

Claire Scanlon and first AD Kelly Cantley. Ellie Kemper's sister, Carrie Kemper, joined the writers' room along with Caroline Williams, Allison Silverman, Amelie Gillette, and Niki Schwartz-Wright. We even got a full-time female camera operator, Sarah Levy, when Matt Sohn was promoted to cinematographer. And in later seasons, actresses Ameenah Kaplan, Catherine Tate, and Kathy Bates joined the cast. The sausage fest was over, and things felt a lot more balanced.

Angela

Jenna and I have this ongoing conversation about who and what we would take with us if there was a zombie apocalypse. I'm not sure why this topic comes up so often, but it does. Perhaps it's our love of survivalist television shows and movies, or maybe it's the fact that we wrote this book during a pandemic. Well, I would take this group of women with me. There is that famous saying, "It takes a village." The truth is it takes a village of women. Over the course of nine years, these women taught me to believe in myself, to trust my instincts, and they showed me what female friendship is all about. I am thankful for the time I had with each and every one of them.

Jenna

I couldn't agree more. I think we should all get together and crash the patio at the Ivy. And bring our own giant cake.

We love ya, ladies!

7

the men
of dunder
mifflin

The women of Dunder Mifflin gave us life. The men gave us headaches. Ha ha. Just kidding. Steve and Oscar were okay. In all seriousness, we loved these goofballs. I don't know if Greg Daniels made kindness a prerequisite when casting men on *The Office*, but as we look at the men of Dunder Mifflin, you will see it comes up quite a bit. *That's what she said.*

Jenna

The star of a television show sets the tone on set, and you can ask any producer what happens when a difficult/insecure narcissist has the lead role. The toxicity and bad behavior trickle down and make a miserable experience for everyone. Lucky for us, we had Steve Carell as our number one. It's hard to know where to begin when sharing about Steve, because my feelings of admiration and gratitude run so deep. With Steve as our leader, we all learned what was okay to make a stink about and what was not. For example: ants in our trailers. Is Steve complaining? No? Ants = Okay. Early morning call times? Wait, Steve has been here since 5 A.M. Gotcha. What about last-minute script pages? Are we stressed about that? Hmm . . . looks like Steve just had to memorize three new speeches in fifteen minutes. We can handle it. Steve never complained. And I mean that. I can only recall three times in the seven years we spent together on *The Office* that Steve expressed frustration. He so rarely cracked under pressure, and no one was under more pressure than Steve. He had more lines in the script, week after week, than anyone. He drove most plotlines. And he was the public face of our show. That meant the bulk of the interviews, photo shoots, and promotional work fell on his shoulders as well.

People often ask me, "What was it like to work with Steve Carell?" I think they expect me to say he was a laugh riot, always joking around and doing bits. This was not the case. Steve was very quiet. I can't tell you how many times we would be ready to start rolling and the director would say something like, "Wait, we can't start until Steve gets here." But he would be there. Usually sitting on the couch by reception waiting patiently. It is hard to imagine you wouldn't notice that you were standing next to Steve Carell, but I guess he and Phyllis share the power of invisibility. None of my memories of Steve are of a person who was overwhelmed or stressed or worried or

maniacally running lines (as I imagine I would have been if I were in his shoes). My memories of Steve are of him casually sitting on that couch discussing his favorite pizza places or the good deal he found at the mall over the weekend, and then killing it when the director called "Action."

Angela

There is a joke in Hollywood that Steve is the nicest man in show business. Those of us who have had the opportunity to work with him know that it's true. Steve is incredibly kind, but he is also incredibly talented. To be on set with him felt like attending the best comedy and improv class in the world. There were several times that I lost my place in a scene because I was just watching his performance. I would forget that I had to act too. For example, in Season 4's "Fun Run" episode, there is a conference room scene where Michael is brainstorming with the group about Dunder Mifflin being cursed. He says maybe they should make a sacrifice to remove the curse and starts listing mythical animals. Steve improvised quite a bit in this moment, and I was mesmerized. Angela Martin was supposed to be sad because Sprinkles died, but I just sat there with this silly grin on my face watching Steve do his magic. Seriously though, you try remembering to "act" while Steve Carell looks at you and says, "Maybe there's some sort of animal that we could make a sacrifice to. Like a giant buffalo, or some sort of monster, like something with the body of a walrus with the head of a sea lion. Or something with the body of an egret with the head of a meerkat. Or just . . . the head of a monkey, with the antlers of a reindeer, with, ah . . . the body of a porcupine."

Jenna

Steve is the most skilled improviser I've ever had the pleasure to work with, most notably because of his patience. Steve is not afraid to let a moment or an idea breathe. He never rushes. And he never breaks. He would stay in character under almost any circumstance. I know a lot of comedic actors who are great at coming up with clever, improvised lines, and this was certainly true of Steve. But what sets Steve apart is his ability to communicate so much through his improvised behavior and reactions. A small moment that comes to mind is in the Season 3 episode "Branch Closing," when Jan must deliver the news that corporate has decided to shut down the Scranton branch. During the shoot, a set of wind-up teeth began to spontaneously chatter on Steve's desk. This was not a scripted moment, just a strange accident, but Steve didn't laugh, and he didn't stop the scene. He grabbed the teeth and reacted as Michael Scott would react in the moment, with a mixture of delight and frustration, and then continued with his scripted dialogue. It was brilliant.

Angela

Steve's superpower is knowing when you are about to break and going for it until you do. I learned that I couldn't make eye contact with him when this was happening or he would destroy me, so I started staring at his neck. After seven years, I learned every inch of it. I could probably draw it for you. Sorry if that is creepy, Steve, but if I looked you in the eye . . . I was a goner. Sometimes I could lean into my character's disdain for Michael to avoid eye contact. In the episode "Women's Appreciation," I had to sit next to Steve in a Victoria's Secret store while he/Michael asked me/Angela Martin what type of undies I'd want. It took all my willpower not to laugh and keep my stern exterior until he improvised this line: "Santa's come early. Santa would like to buy you a pair of panties, little girl." And, well, I completely lost it.

Jenna

I loved any scene where I got Steve all to myself. Some of my favorites include: Season 3's "Diwali," outside on the steps when Michael tries to kiss Pam; "Business School," also Season 3, where Michael is the only person to come to Pam's art show; Season 5's "Lecture Circuit," where Pam joins Michael as he

travels to the other branches to share his
best business practices; the entire Michael
Scott Paper Company arc in Season 5;
and most of all, "Goodbye, Michael" in
Season 7. In our final scene together in
"Goodbye, Michael," Pam runs after
Michael in the airport after she missed him
in the office that day, just before he boards
the plane to be with Holly. When we shot

that scene, our director Paul Feig told me he would be capturing
the scene without any audio and needed the emotions to play out on our faces.
He suggested I run up to Steve and tell him goodbye—not from Pam to Michael,
but goodbye from Jenna to Steve. The first take we did went over five minutes, as
I shared with Steve, from my heart, what working with him for those seven years
had meant to me. On both a personal and professional level, Steve had made
an impact on my life. For instance, when my dad retired, Steve stayed late at
work one day and made a video for him as Michael Scott. We used that video to
kick off the retirement party for my father. So I had a lot to say when the scene
started. I talked. I cried. Steve cried. We hugged. When it was done, Paul said,
"Jenna, that was incredible. This next time, maybe you can do it a little faster."

Angela

Steve wasn't one to give unsolicited advice, but he was more than happy to
offer guidance if asked. He was a person I could confide in both personally and
professionally. For example, I was super nervous about my first guest appearance
on the *Late Show with David Letterman*. Steve was our only cast member at that
time who had been on Dave's show, so I asked him what to do. He told me not
to go for the joke, but to sincerely share a story and keep it honest and real. He
was right! I told a story about my friend in Indonesia whose family rescued a
one-armed gibbon ape. For some reason, the gibbon decided that I was its sworn
enemy, and it used to pee at the window in their breakfast nook whenever it

saw me. I had all the beats of my story planned out, but then Dave threw me a curveball. He asked me why the ape only had one arm. This question wasn't part of my story. I started to panic and then remembered what Steve had told me: "Don't go for the joke." So I answered earnestly and stated that the gibbon had lost its arm swinging on a

power line. This was met with groans from the audience, but it surprised the heck out of Dave and made him double over with laughter.

I also asked Steve a ton of questions about becoming a homeowner. I remember troubleshooting with him about my wonky sprinkler system. In particular, the sprinkler heads by my driveway that shot water at you rather than toward the grass. It was a monthlong saga, and Steve would check in with me about it every week. To this day, he will know what I mean if I tell him that station 4 is finally working properly.

Jenna

So much of our show's success is because of Steve's consistent hard work and emotional balance. There was no drama on our set. And that is 100 percent due to Steve setting a tone of humility and gratitude with his own behavior from the beginning. We all wanted his respect, because we respected him so much.

Now, if Steve was the man who kept us calm, John Krasinksi was the one to pump us up. Every set needs a person who can give you a second wind, and after six hours of shooting the same scene in the conference room, we definitely needed that. Whenever we hit a wall, we could count on John to do an impression or crack a

joke that would reignite our energy. One time, when our boom operator Nick Carbone accidentally dipped his microphone into the shot, John came up with the catchphrase, "You've been Car-boned!" This cracked us up, Nick especially. That started a trend where any time we had to stop a shot, for whatever reason, we would say we'd been "Car-boned!" and Nick would take a bow. On other sets when there are issues that stop filming, I watch as the actors and director get all flustered and irritated. But on our set, we couldn't wait to yell "CAR-BONED!"

Angela

John and I had a few inside jokes that I'm sure drove everyone nuts, like the time we were reminiscing about the Kid Sister doll that was popular when we were children. John insisted I was the same size as the doll and looked just like her. (I actually had a life-sized doll growing up.) If there was a lull in shooting, John would call out across the set, "Kid Sister!" and I would yell back, "Big Brother!" We learned later that Kid Sister's brother was actually called My Buddy, but our silly bit was already cemented. It made no sense to anyone else, but it always made us laugh. John even drew us doing our shtick on a piece of scratch paper. Years after *The Office* wrapped, I was in a toy store and saw a tall doll about my size. I texted a picture of it to him with no caption. I knew he'd know exactly what it meant. He immediately texted me, "Kid sister!"

147

Jenna

John has a great laugh. Something happens to John's body when he breaks. He goes all noodle-y, he wheezes, cry-laughs, and finally his body collapses. I was often standing next to him when this would happen. We'd be doing a scene, trying to hold it together, and suddenly John was literally on the floor. If you'd like an example of this, watch any of the *Office* bloopers, but especially the ones from "Dinner Party" when Michael is showing us his new flat-screen television. When you are making a comedy, it's encouraging to have a person who finds what you are doing so funny that they dissolve into a heap on the ground.

Angela

I met John's family at the *Leatherhead* movie premiere. They are the nicest, tallest group of people you'll ever meet. I instantly understood where John got his good manners. Even with all his success, John is still a sweetheart. A few years ago, my husband and I ran into him at a fancy showbiz shindig. My husband hadn't attended many of these types of events with me, because we met after *The Office*, and he was feeling a bit out of place. I told him we'd find a corner and people-watch, but before we could do that, I heard my name being yelled over the crowd. We turned around and saw John approaching us. He gave me a big hug, and I introduced him to Josh. John literally gave him an even bigger bear hug. Then, like a good big brother would, he told Josh that I was the "real deal" and deserved the best, and he was so happy we had found each other. It was really moving to me and a great icebreaker for my husband at this fancy party. John is the type of person where no matter how much time has passed, you pick up right where you left off.

Jenna

People often ask, "Who is most like their character?" The answer is easy: Creed. Creed is a loveable quirky soul, both on- and offscreen. One of the many things I love about Creed is how he will text Angela and me videos and pictures of cats and babies doing silly things. Or he will hit us with a crazy story. They come out of the blue. With no reason or explanation. *Ding!* Cat Taking a Bath. *Ding!* Baby Playing in Puddle. *Ding!* "I just got mauled by a hairless cat that wandered into my yard!" I love our text thread, and it always brings a smile to my face. Creed is one of those people that lights up any room (or text thread) with his positivity and love of other people.

Angela

Like Jenna said, Creed is quite the character, and we never knew which of his stories were true or which he was making up. (Turns out, the hairless cat story was true!) Luckily, I've spent enough time with him that now I can tell the difference. He gets a twinkle in his eye when he's spinning a tale, but early on, he'd always fool us. For example, while filming "Dwight's Speech" (Season 2), his character gives a shout-out in Mandarin to his friends. We all wondered if Creed could actually speak Mandarin, because in between scenes, he told us he once starred in a hit television series in China. He said  he played a captain, and the show was so popular people would point at him and yell, "Captain Clark!" We hung on his every word. He went on to say, "Yeah, I was actually partially raised in China when I was very little, and now I wake up some mornings speaking Mandarin, but then it goes away." We were riveted. Then he cackled and that twinkle in his eyes appeared. So which part of this story was true? As it turns out, he did star in a TV show that aired in China called *The War of Gene*, but it was filmed in Los Angeles. He never lived in China and cannot speak Mandarin. See what I mean?? But that ability to tell crazy stories so convincingly made for an amazing character, and we loved hearing his tall tales.

Jenna

Before landing on *The Office*, Creed had a very long, exciting career as a musician. He played lead guitar and sang lead vocals with the rock band the 13th Floor, who later became the Grass Roots, from 1967 to 1969. He then had a successful solo career and is still writing music and touring to this day. Knowing about his backstory, I was curious to find out how exactly he landed on our show. He told me that he had been working as a background performer and improviser in sketches for *The Bernie Mac Show*, which Ken Kwapis had directed. When Ken found out that Creed had been in the Grass Roots, he got a little starstruck. Ken is a massive music fan. He sent an assistant to a local record store to buy a vinyl for Creed to sign. The two of them got to talking about music, and Ken gave Creed his phone number and told him to keep in touch. Later, when Creed heard that Ken was directing the pilot of *The Office*, he knew what he had to do. He told me, "Now, I had never ever called anybody like that before, but I called him, as my intuition said, *This feels right. This feels right.*" Creed explained that he was a big fan of the British series and really hoped for a chance to be part of the American remake. Ken talked to Greg Daniels and told him that Creed was a very interesting and funny guy, and a terrific improviser. Greg's approach was, "Well, we'll see what we can do. We can put him in the background and see if we can work him into the mix."

"That's all I needed to hear," Creed told me. It was the break he needed, and he certainly made the most of the opportunity.

Angela

Over the years, Creed has become a close friend. Any of you reading this who follow me on Instagram know that Creed lives at the end of my street. Yes! Creedo (as I call him) is my neighbor! It's one of the joys of my life. I love that we see each other out walking or running errands. Once I heard "Hey, pumpkin" as I walked into our local coffee shop. I turned around, and it was Creed. There have been many lovely summer evenings when we have gone on long strolls together in our neighborhood. We've also maybe had some adult beverages in red Solo cups in hand, but that is neither here nor there. I told Creed my dad used to call this "hitting the sauce trail." Creed loved that, and so occasionally I'll text him, "Should I walk over so we can hit the sauce trail?"

Creed also loves watching documentaries about animals. We once spent an entire evening watching baby iguanas trying to make it to the ocean in the Galápagos. Spoiler alert: There are a lot of snakes trying to eat them, and we kept yelling at the television, "Run, li'l lizard! RUN!" to Creed's utter enjoyment. But my favorite evenings are when Creed brings over his guitar. We'll sit out in my backyard or by the fireplace, and he'll play songs for my whole family. It always warms my heart. You never know what to expect when you are with Creed, except laughter.

Jenna

The other person who blurs the line between real life and his character would be Rainn Wilson. Like Dwight, Rainn is an oddball. He's not a beet farmer, but he does live on a ranchlike home with a zonkey (yep, a cross between a zebra and a donkey) that wanders in and out of the house. Some of my favorite story lines

153

ever on the show were when Pam and Dwight became unlikely allies, as in "The Injury" (Season 2), when Dwight's concussion turns him into Pam's best friend for the day, or "Vandalism" (Season 9), when they team up to investigate who spray-painted obscenities on Pam's mural in the warehouse. This being said, doing scenes with Rainn was never easy. As part of his character, he does a lot of mouth-breathing and juts out his chest like a peacock. The moment of transformation from Rainn to Dwight when a director yelled "Action!" would always make me laugh. The fun part about acting with Rainn is that, unlike Steve, who almost never broke, Rainn broke all the time. Most of my memories of working with Rainn involve us laughing uncontrollably while the crew waited patiently for us to pull it together.

Angela

Folks, I know exactly what Jenna is talking about. Rainn and I were often put in ridiculous situations together. Neither of us are that good at keeping our composure, so Dwangela moments usually ended with us bursting into laughter. Even when Dwight and Angela were splitting up and we had to both be full of regret and sadness, we couldn't stop laughing. One wonderful example is this dinner date scene in Season 4's "Dunder Mifflin Infinity":

DWIGHT: Are you enjoying your vegetarian noodles?

ANGELA: Very much. How's your meat?

DWIGHT: Dry. Delicious.

ANGELA: I heard a joke today.

DWIGHT: Oh, that's funny.

ANGELA: Yes, it was.

Something about Dwight loving dry meat and Angela not knowing how to retell a joke got us every time.

Jenna

Rainn can be gruff, surly, grouchy, but underneath all of that is a deeply spiritual man devoted to being of service. In my darkest times, I can turn to him for love and support. He is a safe place to go when I am confused or searching for answers. He is a great listener. Rather than give advice, he tries to help you find your truth. It is no surprise that since leaving *The Office*, he has devoted much of his time to running LIDÈ Haiti, the foundation he created with his wife, Holiday Reinhorn. Together, they travel back and forth to Haiti supporting a group that educates and empowers at-risk and marginalized youth, with a special focus on adolescent girls. He also created SoulPancake—a media company dedicated to exploring "life's big questions with integrity, heart, and humor." I would say that mission statement captures Rainn Wilson exactly. He is a man exploring life's big questions with integrity, heart, and humor. I could not love him more.

Angela

Speaking of loveable grumps, do they come any more loveable than Stanley Hudson? Leslie David Baker played grouchy sales representative Stanley and was Angela Martin's competition for best eye roll. I loved the way he could take down Michael with a single look. And OMG, Leslie should have won an award for the way he destroyed Ryan in the "Take Your Daughter to Work Day" episode. One of my favorite gems he shouted at Ryan was, "Boy, have you lost your mind? Because I'll help you find it." Whenever they wanted Stanley to go off on Ryan, the writers and directors would let Leslie improvise, and it was always brilliant.

Leslie is nothing like Stanley in real life. He is a joy to be around and a true gentleman. On long shoot days, Leslie always made sure we ladies had chairs to sit in or water to drink. I remember filming outside on a cold night, and he saw me shivering. In between takes, he took off his suit jacket and wrapped it around me. Leslie was always such a fun, supportive friend for us gals. We could show him countless photos of dresses for events, and he would tell us which ones would work and which ones should be a hard pass. He was always right.

Jenna

Leslie and I both love old movies and the glamour of the Hollywood of long ago. I think that's why he was so good at giving advice about award show attire. I loved talking through my outfits with Leslie. Especially when we got to borrow jewelry. Wearing award show bling made us feel like we were back in the days of that old Hollywood glam. I'll never forget the year I was able to borrow a pink diamond ring worth $1 million! I had to sign so many insurance forms. There was even a guard sent to walk the red carpet with me. I only had the ring for one night, but it was so beautiful, I slept in it. I felt like Cinderella the next morning when the jewelry representative came to my house at 9 A.M. and took the ring away. That same year, Leslie wore a stunning, borrowed diamond tie clip. We were both positively giddy about our treasures. We discussed how amazingly lucky we were the whole week prior on set, and Leslie was the first person I found when I got to the event. We compared our diamonds and giggled like little kids in costumes.

156

Angela

Now it's time for me to talk about the two guys I spent the most concentrated hours with on the set of Dunder Mifflin. They are the fabulous Oscar Nuñez and Brian Baumgartner.

According to Merriam-Webster's dictionary, a "clump" is "a group of things clustered together." In offices all over the world, workers are placed into clumps, specifically "desk clumps." And as everyone who has ever worked in an office knows, your desk clump becomes your de facto work family. It was no different for Brian, Oscar, and me, aka the accounting department. Our desk clump had the only glass partition in the whole bullpen. In my mind, I imagined that Angela Martin requested that because Kevin was smelly, and she needed a barrier from the fumes.

We used to joke that Angela and Oscar were bickering parents and that Kevin was their idiot son. Much of the improvisation that we came up with for all nine seasons of *The Office* was based on that single idea. In real life, Brian is more like a childhood pal. You know that friend from the third grade who you are still close with? That's Brian for me. We are both from the South and could relate to being transplants in Los Angeles. We teased each other and roughhoused all the time. He would poke me in the ribs, and I'd

flop down on his lap and elbow him. We would get the giggles during scenes and each blame the other. Once in a scene, he had to walk past me to fake-file some papers, and he bumped into me purely by accident and I went flying. We both lost it laughing, so it became a bit we would do for years.

Jenna

Brian's character was designed to be the least qualified, least competent of the accountants. The ironic thing is that in real life, Brian is a financial wizard. He does all his own accounting. This might not seem all that impressive, but living as an actor is similar to running a small business. You get income from multiple places, and you don't keep all the money you earn—you must pay managers, agents, publicists, lawyers, union dues, insurance . . . the list goes on and on. At a

certain point, most actors turn this bookkeeping over to a business manager to make sure everyone gets paid, including the IRS, and that your savings and any investments are handled correctly. Not Brian. He does it all himself! When I have a question about how union fees and residuals are calculated, I call Brian. A bunch of us do. In fact, we have a yearly text thread that is basically cast members asking Brian about new union rules and tax laws. We love you, Brian. Thank you!

Angela

Oscar was truly my "work husband." On set, we were like an old married couple. Every day around 2 P.M., we would share a Coca-Cola. We just needed a little afternoon pick-me-up, and neither of us could finish a whole one. It happened so organically I don't think either of us ever even spoke about it. One day he had a Coke. I said, "Oh, I could use some soda." He poured me a little from his can, and that was that. Each day, one of us would grab a Coke and two cups and go find the other. We also took walks together in the studio parking lot. Our schedules were similar, and we would often be on breaks at the same time. And so we would take a brisk walk from the Dunder Mifflin set to the warehouse set around the writers' building and down the back alley by the trailers. It made a nice loop.

When I became a mom, Oscar became a set "uncle" to my daughter, Isabel. He would visit my trailer whenever she was there and read her books or be silly and make her laugh. She LOVED him.

Isabel wasn't my only family member who loved Oscar. My grandmother Lena Mae Kinsey, who didn't care for the show because she thought Michael Scott was vulgar, LOVED Oscar. She visited the set with my mother and sisters when they were in town for my baby shower, and Oscar sat and talked to my grandmother through our entire lunch break. She was completely charmed by him. Months later, I went home to visit her in Texas, and sitting on the little side table next to her recliner was a photo of Oscar mixed in with the photos of her children and great-grandchildren! His photo sat on her side table for the rest of her life.

Jenna

Oscar was definitely the mayor of *The Office*. If we had a visitor, he was the first to greet them and would probably walk them to their car when they had to leave. We had many guests over the years. People from various charities, and our own friends and family. People were always nervous when they came for a tour. I get it. Stepping onto the set of your favorite TV show and seeing all these characters in real life can be a little overwhelming. Oscar made everyone feel like they were a treasured guest in his own home. He was always looking to find ways to make another person's experience better. For example, he would offer to take a photo before the guest had to ask. It was a gesture I noted and then stole.

Like Steve, Oscar had extensive improvisational experience, and he never broke. When you put the two of them together, it was magic. The only proof you need of this is the Season 3 premiere episode, "Gay Witch Hunt." The kiss between Michael and Oscar in the conference room was not scripted. It was conceived of and masterfully executed on the spot by Steve and Oscar. None of the rest of us knew it was coming. The tension, the dialogue, Oscar's reaction, the surprised look on all our faces, it was all born in that moment. There was one take. We cheered them at the end, they were so brilliant.

Angela

Before we move on, I have to share one of my favorite things about the accounting department—our standing accounting dinners. Although our characters would NEVER have socialized outside of work, in real life, we truly enjoy one another's company. For years we have had regular "accounting" dinners, just the three of us going out for surf and turf. Brian finds the best spots and makes the reservations, and Oscar always insists on getting the five-tier appetizer tray that takes up the whole table. And even though it's harder to get together these days with our careers and our growing families, we still meet up. I love these two guys!

Jenna

While those guys were the main fellas of our acting troupe, we also had writers B. J. Novak and Paul Lieberstein popping in from time to time. Before joining *The Office*, Paul had built an extensive and impressive career as a writer on many shows, including *King of the Hill*, *The Drew Carey Show*, and *The Bernie Mac Show*. He had no experience as an actor. None whatsoever. But for "Diversity Day" in Season 1, Greg Daniels needed someone to deliver one line as HR representative Toby Flenderson. He asked Paul if he would step in. Paul reluctantly agreed. He was trying to humor Greg's desire for the writers on the show to mix with the actors. I'm pretty sure he thought it would be a one-time thing. The result was so funny that Greg started writing more and more interactions for Michael and Toby, eventually leading to Paul having a regular acting job on the show. His ability to calmly endure Michael's abuse without breaking was legendary.

When Greg left his full-time position as showrunner to launch *Parks and Recreation* with Mike Schur, Paul took over as showrunner along with Jen Celotta. I would often see him running back and forth from the writers' offices to hair and makeup, then back to the set or the editing rooms . . . he was everywhere. In the early seasons of the show, before Paul was so busy, I'd go over to his office during long breaks in filming. I loved scanning the writers' notecards on his wall in hopes of getting a glimpse into a future story line. I'd plop down on his couch and start jabbering away, sharing about some funny thing that had just happened on set. Eventually, I'd be called back to work, and I'd bounce out the door again. Paul barely got a word in edgewise. I don't know why I chose to do this with Paul and not any of the other writers, but looking back I think he was the only one who was too polite to kick me out.

Angela

B. J. Novak was the first person hired on *The Office*, as both an actor and a writer. His character of Ryan Howard has quite the journey from a temporary employee to the vice president of the northeast region and director of new media to then being convicted of fraud and yet somehow making his way back to Dunder Mifflin. My first impression of B. J. was that he was very smart and very honest. Of everyone on set, B. J. was the one who would give you the straight truth. He'll tell you you look amazing but will also let you know you have some food wedged in your teeth. He is also a very classy guy. For example, he wasn't able to attend my fortieth birthday party, but as I got ready for the party, a small wooden crate was delivered. Inside was a fancy bottle of champagne and a beautiful card from B. J. wishing me a happy birthday.

Another time, when we were all in NYC to do press and we had no idea where to eat, B. J. offered to make reservations and then took Jenna and me out for dinner. The meal was delicious, and we had a fantastic time. My favorite moment of the evening was when we stumbled onto the topic of "encounters with celebrities" from our childhood. Jenna shared a story that when she was ten, she read a poem she wrote about the St. Louis Cardinals on the local St. Louis radio station. I shared that when I was eight, my parents took me to see Kool and the Gang, and the band singled out our group. B. J. casually mentioned when he was twelve, he played Scattergories with Michael Jackson at a dinner party he attended with his parents at Deepak Chopra's house. Um, whaaaaat??? We would then learn that B. J.'s dad is a successful author, and they often went to dinners with eclectic gatherings of artists.

Jenna

Pam's journey would not have been complete without Roy, and my time on *The Office* would not have been complete without David Denman.

David played Pam's fiancé, Roy Anderson, for the first three seasons, and I'd like to use this book as my chance to tell the world that David Denman is not like Roy in any way. He's the BEST, and I adore him. We both come from theater backgrounds and love playing Texas Hold 'Em and so became instant friends. Onscreen, we had to be awkward and sour to each other, but offscreen it was another story altogether. In fact, it always comes as a surprise to people that David was one of my closest friends outside of the show. We played in weekend poker games together all the time, often going head-to-head calling the other's bluff. We also went on couples' dates, and he was my de facto plus-one for show-related events in the early days when we weren't actually allowed to bring a guest. While David didn't mind playing the "bad guy," I hated how people would react when they saw us out in public together, sometimes even shouting out rude remarks. David didn't take it personally, but it made me mad. I would want to shout back that David was a wonderful human being. He'd just laugh and say it was a sign we were doing a good job.

Angela

Roy worked in the warehouse, which was managed by none other than Darryl Philbin, played by Craig Robinson. As the series continued, Darryl became the assistant regional manager, moving into the bullpen upstairs and becoming a much greater presence on the show.

As a cast, we were thrilled to see more of his character, because Craig was so much fun on set. There was always a chance that he and Kate would burst into an improvised song. I remember in the Halloween episode of Season 8 ("Spooked"), we had been doing a conference room scene for most of the day and were all starting to get loopy. In between takes, Craig started to make up a song about the fog machine we were using, and Ellie, Ed, and Kate all joined in. It was nonsensical, but conference room scenes did that to us—being trapped in that room for long periods just inspired silliness. I have video of that day, and it never fails to make me smile. The song they improvised went something like this:

> *"We got the fog machine, and you know*
> *We lookin' really mean*
> *In our costumes that's for Halloween*
> *We got the candy and the tricker-treaters*
>   *for the scene."*

It went on for a while and only stopped when our assistant director told us it was time to start shooting again. And if there was a keyboard around, forget it. Craig would put on a full concert!

Jenna

Literally everything Craig did on set made me laugh, especially the scenes when Darryl confronts Michael. Darryl was the only one in the office that could flat-out say no to Michael Scott. I remember the scene in "Back from Vacation"

164

(Season 3) when Michael accidentally emails Darryl a photo of a topless Jan from his vacation. When he realizes what he's done, Michael runs down to the warehouse, only to find Darryl eating a full plate of food with his feet up on the desk. Michael begs Darryl to delete the photo, but Darryl just says, "I'm kinda busy here, Michael." It's an amazing moment. The plate of food was not in the script. Craig grabbed a plate from our snack table to give an added button to the scene. It was perfect comedy. I also loved how in later seasons we got to meet Darryl's daughter, and that after a few torturous years with Kelly he found love with Val and moved to Philadelphia to start a new business with Jim. Those story lines showed off the softer side of Darryl and were perfectly suited to the big-hearted man that is Craig Robinson. But my favorite memories of Craig are of our on-set sing-alongs. They were joyous, just like Angela described.

Angela

We can't close out this chapter without talking about a total sweetheart—Mr. Ed Helms. No one else could play the role of Andy Bernard, prep-school WASP and a cappella–singing salesman with anger management issues, more perfectly than Ed. I think he made me laugh harder than anyone else on set, and that is saying a lot. We had many great scenes together, but for me the most fun happened between scenes. We brought out the goofiness in each other. We used to make silly sounds to accentuate a story or pretend to be wacky characters with ridiculous accents. We would do these "comedy" bits for hours. I feel like in a different life, Ed and I would have been writing partners in some zany traveling sketch comedy show. The Andy/Angela romance story line happened to coincide with my real-life pregnancy. As a result, I did a lot of scenes with Ed while I was VERY pregnant, and he always took such good care of me. And for whatever reason, whenever Ed was talking to me, my daughter would start to kick in my belly. During the dinner scene of "Dinner Party," we were seated side by side at the table, and it was like Isabel was running a marathon. While we were filming, I subtly grabbed Ed's hand and put it on my belly. Ed's eyes got SO big, he looked at me and whispered, "Oh my God!"

During breaks, you could often find Ed playing the banjo. Our trailers were side by side, and I used to walk over and listen to him strum away. Near the end of my pregnancy, I would get sleepy and doze off to the sound of his banjo. It will forever be a soothing melody to me, because it brings me back to such a happy time. I even changed my alarm clock setting to bluegrass music because I have such fond memories of waking up from my pregnancy catnaps to Ed's playing.

Jenna

I LOVE the banjo. (My husband, Lee, and I had a bluegrass band play at our wedding.) I'd always open my trailer window so I could listen to Ed play. I especially loved when Creed would bring his guitar over and they would play together. I think my favorite scene I shot with Ed was from "The Convict" (Season 3), when Andy sings "Rainbow Connection" to Pam while playing

the banjo. I had to pretend like Pam hated it, but I personally loved being serenaded.

When my son, Weston, was born, Ed sent over a child-sized wooden banjo as a gift. A few years later, he sent a real one. Ed also invited Weston and me to be his special guests at the Bluegrass Situation music festival one year at the Greek Theatre. We got to hang backstage with Ed and the other musicians. It was so much fun. Despite Ed's best effort, my son chose the drums over the banjo. But I'm just so tickled we have two banjos from Ed Helms. Ed is a caring, thoughtful, and very funny man and also a proud dad. When Ed's film *The Hangover* came out and he was catapulted into the realm of big-time movie star, I swear it didn't change him one bit. He is just as considerate and humble as always.

Angela

All these guys filled out the world of Dunder Mifflin so perfectly. And over the years they have made us laugh and been there for us when we needed a sauce trail companion, advice on our taxes, or a tutorial on *Madden Football*. They made coming to work a blast in a million ways. Not too shabby for a sausage fest.

We love ya, fellas!

8

award shows and hollywood parties

By Season 3, our show had hit a groove. We were no longer worried about the prospect of being canceled at any time. Our ratings increased, critics had come around, and we began to be nominated for awards.

As the popularity of the show grew, so did our social calendar. We started getting invited to all sorts of things: movie premieres, charity events, random "parties" thrown by magazines, and even fancy award shows. They don't teach you how to pick a gown and pose on a red carpet in acting school. There is no training for how to suddenly be around *really* famous people without totally losing your cool. Or how to adjust to being famous yourself! We had to learn these skills as we went along, and it was not without hiccups. But luckily, we had each other. We failed and succeeded together. Let's start at the beginning—before we hit the groove, back when we were still learning.

PAWS AND PRUNES

Angela

When I daydreamed about becoming an actress, I couldn't help but imagine myself in a gorgeous gown on the red carpet. The "red carpet" has been synonymous with royalty for centuries and became a permanent fixture in Hollywood at the Academy Awards in 1961. Did you know that the Oscars red carpet is 50,000 feet long, weighs over 630 pounds, and takes weeks to set up?! I could not wait to walk my first red carpet! I wondered about which designer I would wear, who would do my makeup and hair, whether I would don any fabulous (borrowed) jewels. So imagine my excitement when Jenna invited me to my first red-carpet event! We had just started shooting Season 2. Her agent sent her the invitation, and Jenna asked if I'd be her plus-one. Jenna told me that the event was to be held at the Loews Hotel in Beverly Hills. Beverly friggin Hills! We were at lunch when she opened the envelope. I was sure I was going to find something printed on gilded paper and tied with ribbon, but as Jenna handed me the invitation, the first image I saw was a dog.

Jenna

! probably should have told Angela the invitation was for an animal charity event. She looked a little confused as she read it. The event was called Paws for Style, and the money raised would go to the Humane Society. I was invited to bring my dog, Wesley . . . that was the "paws" part. The "style" was a runway show where celebrities walked a catwalk with their dogs, but the *dogs* were the ones in high fashion. There you have it: Paws for Style. Just to be clear, Wesley and I were not part of the fashion show. Instead, we were invited to watch the fashion show and mingle afterward at a cocktail party. The invitation read "Upscale Casual. Red Carpet Upon Arrival."

Angela

So it was official: Paws for Style was to be my red-carpet debut. And even though I wouldn't be wearing an evening gown, I was very excited. It was time to go shopping. To prepare for the event, I bought a turquoise tank top at Target and another turquoise tank top from the Gap, and I layered them. I layered two turquoise tank tops. Why did I layer two turquoise tank tops? I cannot answer this question, because I do not know. I thought I looked cute. Then I added a pair of white jeans and a little turquoise corduroy purse (both also from Target). For shoes, my mom gave me a pair of her very tall wedge heels. They were a size too big, and I could barely walk in them, but I was determined. I did my own hair and makeup. I was red-carpet ready!

Jenna

I spent very little time on my outfit (something I think you can tell from the photos). I was most concerned with how I was going to bring my thirty-pound terrier mix rescue pup, Wesley, to a red-carpet event. Now, Wesley was a good dog. He had lots of energy, but he was sweet and obedient. Even still, it is not easy to navigate a party with even the most well-behaved dog on a leash. Especially when the entire party is filled with dogs on leashes. But I didn't think that far ahead when I RSVP'd. I just thought it would be an interesting night out—so off we went.

Angela

The event took place on July 19, 2005, and the headliner was Paula Abdul. Not only was her music a fixture in my teen years, but *American Idol* Season 4 (which she hosted) had just finished filming, and Carrie Underwood had won. I had LOTS of questions for Paula. Jenna drove that night, and our first hiccup was finding parking. No one told us where to park. This is when we learned that most celebrities hire limos or car companies to drop them at the door of these events. We did not. We had Jenna's Volkswagen Jetta, and we needed to park close because I could barely walk in my three-inch wedges. And Jenna had her dog.

Jenna

As it turns out, the hotel was actually in the heart of Hollywood, not Beverly Hills. (I think they fudged the invite.) I remember circling the block looking for a spot on the street because it cost a fortune to park at the hotel. I'd only just paid off my credit cards and I could hear my dad's voice in my ear telling me there was no way I should pay $35 to use the valet service at a fancy hotel. We finally found a spot and Wesley promptly peed on the tree by my car. I was happy about that, because now it was less likely he would pee on the red carpet. As we walked up to the event, I watched Angela's face fall. There were photographers taking photos, but the red carpet was actually a faux wood walkway. I'm guessing this was because of the dogs, as it was easier to clean up accidents on this surface than an actual carpet. Then we saw Paula Abdul. She was getting set to walk the wooden "carpet" with her three Chihuahua mixes all dressed in cute sweater outfits. Paula was very friendly. She greeted us with a big smile, and our dogs sniffed each other's butts. My teenage self, who had memorized all the dance moves in her video "Straight Up," was fangirling big-time. I really wanted a photo with her, but was too shy to ask.

Angela

So there was no red carpet. I shook it off because Paula Abdul was standing right in front of me. We watched as Paula and her dogs posed for photos. She was clearly a pro. She would turn from side to side and pop her leg out and put her hand on her hip. She was amazing. Effortless. Even with three dogs. I was taking mental notes.

And then it was our turn.

Jenna

I went first. I started by walking Wesley down the "carpet" on his leash, but a photographer yelled, "Hold up your pup!" Wesley was one of those dogs that was small enough to carry, but too big to hold gracefully. I had to give Angela my purse and pick him up with both arms. It was beyond awkward.

Angela

I thought Jenna did great. I mean, she *was* holding a dog. Then it was my turn. It was time for my first red carpet (that was actually a wooden floor). I took a deep breath and stepped in front of the photographers. I intended to do my best Paula. Turn, leg pop, hip, smile! Repeat! But I was afraid to blink or move. I stood there, stiff as a board, holding two purses and staring blankly for an uncomfortably long time. They actually had to usher me off because I was holding up the line. I learned the reason they call a red carpet a "step-and-repeat" is that you are supposed to keep moving. I was doing more of a "step-and-stare."

Jenna

But look at us! We did it! Our first BFF red carpet was in the books. The dog fashion show was adorable. We had a great time mingling with the other guests and their pups, although we could only stay two hours because that was the limit on the meter for my car.

Angela

As Jenna said, we had done it. But we also agreed we could do better. But how do you get better at something like this? Practice! I started practicing poses and realized I had no idea what to do with my hands. I looked through dozens of magazines featuring celebrities at events and made note of different hand placements. The "one hand on hip," "both hands on hips," "both hands by your sides," "one hand on the thigh," and "both hands clasped in front" were all options. After trying them out in front of my mirror, I decided "both hands clasped in front" was the way to go.

Jenna

My research provided us with this nugget: I read that the reason Mary-Kate and Ashley Olsen always look so cute in red-carpet pictures is because they say the word "prune" while the photographers are taking the shot. (Who knows if this is really true. But that's what I read.) The idea is that it gives you the perfect mix of pouty and sexy. We decided at our next press event that we were going to say "prune" while our picture was being taken and clasp our hands in front of our bodies.

Angela

We were sure this was the magic we needed to look amazing, and we had the perfect event to try our theory. Jenna and I were invited to *US Weekly*'s Young Hollywood Hot 20 party on September 16, 2005. We went to the mall and bought party dresses. The hair and makeup folks from *The Office* got us ready. They even put a shimmery lotion on our arms and legs. We looked so good! We still drove to the party in Jenna's Jetta, *but* we figured out where to park before we left. We were going to nail this one, guys.

When we got to the party, the red carpet was abuzz with activity. Jenna went first, and I could see her saying "prune," but she wasn't clasping her hands. I wasn't sure why. Soon it was my turn. I remembered to move and blink. Things were going great. But when I went to clasp my hands, I realized I was holding my purse. I didn't factor my purse into the "clasp pose." Dang it! I began to panic and awkwardly put my hand on my hip. In my head I was saying, *Too low! Too low! You're putting your hand too low!* But it was too late. I was so worried about my arms, I forgot to say "prune."

Jenna

The next day we were so excited to see our photos. I did the whole red carpet saying "prune," "prune," "prune," and in every photo I either look constipated or pissed-off. I did not master the "prune." Angela hated her arm placement, but at least she was smiling. The night wasn't a total disaster. I thought we still looked cute. But we didn't look like Paula, Mary-Kate, or Ashley. We'd get there eventually.

AWARD SHOWS AND FAMOUS PEOPLE!

Jenna

Our first invitation to an award show was for the 2006 Golden Globes. It was January, and we were halfway through shooting the second season of *The Office* when Steve Carell was nominated for Best Actor in a Television Series. Our ratings were low and we were on the verge of cancellation, so this nomination was incredible for the whole cast. It created a great deal of publicity for the show, which meant possibly more viewers and perhaps the chance to stay on the air.

But as Steve was the only one nominated, he was the only person invited to attend the actual award show. The rest of the cast was invited to watch the show live at the NBCUniversal viewing party nearby. We were not allowed a plus-one but were thrilled to attend what I called the "Award Show Adjacent Event."

In the weeks leading up to the Award Show Adjacent Event, my agent asked a stylist if they could arrange for me to borrow a dress. I didn't get any choices. I received one black dress at my house. It fit. I wore it. My friend knew a jeweler who worked out of her home about forty-five minutes away from me in Calabasas. I went over one afternoon, and she let me try on different necklaces and earrings. I ended up borrowing a pearl choker. The Golden Globes were on a Monday evening, and, after working all day shooting the show, the hair and makeup team from *The Office* offered to quickly transform the cast for

the party. I remember my hairdresser Kim Ferry suggesting an updo as the best way to quickly restyle my hair from Pam to glam. I arranged for a limo to pick up Angela, Kate, Paul, and me at the set (no more circling the block for parking) and drive us to the viewing party.

Angela

I splurged and got my first ever spray tan and bought my dress at Macy's. Since we went straight from work to the party, I just kept my "Angela Martin" ponytail from the episode we were filming that week. When we arrived, we quickly realized that the NBCUniversal viewing party was on the roof of the parking garage for the hotel where the actual Golden Globes were taking place. I called it the "Parking Lot Party." NBC put up a huge tent and laid down a large carpet, but on the edges of this outdoor room you could still see the white lines for parking spots. Around the perimeter of the tent were pleather benches and TVs mounted in fake silver frames. The first thing I noticed was there were no bathrooms. (I am the person who always scopes out the bathroom right away. I pee a lot.) I would spend the next two hours looking for a bathroom. The party was filled with network executives and agents. I'm pretty sure we were the only actors in attendance. And since

The Office had been on less than a year, people didn't know the show or us that well. There was a tiny red carpet just before you stepped into the party. No one shouted our names for a photo. I had brought my own camera and asked Paul to take a picture of Jenna and me. I thought that this Parking Lot Party might be our first and last experience with a Hollywood award show.

You had to cross a bridge from the parking garage to the hotel to get to them. It was a hike, so I asked Jenna to go with me. What we didn't know was that this corridor was also being used by the guests of the actual Golden Globes to leave the show. So there we are swimming upstream against movie stars like Russell Crowe, Keira Knightley, Judi Dench, Terrence Howard, and more. We dove into the bathroom erupting into laughter and bumped right into Rhona Mitra. I was a fan of hers from her show *The Practice*, so of course I asked for photos . . . in the bathroom! (Yep, I was *that* person.) The whole evening was full of hilarious and ridiculously awesome moments. It was one of the most amazing nights of my life.

Jenna

Without a doubt, it was one of the most joyous nights of my life as well. We closed that party down, dancing, drinking, and posing with Steve's award. Steve kept saying over and over that he couldn't have done it without us. He was so gracious. Steve remained the same wonderful Steve after his win, but the energy surrounding the show started to change. We were on people's radar now.

Angela

The show really skyrocketed in popularity after we won an Emmy for Outstanding Comedy Series in September 2006. Once again, we were not the favorite to win . . . but we did! Our struggling show had now won two major awards in one year. Journalists started coming to set wanting to do stories on us, *Access Hollywood* showed up for interviews, and people learned our names. The change was real, and fast.

Jenna

I'll never forget the time we were eating outside on the patio of a restaurant in North Hollywood when someone screamed from the passenger side window of a passing car, "JENNA AND ANGELA, WE LOVE *THE OFFICE*!" Or the time we were shopping in the seasonal aisle at Target and heard someone humming the *Office* theme song over our shoulders. After nearly two years of working on the show in relative obscurity, we were suddenly popular.

Angela

During the run of *The Office*, the cast and crew received a combined total of 163 award nominations and thirty wins. As a cast, we took home two Screen Actors Guild Awards, one Primetime Emmy Award, and a TV Land Award.

And now, after attending so many of these events, we learned a few tips and tricks we'd like to share with you.

I don't want to say that Jenna and I have the whole "fancy Hollywood award show" routine down, but by the end of our nine years on the show, we could blend into the red-carpet crowd without looking like total idiots. And we always had a really good time. So, should you find yourself at one of these gala shindigs in the future, here is . . .

THE OFFICIAL *OFFICE* BFF GUIDE
TO HOLLYWOOD PARTIES
#1: Eat

Jenna

One thing all award shows have in common is that they are very, very long. Eat before you go. We cannot stress this enough. There is usually very little food but ample amounts of adult beverages. This can be a problem.

Angela

At the Emmys, you sit in a traditional theater, as if you were attending a play. Once inside, they do not serve any food or drinks at all. At the Screen Actors Guild Awards, they do serve a meal, but I swear it's never enough. It's like a meal for a toddler. It is tiny. EAT BEFORE YOU GO. I DON'T CARE HOW TIGHT YOUR DRESS IS.

Jenna

I do not like to be without food. Ever. But certainly not at award shows. The red-carpet portion of these events starts in the midafternoon. You are on the red carpet by 3 P.M.; the event starts at 5 P.M. There is no dinner. The after-parties usually have food, but you won't get to those until at least 9 P.M. I usually try

110162

THE 14TH ANNUAL SCREEN ACTORS GUILD AWARDS
SHRINE EXPOSITION HALL
SUNDAY, JANUARY 27, 2008
3:30 Cocktails
4:30 Doors Close
4:45 Show Begins
5:00 LIVE Broadcast
7:00 Post Awards Gala
LIVE ON TNT & TBS
PRICE: $600
Black Tie

ANGELA KINSEY

Table 07   Seat 12

CW86P

TICKETS ARE NON-TRANSFERABLE, NON-REFUNDABLE, AND NOT FOR RESALE.

to pack a snack. (Yes, I'm that lady. I am not embarrassed to pull a protein bar out of my purse while chatting with Tom Hanks. I'm just not.) The only problem is that those fancy evening bags are usually the size of your hand. I've gone to events where I've had to choose between bringing my phone or a granola bar. This creates a major dilemma for me. I need my phone. I also know what happens when I get hangry.

Angela

For Jenna to say "I don't like to be without food" does not properly communicate what this woman is willing to do when she is hungry. You know in the "Dinner Party" episode when Pam says, "I just want to eat"? That was 100 percent based on Jenna in real life. Let me provide you with an example: It was the 2010 Emmys, and *The Office* was nominated for Best Comedy Series. We were all starving, because despite the advice emphatically shared above, none of us followed it. During a commercial break, Jenna turned to me with a fire in her eyes and said, "Let's go look for food." This was not a suggestion. She was giving marching orders. We gathered our dates, Jenna's husband, Lee, and my friend Michael, and off we went.

First, we checked the bars in the lobby. No food. Then we went to the back of the ballroom near the bathrooms. No food, but I did see Ann-Margret and Alexander Skarsgård. That was pretty cool, but Jenna had no time for chatter about celebrity sightings—she was on a mission. Jenna found a young gal wearing a staff blazer and a headset, holding a clipboard. Bingo. Headset Gal quietly said something into her headset mic and then motioned for us all to come quickly. Headset Gal was surprisingly agile and fast. We were practically running down a long hallway to keep up with her. She led us around a corner to a security guard standing by a big thick curtain. Headset Gal whispered something to him, and he quietly ushered us behind the curtain. There we were greeted by an elegant older woman in an evening gown who was also wearing a headset and holding an even fancier-looking clipboard. The room was dimly lit, and my eyes took a moment to focus, but it was clear that she was important. She sternly whispered for us to be *very* quiet. I nodded. I did not want to piss off this woman. Elegant Headset Woman pointed us toward a table of food. Jenna pounced, piling cheese and salami on a plate. I looked around for Michael and Lee, but they were nowhere in sight.

I went to the back to the big curtain and found them standing with the security guard. Michael and Lee apparently weren't allowed anywhere near that food. I motioned to Jenna and pointed to Lee and Michael, but she just kept eating. I was finally able to convince the security guard to let our dates in, and we went to find Jenna. She had moved on from the charcuterie table to the dessert table. She handed the three of us giant chocolate chip cookies and never broke stride, chewing the entire time.

It was then that I realized that not only were we in a private greenroom for Emmy presenters and nominees, but this room was actually just a curtained-off section situated right on THE STAGE. Let me repeat. WE WERE ON THE ACTUAL EMMY STAGE! That is why it was so dimly lit. The show was literally going on just a few feet away, and we were stuffing our faces with chocolate chip cookies. No wonder they kept telling us to keep quiet!

There were only a handful of other people in the greenroom—Laurence Fishburne was about to present an award. As I took the last bite of my cookie and started in on a plate of cheese, I felt a gaze come over me. I briefly made eye contact with Mr. Fishburne. He leaned over to a man seated next to him and whispered something along the lines of, "Who the fuck are these assholes?" I whispered to Michael, "Did Laurence Fishburne just call us assholes?" He fervently nodded yes. I took that as a sign that we should wrap it up.

Jenna

I missed this exchange entirely. I was too busy going back for seconds of salami. Lee whispered that we needed to go, and he seemed to mean it, so I grabbed a banana and we tiptoed the heck out of there. When we finally got back into the hallway, we burst out laughing.

Angela

Only Jenna would find a way to muscle us onto the actual Emmy stage for snacks. I'm sure Laurence Fishburne will never read this, but just in case: We're very sorry. We were those assholes shoving cheese and cookies into our faces while you were preparing to go on the Emmy stage. Also, to the Television Academy: Can you please consider adding a snack table by the bathrooms for future ceremonies? Be sure to include the giant chocolate chip cookies. They were very good. Thanks.

Jenna

This is a true story, and I'm not in the least bit ashamed. In fact, I am proud of it.

#2: Never Pee Alone

Angela

Finding a bathroom is tricky. You will likely have to walk a VERY far distance and climb a stupid amount of stairs in your ridiculously high, uncomfortable heels to find a bathroom. You might get lost and find yourself in a random hotel corridor with a rollaway bed. You'll need your BFF to document the moment if the lighting is good.

187

Ladies, listen to us. You need a bathroom buddy. And not just to take photos. If you've ever gotten married, you know what it's like trying to pee while wearing your wedding dress. You need someone to hold up your dress, your purse, probably your shoes, and help you get your Spanx down and then back up again. Here's something else they don't teach you in acting school: If you win an award, you have to carry it around all night. That means you also have to carry it to the bathroom and either set it on the ground OR ask your bathroom buddy to hold it while you pee.

Visiting the bathroom is a MUST for other reasons, even if you don't have to go. One of our favorite parts of award shows is the bathroom. You can see tons of A-list movie stars in line for the bathroom. It was while standing in line for the bathroom that I found myself next to ANGELINA JOLIE, THE MOST BEAUTIFUL WOMAN IN THE WORLD. We didn't speak to each other, but STILL. It's also fun to see a SAG award or an Emmy sitting on the sink while someone washes their hands. In summary: Go to the bathroom. Bring a buddy.

#3: How to Avoid Wardrobe Mishaps

If you attend enough of these events, you will eventually have a wardrobe mishap. It's destined to happen. When it happens to you, perhaps it will bring you comfort to know . . . we've been there.

Jenna

Mine happened early. It was August 11, 2005, and Steve had invited the entire cast to the premiere of his movie *The 40-Year-Old Virgin*. We were very excited to attend the premiere as a cast and support our friend for such a big movie opening. Our wardrobe designer helped me find a dress and some gold vintage shoes to match. I felt very stylish. The dress was unusual. It had a teal silk slip covered in blue-green printed lace and a wide, bright blue ribbon that sat on my hips and hung down to my knees in the front. Imagine a mermaid dressed as a flapper from the 1920s. The premiere was on a Thursday evening. We went after a full day of work. I only had about twenty minutes to get ready before I had to be on my way. In my rush to get ready, I'd forgotten to use the restroom. When I arrived at the event, the first thing I did was run to the bathroom. I was VERY CAREFUL not to pee on the long blue ribbon. I mean, that would have been a disaster. I held it above my head. Mission accomplished. No pee on ribbon. I reapplied some lip gloss, checked myself in the mirror. I looked great. Time to hit the red carpet. I walked, I posed, I felt sassy in my dress. I even did an over-the-shoulder pose! Lucy Davis, who had played Dawn in the British *Office* series, was there. We posed together. What a night. Once inside, I found my seat between Rainn and John. I waved to Angela a few seats away. When I sat down, something didn't feel right. I could feel the fabric of the seat directly on my bottom. I thought, *Huh, this feels odd.* I reached my hand behind me, and I felt lace, and then skin. No slip. WHERE WAS THE SLIP?!? I'll tell you. It was tucked into my underwear.

It was in this moment that I realized I had just walked the entire *40-Year-Old Virgin* red carpet with my slip tucked into my underwear with only lace and a sash hiding my undies. But wait. There is more. I was not wearing cute undies. I was wearing what Angela calls "laundry day undies." They were from a Target variety pack and featured a silly butterfly-and-flowers print. From the front, the big blue sash (that I'd worked so hard not to pee on) saved the day. But there was nothing saving the sassy over-the-shoulder shots.

Angela

My wardrobe mishap was at the 62nd Emmy Awards. For the first time ever, a designer had offered to loan me a dress for an event. It was a beautiful strapless couture gown by Romona Keveza. It had a long train. I felt very fancy. I had never had to maneuver my way down a red carpet with a train before. It was more complicated than I thought. As I went down the red carpet, I would pick up my train and carry it to the next section of photographers and then let it down to pose. I quickly realized I had a whole evening of train maintenance ahead of me. I didn't care. I loved my dress. I watched as Jenna breezed her way down the carpet in her no-train dress and waited for me at the end so we could enter the event together. I had only one bank of photographers left, so I felt confident. I took a step but couldn't seem to move. I was stuck on something. I took an even bigger, bolder step to try to free myself when suddenly my dress was violently yanked down! I had been standing on my own dress with one foot and yanking off my dress with the other. My boobs nearly popped out! I immediately doubled over and grabbed my chest. *Flash flash flash!* It was all captured on film. Nearly every photo from this red carpet is of me fighting with my dress. I'm not saying you shouldn't wear a dress with a train on the red carpet, but definitely practice walking at home before you go.

#4: Take a Lap

Take full advantage of the commercial breaks. During those minutes, everyone gets up and mingles. The room is basically a sea of your favorite stars chatting, laughing, and being fabulous and famous with one another. Get out there and enjoy!

Angela

Jenna loved walking around during the commercial breaks. She called it "taking a lap." I don't like mingling during the commercial breaks, but she always insisted. It's enough for me to have walked a gazillion miles in my fancy dress and awful shoes to find a bathroom. After those adventures, I just want to kick off my high heels, eat one of the three peanuts that have been graciously placed on the table, and drink one of the five bottles of wine. But if you are with Jenna, she will say, "Come on! This is the freaking SAG Awards! Let's take a lap!" She's very persuasive. And so off we would go.

Jenna

My mom told me I had to take advantage of these situations. "You don't know how long you'll be invited to these parties, Jenna. Make the most of them!" So yes, I wanted us to mingle. Everyone table-hops, and commercial breaks are a great opportunity to meet people. Plus, there are often television stars *and* movie stars in attendance at these events. So I would make Angela put her shoes on and walk around the room with me. I also had a strategy on how to walk up to celebrities you didn't know. First of all, you have to be smiling as you approach them, and then right as you get close, begin to laugh. Continue to stand there and laugh, and then say hello. I am telling you, this works. That is how we met Meryl Streep!

Angela

This is one of Jenna's proudest accomplishments of all the award shows we attended. Early in the evening, she spotted Meryl Streep, and she was laser-focused on meeting her. We began doing our laps around the room, but with no luck. I thought Jenna might have given up and I'd get to eat some peanuts, but then Jenna saw Amy Adams talking to Meryl. My BFF leaped out of her seat and began to drag me across the room. She said, "Angela, come on! Come on! This is our chance. We know Amy! We'll walk up to Amy, and she'll introduce us." As we got closer to them, you could tell they were mid-conversation. And then the lights started dimming, signaling us to return to our seats because the show was about to resume. I started to backpedal, but Jenna was determined. That's when on the fly, Jenna came up with her "walk up laughing" plan. I didn't have time to think it through; we were about to be right next to them. Jenna stepped forward boldly laughing, and I trailed behind half-assed laughing. And I'll be damned if Amy didn't turn and smile and introduce Jenna to Meryl Streep! Then the lights dimmed again, and everyone dispersed. I never met Meryl.

Jenna

You came *very* close to meeting Meryl. Can we just take a moment to acknowledge that my plan worked?! The "lap around the room laughing" approach is a winner!

Meryl looked at me right in the eyes and smiled. She said my name, and I'm pretty sure she glanced over my shoulder at Angela. We sort of met Meryl Streep, and no one can take it away from us. I'd just like to say, I feel like this chapter is making it very clear that I am the best person in the world to attend an award show with. You will get food *and* meet Meryl Streep. As a huge bonus, a photographer captured this moment and now we can treasure it forever.

#5: Play It Cool

Angela

Be prepared to be approached by famous people. It's true—sometimes the tables turn. And sometimes super-famous people want to meet you or get a photo with *you*, instead of you fake-laughing your way into a Hollywood royalty photo op. If you're like us, this will blow your mind.

Jenna

I will never forget the time I was crossing the room at an Emmys party and ran right into Sally Field. Like, literally ran into her. I was mortified. I said, "Oh my goodness! I'm so sorry!" She said, "Jenna Fischer?" And I said, "Sally Field? You know my name?" And she said, "Oh yes! I am a huge fan." I played it cool and said something like, "Oh my goodness, that means so much to me. I just love your films!" She gave me a hug and told me she couldn't wait to see more of my work in the future. She walked away, and then I pooped myself. Not literally, but metaphorically. Guys, Sally Field was one of my idols growing up. There were three actresses I studied: Debra Winger, Shelley Long, and SALLY FIELD. And she had just told me SHE KNEW ME and was a FAN?? When I got home that night, I called my mom and woke her up (it was after midnight in Missouri) and screamed, "SALLY FIELD KNOWS ME!" I knew my mom would get it. And she did. She started screaming with me and said, "Oh, Jenna! That is just so cool! I remember taking you to watch her movies over and over again!" (I'd just like to point out these are exactly the types of experiences my mom didn't want me to miss out on by refusing to mingle.)

Angela

Of all of the famous folks I've met, the one encounter that took me completely by surprise didn't actually happen at an award show or a fancy party, but rather in a Southwest Airlines terminal. Back in March of 2018, my tall friend Rainn Wilson was set to host an event in San Francisco for the Tahirih Justice Center. (They are an amazing nonprofit organization that helps immigrant survivors fleeing gender-based violence.) Due to a scheduling conflict, Rainn was unable to attend, and he asked if I could step in for him. After hearing the stories of the women Tahirih has helped over the years, my answer was an enthusiastic yes. It was an amazing night, and I am still in awe of what this organization does for others. The next morning, I had an early flight back to Los Angeles out of San Francisco International Airport. While my husband was looking for coffee, the airline announced that it was time to board the plane. I grabbed our carry-on luggage and went to stand in line, when a shy young gal in a hoodie sweatshirt and baggy orange pants walked up to me and asked if I'd take a photo with her. I said of course and a big smile came across her face. She introduced me to her brother, Finneas, and he snapped a few photos of us. She was such a sweetheart, and even in those few moments I was charmed by her. She told me thank you and we said goodbye. My husband walked up (with coffee and a donut—bless him) and asked me who she was. I said I didn't know, just a lovely *Office* fan. We got on the plane, and I didn't think much more about it until a few days later,

when I suddenly noticed I'd been tagged a gazillion times in a photo of me and the sweet gal from the airport. That gal was Billie Eilish. If I wasn't a hundred years old, maybe I would have recognized her when she approached me. The photo she posted of us, as the kids say, "went viral." I immediately downloaded her music and was blown away by her voice! Billie, not only are you crazy-talented but you also share the same name as my sister and my dad (so you are already a winner in my book!). And you made me seem cool to my kids . . . so thank you!

#6: Share This Moment with Someone You Love

Angela

One of my most cherished memories is when I took my dad to the Emmys in 2009. I wasn't sure what he would make of the whole award show scene. My dad had grown up on a ranch in rural Texas and in his early twenties began a career working on oil rigs.

Suits were not part of his job description.

Despite his rugged lifestyle, my dad was a devoted family man. My mom, my sisters, and I were his whole life. When I told him that I wanted to move away from home to become an actress, he cried. He couldn't imagine me so far away, and he struggled with my career choice. But true to his loyal heart, he became my biggest champion. My mom shared with me that he was so thrilled when I asked him to be my date to the Emmy Awards that he bought their plane tickets that very day. He and my mom made a deal that he would go to the actual awards with me, but that she would be my date for all the pre-show parties. He didn't want her to feel left out.

Mom put together her outfit pretty quickly, but Dad agonized over the "perfect" suit to wear. They drove twenty-five miles to the nearest Jos. A. Bank men's clothing store so he could go suit shopping. My dad never met a stranger, and Mom said he told everyone he was going with his daughter to an award show in Los Angeles. On the day of the Emmys, he couldn't stop smiling. He chatted up the hair and makeup gals, he chatted up our limo driver, he chatted up the award show staff as we waited on the red carpet. Thanks to my dad, several people learned our whole life story before the ceremony ever took place.

As I walked the red carpet, photographers were yelling out my name. My dad was beside himself. He couldn't believe that all those people knew my name.

Then a photographer asked me who my date was, and I said my dad and gave his name, Bill Kinsey. As we turned a corner to the next bank of photographers, one of them called out, "Mr. Kinsey! Bill! Over here!" My dad's eyes got big as saucers, and he enthusiastically waved back. He was so tickled.

During the ceremony, we were seated next to Jenna and Lee, and in the first commercial break they got up to mingle (that classic Jenna move). Well, they didn't make it back to their seats in time and were temporarily stuck outside the theater until the next commercial break. Two strangers promptly took their place. My dad was worried and leaned over to me and said, "We've got a couple of hitchhikers." He was convinced these interlopers had stolen Jenna and Lee's seats. My dad politely whispered to the seat fillers that those seats were taken, and they needed to find other ones. He then put my purse and program on Jenna and Lee's seats so no one else would take them. I had to tell my dad that they were actually doing their job. Seat fillers are hired by award shows to make sure whenever a camera sweeps the audience that *all* seats are filled. When the actor comes back, the seat fillers return to the wings. Well, that was more than my dad could wrap his mind around. He had endless questions for me about seat fillers for the rest of the night.

Jenna

I remember this very clearly, because the first time I went to an award show, I thought people were stealing our seats too. Being at these big events can be overwhelming. Especially for someone who is more of an introvert like I am. I know we've shared a lot about my bold drive to make the most of these evenings, but I was only able to do that because I had Angela by my side. She gives me courage. She also keeps me safe, both emotionally and physically. There is no better example of this than the time she quite literally had to scoop me off the floor at a press event for *The Office* in New York City.

It was May 2007, and we were in New York promoting the Season 3 finale of the show. During the day, we did interviews and participated in a live presentation to advertisers. In the evening, there was a meet-and-greet "party" where actors from different shows mingled with press and advertisers as a way to build up publicity and ad revenue. As Angela would say, "It's work, but it's fancy work."

On this particular evening, the party was at a club called Buddakan. The venue has two floors separated by a long marble staircase. We entered on the top floor, where there was a small bar with drinks. The staff was serving a pineapple daiquiri type cocktail. I'm not much of a drinker, but I love a fruity beverage in a novelty glass, so I grabbed one. To get to the main part of the event, you had to go down the long set of marble stairs. I had my fancy drink in my hand as I did my best to walk down the stairs. I took one sip of my daiquiri and something terrible happened. My foot slipped out from underneath me, and I went crashing down on the edge of the stairs. Hard. To add insult to injury, I also threw my drink in my own face. I was sitting on the ground, covered in daiquiri, and feeling like I might vomit when the room started to spin. A bouncer came over and immediately started treating me like a boozy Hollywood starlet. I tried to explain that I hadn't even had a full sip of my drink. That in fact, it was all over my head. But I was disoriented. I was probably slurring my words. He picked me up and whisked me away to a back room. Angela followed. I told her my back hurt and I didn't feel good. She lifted up the back of my shirt and immediately said, "Call an ambulance."

Angela

I was behind Jenna on that staircase, and I saw her go down. Someone had spilled something on those stairs, and they were slick. Jenna was wearing wedge high heels, and she turned her ankle. When she fell, I couldn't stop it. I saw it all happen in slow motion right in front of me. Her back was purple and swollen, there was a small cut and some blood. It did not look good, and I was scared.

Jenna

I only remember bits and pieces after that. I remember being loaded into an ambulance. I remember getting morphine and an X-ray. I definitely remember that Angela was by my side the entire time. Even when the nurses came in to give me a catheter, she stayed. I remember being asked, "Would you like your friend to step out while we give you this catheter?" and answering, "Not only would I prefer she stayed, I'd like to hold her hand."

Angela

There was no way I was leaving her for a second. I climbed into the back of the ambulance and told them, "She has no family here, and she's going to an emergency room in a city that's not her own. I am not going anywhere. You are stuck with me." They didn't mess with me after that.

Jenna

I vaguely remember something about a man being handcuffed to the bed next to me.

Angela

Oh yes. The police walked him in, and he was very surly. They handcuffed him to the chair next to your hospital bed and left. I shut the little curtain around us but if I hadn't been there to do that, Jenna would have been staring at a surly drunk guy for hours!

Jenna

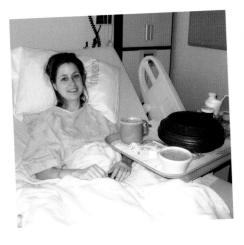

Eventually I was admitted and moved to a room. Angela took up residence in the chair next to my bed, and we drifted in and out . . . or at least I did. But I'll never forget the doctor coming in to give me my X-ray result. He said, "The good news is you're going to walk again." I said, "Well, that is good news. However, it feels like there is a lot of bad news if you are leading with that." As it turns out, I had fractured four of the transverse vertebrae in my back. If you're going to have a back injury, I guess this is the best one, because it will heal on its own, similar to a broken rib. And motion is the best thing for it. So even though walking and moving were painful, I was encouraged to do it. I was told I would be discharged in the morning but that I was not allowed to travel for at least two weeks.

Angela

Here's a crazy twist to the story: NBC had put the entire cast up at the Ritz-Carlton for the two days that we were doing press. We had been so excited! Talk about country mouse come to town—we were at the fancy-schmancy Ritz-Carlton facing Central Park. Well, when Jenna broke her back, NBC had to extend her stay for two weeks!

Jenna

That's right. I lived at the Ritz-Carlton for two weeks with my broken back. Angela stayed with me for the first week. My family headed out to New York to help me, but they needed a few days to get there. My *Office* castmates all

came by to visit as I recovered. When Creed stopped in, the three of us watched *The Larry Sanders Show* together. Laughter really is the best medicine.

After my accident, I couldn't shower for several days. That fruity pineapple drink I'd thrown all over the left side of my head got very smelly. I mean I was gross. I'm sorry you had to live with that, Ange.

Angela

I think every friendship has milestone moments that forever bond you. Trying to wash rotten pineapple daquiri out of your friend's hair before gently lowering her onto the toilet is definitely one of those moments.

Jenna

Yeah, that's best friendship right there. That brings us to . . .

#7: Have Fun!

Definitely dance the night away with your friends and castmates. The *Office* cast always took over the dance floor at every event. Don't be afraid to dork out. And if dancing isn't your thing . . . have fun in other ways. Stage a fight or jump into the pool in your evening dress. We've done it all.

Angela

Whether it was at the Emmys or SAG Awards or NBC publicity parties . . . we were the center of the action in those days. During the after-party for the 2009 SAG Awards, Creed jumped onstage and sang with the band. No one cuts a rug like Craig Robinson. And any time they played Beyoncé's "Single Ladies," Jenna, Oscar, and I took to the dance floor to re-create the music video.

To understand how passionately we took over a dance floor, one only needs to gaze upon Jenna's expression the night we ruled the 2006 NBC press party in New York City.

BTW, Jenna and I are totally sober in this photo. We are just that happy to be crushing it on the dance floor.

Jenna

One year, we decided to stage a fight in the middle of the after-party for the SAG Awards. We'd been joking about how no one believed that our cast were actually all friends in real life and that our show was drama-free. Rumors of infighting on the sets of *Desperate Housewives* and *Grey's Anatomy* were big tabloid fodder at the time, and it felt like reporters were looking to find more of these stories anywhere they could. Several of us had journalists corner us on the red carpet and say, "Come on. You guys *really* all get along? There must be something you aren't telling us." By the way, I always found these questions so funny. First of all, there really was no drama. But if there was, would we have shared about it on the red carpet?? Could you imagine their faces if I'd said, "Oh, I've been wanting to talk about our on-set drama for years, thanks for asking . . ." Anyway, we were joking that we should stage a huge fight just to see what would happen. So we did.

Nothing happened. No one believed it. In fact, during our time on the show we were rarely the subject of tabloid gossip. When we were, it was comical. I remember reading a story in the *National Enquirer* trying to imply that John Kraskinski and I were secretly dating. Their proof was a report from an "inside source" that we ate lunch together alone in my trailer every day. When I showed the article to John and Angela on set, we all laughed so hard. John said, "They meant Angela! You eat lunch with Angela every day!" As funny as it was, I'll admit it was weird to read a

100 percent false story about myself in a tabloid. Growing up, I always knew that not everything you read was true, but I figured there must be *some* element of the story that was true or they couldn't print it. But no! In fact, that wasn't the only time it happened to me. A few years later, *Star* printed a story about how I was dating David Spade. There were all kinds of details from "a pal" of mine about how we'd met at a party—he'd made me laugh, and we started dating. The "pal" even made sure to add that the relationship was "just light and fun." Guys. Not

only was I not dating David Spade, I'd never met David Spade! It was so bonkers! Years later I ran into him, and we talked about the fake story. He told me he got in a lot of trouble from that article with the girl he was actually dating at that time. Ironically, while all these totally fake stories were being written, Angela jumped into a pool in her cocktail dress during an after-party and no one wrote a word.

Angela

Not jumped, dove. I proudly dove into that swimming pool in my cocktail dress. Brian and I had been to several parties that night and our last party was poolside at the Hollywood Roosevelt Hotel. It was a beautiful night, and steam was coming off the heated pool. I watched this dapper guy in a fantastic suit casually stroll down the steps into the pool and then his date followed shortly after. Imagine two beautifully dressed people lounging on the steps of a swimming pool. It looked glorious. So I took off my red high heels and handed them to Brian. He asked me where I was going and I said, "To the deep end." I walked the length of the pool and stood at the deep end as a crowd gathered around me. I leapt in the air and dove headfirst into the pool. When I came up for air the entire party applauded. I highly recommend swimming in a cocktail dress, the fabric billows around you in the water and you feel like an underwater fairy princess. However, bring a change of clothes because the damp car ride home is not so magical.

Jenna

If we can leave you with anything it's this: If you have the chance to be at fun events with your friends, CELEBRATE, DANCE, ENJOY! Do not waste time being "too cool for school." Own the moment. Own every moment. Like my mom said, these moments won't last forever. And when they are gone, and you aren't with your friends, you won't regret the time you spent dancing your face off or swimming in a cocktail dress or walking up to Meryl Streep laughing. Trust me.

9

jam

by Jenna

Jim + Pam = JAM

Imagine walking into a room, a song starts playing, and suddenly you and a complete stranger begin to dance in perfect unison. That's what it felt like when I first read my scenes with John Krasinski at our audition for *The Office*. From the moment we met, it was like we shared the JAM brain. We instantly clicked. John and I have both shared that when our agents initially gave us the news that we'd been cast on the show, our first questions were "Did Jenna Fischer get the role of Pam?" and "Did John Krasinski get the role of Jim?" We knew our best shot at doing this job right was doing it together. John Krasinski is like family. I feel so fortunate to have worked with him for nearly ten years, bringing the story of Jim and Pam to life.

In real life, John and I are both happily married to other people; John to Emily Blunt, me to Lee Kirk. (In fact, we got married within one week of each other in July 2010. And now we both have two kids.) I always say, he found his Pam, and I found my Jim.

John, Emily, Lee, and I are all good friends. I adore Emily. Actually, I more than adore her, I admire her. She's a force. She's also engaging and funny and giving. When my family briefly relocated to London while I filmed the British television series *You, Me and the Apocalypse*, Emily put together a list of fun things to do in London with my kids. And after we arrived, John and Emily took us to dinner, and later we all met up for playdates. It made the relocation so much easier on our family because we were with such close friends. Before we had families, we did all kinds of things together, from late-night dinner parties to traveling together. If you ever get the chance to spend time with John and Emily, be prepared to laugh. A lot.

These days, John and Emily split their time between New York and London, so we see them less frequently. But when John made his stage debut at the Public Theater in 2016 in the play *Dry Powder*, Lee and I flew in to see it. John and Emily had come to support me when I had my off-Broadway stage debut, so I knew what a big deal this was. We had to be there. John was great, of course. Nowadays, whenever any of us pass through the others' city, we make it a point to reach out and see one another. John and Emily are enthusiastic cheerleaders, amazing hosts, and just all-around lovely people.

I could go on and on about how much our friendship has meant to me over the years, but let's get to why we are here. Let's talk JAM!

Jim and Pam's connection is obvious from the start of the series. Although Pam is engaged to Roy, she spends most of her day talking and flirting with Jim. It is only a matter of time until these two get together, and the

207

writers did such a wonderful job of crafting the slow evolution of their relationship. Greg made sure there was always one Jim and Pam moment per episode. It was either a moment of connection—something as simple as a glance across the conference room or a prank they play on Dwight—or a moment of disconnect, like when Jim doesn't give Pam a gift for Valentine's Day. Scenes with Jim and Pam got a lot of attention on set. We would shoot and reshoot these moments, making tiny adjustments, until we got them just right. Often the rest of the cast had to wait hours for us to finish. Sorry, guys!

John and I were equally invested in the Jim and Pam story. Our connection to the characters was natural, so we could easily feel our way through a scene on instinct alone. But we also had a lot of discussions about these moments, breaking them down intellectually too as part of the story. A good example of this was our very long discussion during the "E-Mail Surveillance" episode (Season 2): Does Pam sit on Jim's bed when he gives her the tour of his bedroom? And if so, when? Sometimes we'd discuss a moment back and forth, over and over, until one of us would finally say, "Wait, I got it! I got it!" The cameras would start rolling and the other would instinctively know what to do. Creating those scenes was exhilarating. And when we'd created something special, we knew it.

When I think back on our journey there are certain moments that stick out for me. One of my favorites is from Season 2, "The Client." In that episode, Michael goes to Chili's with Jan to woo a big potential client. Back in the office, Pam finds a movie script Michael has been writing—the infamous *Threat Level Midnight*. The employees all gather in the conference room for a hilarious table read. Afterward, Jim makes Pam grilled cheese sandwiches, and they eat together up on the roof. To me, it's their first dinner date.

Shooting that scene on the roof is one of my fondest memories of the show. We shot on the actual roof of our soundstage, and the only people permitted on the roof were Greg Daniels, Paul Lieberstein, our first assistant director, a boom operator, the director of photography Randall Einhorn, John, and me. It was a warm summer evening. The only "set" was two folding chairs, a candle, and delicious grilled cheese sandwiches. We took our seats, and the scene began. Off in the distance, Rainn and Brian (aka Dwight and Kevin) set off fireworks. Unfortunately,

the fireworks were so tiny, we could barely see them from the rooftop. Greg told Rainn and Brian to jump, yell, dance around, anything to make the scene more visually interesting. The guys did their best, screaming and waving their arms, which makes the scene very funny. But this episode was significant in other ways. When *The Office* was picked up for a second season, the network only ordered six episodes. "The Client" was episode number seven, the first in our extended order. A big part of my bond with John arose from the fact that *The Office* was each of our first series. I remember turning to John and saying, "We are really on this TV show," and he smiled. He got it. I didn't want the scene to end.

Jim and Pam's flirtation ultimately culminates with a kiss during the Season 2 finale, "Casino Night." We can't have a chapter about Jim and Pam and not talk about that kiss on "Casino Night." I've been told it's one of the most romantic moments in TV history, and I'd have to agree!

But there is a different scene from "Casino Night" that John and I were most focused on. It is before the kiss, in the parking lot, when Jim tells Pam he is in love with her. Everyone agreed that the parking lot scene would set everything in motion. If we didn't nail it, the kiss wouldn't matter. Because our director Ken Kwapis felt it would be the most challenging from an emotional standpoint, he moved the parking lot scene to the end of the week's schedule. Yes, we shot the kissing scene BEFORE the confession in the parking lot! How crazy is that?

When it was time, it was at the very end of the day. The entire cast had been sent home. We gathered in the parking lot, where we must have talked about the scene for an hour before we began. Greg and Ken discussed where the cameras should be, if Jim and Pam should know they are being filmed, or if the cameras should be hidden in a "spy shot." We all spent time discussing the dialogue, eventually deciding that Pam should be in the middle of teasing Jim when he shocks her with his confession. So Pam's lines—"Oh, do you want me to take your money now? Or I could take it later or when do . . ."—were all playful banter that we came up with on the spot. Ken told John to cut me off at a different point in each take, so that I could never be quite sure when Jim would say "I'm in love with you." It was a brilliant idea that worked perfectly. I was completely surprised every time.

Later in the scene, when Pam says, "I'm really sorry you misinterpreted our friendship," John improvised the line "Don't" and started to cry. This took me off guard, and I could feel the blood flush my face. It was so hard to stand there while John cried as Jim. I felt horrible rejecting him this way—even fictionally. John's performance was brilliant. He broke all our hearts in that moment. After the scene was over, I wanted to rush over and say, "I'm sorry, I'm so sorry!"

As for the kissing scene, John confessed that it was his first onscreen kiss. I had done a couple of kissing moments with David Denman (who played Roy), but those weren't the kind of swoony, romantic kisses that this scene required. Up to this point, my only romantic kissing scene had been in a movie called *Born Champion*, one of my first acting jobs. But of course, that kiss in no way compared to this one. It seemed like everyone in the cast, crew, and viewing public had been waiting to see Jim and Pam kiss, and we had to get it right. We asked questions: How big should the kiss be? How long does it go on? How much does Pam kiss Jim back? But we never rehearsed the scene. Everyone agreed we should let even our first attempts at this moment play out while the cameras were rolling.

On the day of the shoot, John and I were both very nervous. We didn't want to mess up this pivotal moment and let everyone down. Understanding the stakes involved, Ken planned to keep things casual and act like it was just another day of shooting. His plans were foiled before the day even began when the entire cast and crew were handed the shooting schedule for the day, which had been printed with ***"JIM KISSES PAM!!!"***—bold, all caps, italics, and three exclamation points— across the top.

To create the right mood, Ken brought me to set without John, to walk through the scene alone. This approach was different from how we normally did things. It was strange being on set by myself with the lighting moody and dark. There was a long discussion about where I should stand. "Wouldn't I just stand at reception?" I asked. I was told there were concerns about this placement because the reception desk would block too much of the action, as the plan was to hide the camera in the kitchen and shoot secretly through the blinds in a spy shot. (Actually, they called it a "super-secret spy shot.") Eventually, we settled on Jim's desk. We worked out how I could position myself with the phone, allowing for the camera to read some, but not all, of my reactions. Ken felt that having my reactions partially blocked would create suspense. After my location was chosen, I was told to go back to my trailer and wait. This was also a very strange request. We never sat in our trailers alone between scenes. As I'm sure you've gathered by now, we were a social bunch. But I did as Ken asked and went to my trailer to wait.

Meanwhile, John was going through a different experience. He was never brought to set for a walk-through rehearsal at all. Instead, he was left wandering around the backstage area alone, wondering where we'd gone.

When Ken Kwapis came on *Office Ladies*, we asked him why he made the decision to keep us separated like this. He explained that since we hadn't yet filmed the parking lot scene, he wanted to manufacture some of the tension that our characters might be feeling when the kiss happened and decided that separating us might do just that.

Well, the plan worked. Oblivious to what was happening, John was suddenly called backstage and told that the scene was ready to roll, having no idea that I'd been placed at his desk. He was instructed to wait for Ken to call "Action," walk in the office, find me, and do the scene. He had no idea where I'd be in the room, which is probably why his reaction to seeing me at his desk is so genuine.

After all this buildup, I hoped we'd get it right. I remember my heart was pounding as I waited for the scene to begin. I heard "Action," John appeared, and we filmed the scene. We only did three takes. I'll never forget the smile on Greg's face when we wrapped that day. He knew we'd nailed it.

But as wonderful as it was, Jim and Pam's kiss does not result in them getting together. Pam says she still plans to marry Roy, and Jim transfers to Stamford.

Argh! And even though Pam eventually breaks her engagement with Roy, Jim and Pam spend most of Season 3 estranged. It isn't until the "Beach Games" episode, written by Greg Daniels and Jen Celotta, that Pam gets one step closer to a relationship with Jim. But first, she takes a stroll across some hot coals.

When I spoke to Greg about this episode, he told me the early obstacle to Pam and Jim being together was Roy, then it was distance, and then it was Karen. He wanted the final obstacle to be Pam's internal struggle, overcoming her timidity and willingness to accept less than she deserved in life. His vision was to have Pam reveal the same type of courage that Jim had shown in the Season 2 finale, "Casino Night." But Greg did not want this important moment to happen in the Season 3 finale. "The trick was to bury it inside the 'Beach Games' story so you didn't see it coming."

When I first read the script for "Beach Games," Pam's final speech made me cry. Everything comes pouring out of her. She confesses her sadness that people didn't come to her art show. She reveals her feelings for Jim and how much she misses him. But most of all, she shares the big truth, which is that while there were many reasons to call off her wedding to Roy, the true motivation was her feelings for Jim. It was absolutely perfect.

People often ask if that speech was improvised. Nope. Not one word. Jen Celotta told me that while she had cowritten the episode, Greg wrote Pam's speech himself. I memorized it and delivered it word for word. I knew how important this moment was for Pam and believed that the better I knew the material, the more I could focus on my performance. I wrote out notes in my script, recalling moments in my life when I had experienced a rush of adrenaline like the one Pam would be feeling after walking over the coals, and how that elation would drive me (and her) to be impulsive. I wanted her speech to feel pieced together

PAM: Hey, I want to say something. I've been trying to be more honest lately, and I need to say some things. I did the coal walk. You couldn't do that Michael, so maybe I should be <u>your</u> boss. I feel really good right now. Why didn't any of you come to my art show? That kind of sucked because I invited all of you. It's like sometimes some of you don't even act like I exist. Like, Jim, I called off my wedding becaue of you and now we're not even friends, it's just weird between us and it sucks. I miss you. You were my best friend before you went to Stamford. I miss you. I shouldn't have been with Roy and there were a lot of reasons to call off the wedding, but the truth is, I didn't care about any of the reasons until I met you. And you're with somebody else now, and fine, that's whatever . . . My feet are starting to hurt like hell, and I just wanted to tell you, Jim, and everyone here in this circle, I guess, that I miss having fun with you, not the other people in the circle so much, anyway I am going to walk into the lake now. Good day.

in the moment while also revealing she had spent many sleepless nights going over these feelings and these words in her head. I thought of the Academy Awards, when an actor who's been a longshot is suddenly the winner, finding herself onstage, speaking from the heart while also patching together a speech she's been practicing since she was a little girl.

People also ask me if I really walked across hot coals. I wish I could say I did, but the coals were not heated. Our crew did an amazing job of making them look real. They dug a hole in the ground and wired a giant flickering light box with yellow and orange gels to make it appear as if the coals were burning. They then covered the box with lava rocks, adding gas lines on either side of the path with tiny flickers of real fire. I was directed to make sure I stayed in the center of the path since the flames on the sides were in fact very real.

The coals weren't hot, but they did hurt. Imagine scattering a bunch of Legos on the ground and then walking over them. That's what it felt like. By the time I was set to deliver Pam's big speech, the temperature had dropped, I was quite cold, and my feet were throbbing. And like Pam, my adrenaline kicked in. I walked up to my castmates and steadied myself to speak.

This was my first experience with being the center of attention in a scene. In three seasons, Pam had never been in the center of the action. Most of my acting career had been spent in supporting roles. And here I was, all eyeballs on me. This was my glimpse at what Steve did every single day, every single week. I was so nervous. I wanted to nail this moment for our gal Pam.

I can't remember how many takes we did of the speech, but I do remember that Greg had come to set to watch the filming. Greg, Harold Ramis, and Jen Celotta all hovered over little video monitors in a tent next to where we were shooting. After the first take, I looked over to the tent, and they were all peeking out smiling. Jen gave me a big smile and a thumbs-up. I was able to relax a little after that.

This scene was the start of a major shift for Pam. It was the moment she took charge of her own life. And for me, it was a personal milestone as an actor. Just like

Pam, I gained confidence that night too. My most treasured moments playing Pam were the times like this, when our lives intersected perfectly, and we both found our voice together.

Another big production moment was Jim and Pam's engagement. Greg Daniels decided Jim should propose to Pam at the end of the Season 5 premiere episode, "Weight Loss." Why did Greg embed such an important plot point in the premiere episode? Because he didn't want the viewers to see it coming. (You might be noticing a trend? Greg liked to do that.)

Greg wanted the proposal to feel special, but he also wanted it to feel like Jim made the decision without a lot of planning. This inspired his idea for the location of this scene, a gas station along the freeway between Scranton and New York, in the rain.

We based the station on one that Greg Daniels had traveled to as a kid along the Merritt Parkway in New York. But instead of flying us there, our production designer Michael Gallenberg and his team built one in the parking lot of a Best Buy in Los Feliz, California. (Yes, you read that right.) They used Google Street View to capture images of the Merrit Parkway station, then built one to match. The interior of the gas station is a series of high-definition photographs. Those soda bottles and cereal boxes inside the window are not real, folks! To create the illusion of traffic, a four-lane parkway was constructed, and stunt drivers were

brought in to drive all varieties of cars, trucks, and semis in a giant circle around the set and in front of the cameras. Our production manager Randy Cordray hired thirty-five precision drivers who went around us at 55 mph. I could feel the wind from the vehicles as they zoomed past. On top of all this, rain machines were brought in. It felt like I was on the set of a major film production, like maybe Vin Diesel was driving by in one of those cars about to start a chase sequence. After we shot the scene, the team sent the footage to a special effects company that replaced the California mountains in the background with tall, East Coast trees and foliage. This was the single most expensive and elaborate scene we shot during the entire run of the show. They had only nine days to scout, design, and build the set. The fifty-two-second scene cost $250,000 to shoot.

Now it was time to get these two hitched. Jim and Pam's wedding created some of my favorite offscreen moments, especially when we filmed at Niagara Falls. This was the only time I ever traveled outside of California to shoot something for *The Office*. And it almost didn't happen. The original plan had been to send a camera operator to shoot footage of the falls and then insert John and me via green screen from a soundstage. Our line producer Randy Cordray was not on board with this idea. He fought very hard to have John and me travel to Niagara and shoot the scene on one of the Maid of the Mist boats. This was not an easy task, as Niagara Falls straddles the United States and Canada. Getting permission to shoot on the boats was complicated. And the budget to make it happen was very tiny. But he was determined to make it work.

About three weeks before the shoot, Randy went to Niagara, New York, for a technical scout with director Paul Feig and cinematographer Randall Einhorn. They rode the Maid of the Mist a few times to plan how they might shoot the scenes on the boat. Randy secured permission to do the shoot, but there were a lot of rules. One being that we could not rent out the entire boat. We could only reserve the front. Second, the boat would not be allowed to go off course. Finally, the rest of the boat would still be filled with tourists.

During their scout Randy, Paul, and Randall timed the trip out to the falls and back. They needed to calculate how much dialogue we could realistically shoot in one trip and so how many trips were needed in total. It was decided we would reserve eight trips to the falls. Four in the morning, four in the afternoon.

Another concern was the water. You get sprayed from the falls depending on the time of day and the wind. While they didn't get too wet, Randall was concerned he wouldn't be able to shoot against the white falls with the spray of the water using our usual high-definition digital cameras. So Randall requested a 16 mm film camera fitted with a special motorized rotating filter that literally spun the water off the lens.

The production budget only allowed for a small group of us to travel for one day of shooting on the Maid of the Mist. Our little group consisted of John and me, of course, joined by Mindy Kaling, who cowrote the episode; our director Paul Feig; Randy; Randall; and a small skeleton crew. On our first night in town, we all went out for dinner together. It was the cast and crew around a large table, laughing over some shared chicken wings. The folks in town were so excited to have us there that they gathered outside the restaurant to meet us. Since we normally shot in such an isolated area, it was fun to be out in the world seeing the impact and enthusiasm for the show.

The hotel where we were staying had a lot of fun with the fact that Jim and Pam were getting married. When I first arrived in my room, the hotel had left a "wedding basket" for me. It had a variety of chocolates, candies, flowers, champagne, and two champagne flutes with hearts on the stems. They were so cute I kept them. The one bummer was that my bestie Angela wasn't with me on this trip to share all the fun. I had to eat all the chocolates myself!

The morning of the shoot, I had to arrive almost two hours before John, at 5 A.M., to get my hair done and do my fancy wedding makeup. When John finally arrived, he was very sick with the flu. He couldn't keep anything down. But we couldn't change the shoot schedule. And we had to fly back the next day. I felt so terrible for him. It was clear he was miserable.

At 9 A.M. we boarded the boat and were handed blue Maid of the Mist parkas. The boat captain made an announcement, telling everyone to "expect a little spray by the falls." We loaded our group into the front of the boat as planned. Since we were only allowed so many in that space, Randy volunteered to play the minister who marries Jim and Pam. One ticket for double duty of actor and production manager. To fill in the background, we brought on family members of the cast and crew. Greg Daniels's assistant, Mary Wall, was from the area, and her family volunteered to ride with us. Brian Baumgartner's parents, Bruce and Cherry, happened to be on vacation in Rochester, New York, with plans to visit the falls the same day we were shooting. They stopped by the set, and Paul Feig talked them into coming along for the shoot. You can see them walking right behind Jim and Pam as we board the boat.

Because the rest of the boat was filled with paying customers watching us film, we were all very concerned that this particular plot point would leak. No one was allowed to come to the front where we were filming, but they were free to take photos and videos. So before every journey, John and I gave a little speech, posed for photos, and asked people to help us keep the secret. Amazingly, the secret never got out!

We tried to get as much footage of the wedding scenes as we could on the first trip out to the falls while we were nice and dry, just in case we got wet when we arrived. Well, it's a good thing we shot the wedding footage on that first pass, because I got SOAKED when we floated by the falls. John got a little wet, but I got DRENCHED. It was like people threw buckets of water on me for ten minutes. My hair was sopping wet, and I had eye makeup running down my face. You know that beautiful moment at the end

of the wedding montage where the camera is on our backs as we look toward the falls, Pam's head on Jim's shoulder, and then Jim turns and smiles to camera? That shot happened because I couldn't turn around or have my face on camera. It was the only thing we could shoot on the way back to the docks.

We went back on shore and regrouped. The hair/makeup/wardrobe team attempted to dry us off and redo my hair and makeup as best they could. Then we went out in the boat again. Same thing. Sheets of water. I remember thinking, *We are supposed to pass BY the falls, not UNDER the falls, right?*

Besides the water, our other big concern that day was the wedding kiss. Everyone was afraid I'd catch John's flu. John was especially protective of me. But we also knew you can't film a wedding scene without a kiss, so we got creative with the angle of the shot. I put Polysporin up my nose, John pursed his lips tightly, we held our breath, and I basically kissed his cheek. We hoped that by intercutting that with a great kiss back at the church, no one would notice the cheat.

We got back to the docks again. I was beyond soaked, and John was still reeling from the flu. After just two trips, they felt we'd gotten what we needed. Thank goodness! Lunch break was called for the crew, and I went back to the hotel to shower and get completely redone while John rested. We had only a few other scenes to shoot of us arriving to the hotel, and then we would be done for the day. That's when Randy popped his head into the hair and makeup room. "Umm . . . how do you feel about getting back on the boat?" What. He explained that Randall had found a little water in the camera and while they were pretty sure we could use the footage, it was important to take one more trip just to be sure we had what we needed. I thought John was going to die, but as miserable as he was probably feeling, he didn't complain once.

The afternoon trip went much more smoothly thanks to some sweet-talking from Randy and an awesome boat captain. Randy got to chatting with the actual captain, a super-nice guy and fan of the show. The captain said, "Man, you guys got soaked this morning, didn't you?" Randy laughed, telling the captain that management had made it clear that there would be no special alterations of the run just for our shoot.

The captain was shocked. "What?!?! They don't drive this boat, I DO!" So Randy gently suggested that maybe he could pause the boat a wee bit farther from the falls and keep us out of the wettest part of the spray. The captain was all too happy to help us out. "Heck yeah, I'll do anything you guys want!" Thank you, real boat captain! This time as we approached the falls, we were hit by a light mist, and a rainbow lit up the sky. Jackpot!

Later in Season 6, Pam has their baby. It's a two-part episode called "Delivery." In Part 1, Pam goes into labor at work but refuses to leave because her insurance only allows a certain amount of hospital time. Eventually Jim gets her into the car (with Michael), they head to the hospital, and Jim and Pam's daughter, Cecelia "Cece" Marie Halpert, is born. Want to hear something adorable? We named Jim and Pam's baby after my niece, who had been born the week prior to shooting the episode. I had asked the writers and they agreed. I didn't tell my sister. I waited patiently for the episode to air so it would be a surprise. My sister called me freaking out that night, she was so touched by the gesture. The baby photo of "Cece" that went on my desk was a photo of my niece. (My niece loves knowing this little tidbit.) Fans get so tickled when I walk around with the real CeCe and call her name.

In Part 2 of "Delivery," we are in the hospital room with Jim and Pam as they navigate their immediate postpartum life. At the time, neither John nor I had kids, so we peppered the parents in our cast and crew with questions about how to make these scenes most authentic. I think we did a pretty good job, but I never looked as good as Pam does in these scenes. My hair was a hot mess for days after giving birth to both of my kids.

One of the scenes in the hospital room involves Jim and Pam struggling to swaddle baby Cece. The scene, as written, went like this:

The baby is crying. Jim and Pam fumble around at swaddling, not really knowing what to do. Jim thinks he's done it, only to pick up the baby and have the swaddle fall off. The baby cries.

John and I were thinking it would be pretty easy to *not* swaddle a baby since we'd never really done it before. But here's the thing: John Krasinski was instantly an amazing baby swaddler. He couldn't *not* swaddle the baby. I mean, as much as he tried to botch the job, every time he picked up the baby, it was perfectly swaddled and happily cooing in his arms. This went on for multiple takes. The producers said, "John, STOP swaddling the baby." To start the scene, they would put a perfectly swaddled baby into the bassinet. On "Action," they undid the swaddle, and the baby would naturally get upset and cry. This killed us. (Even though the baby nurse assured us the baby was okay, we didn't like hearing the baby cry.) I think John's natural fatherly instincts kicked in, and he needed to swaddle that baby on some deep primal level that couldn't be quelled. He was engaged to Emily at the time. I remember watching the whole thing and thinking, *This guy is going to make a kick-ass father.* Emily chose well.

Another fun thing about this episode was that my now husband, Lee Kirk, got to play Pam's lactation consultant, Clarke. Before we started shooting the episode, Paul Lieberstein, who was now our showrunner, pulled me aside and told me that the writers had a funny idea for a story line but wanted to run it by me first to make sure I was comfortable. He said that Pam would struggle with breastfeeding, and the hospital would send a male lactation consultant. He said they thought it would be funny if this male nurse had to be massaging Pam's breasts in front of Jim, who would be struggling to act like it was no big deal. (I guess this was based loosely on one of the writers' real-life experiences.) He told me that to make me more comfortable, maybe my real-life fiancé Lee could play the role. That way, a stranger wouldn't be fondling me during the shoot. I told Lee, and he said he was game to give it a try. Lee came in for an audition and was given the part. At this point, John and Lee were already friends, so we had a blast. It was a blessing and a curse to have Lee there, because we couldn't stop laughing.

220

Jim and Pam go on to navigate a lot of things in their lives: new jobs, more children, a long-distance marriage. But they always seem to find their way. I love their journey from coworkers and friends to husband and wife to parents. I'm grateful that Greg Daniels had the courage to let their whole relationship play out on the show. So often, we only see the courtship phase of relationships portrayed in Hollywood, not the marriage with all its ups and downs. I remember talking with Greg after Jim and Pam got married. A lot of people were worried that fans would lose interest in Jim and Pam once they got together. But Greg had confidence in us. He said that for the first part of the series, Jim and Pam are kept apart through a series of obstacles that they eventually overcome. And now that they were married, we could watch them tackle new obstacles together.

Don't worry; it's a fake baby!

Throughout the series, John and I fought very hard to never have any infidelity in the Jim and Pam relationship. When Pam went to art school, there was talk that maybe she would fall for her art school friend Alex, played by Rich Sommer. Later, when Pam was on maternity leave, there was a story line where her temp replacement, Kathy, hit on Jim. And in the last season, the boom operator Brian takes a shine to Pam. But

221

in all these cases, Jim and Pam were faithful to each other. We felt that Jim and Pam could come back from many things—such as Jim investing their savings in a company without telling Pam—but infidelity had to be off the table. A series of breakups and makeups would leave the audience exhausted and unsatisfied.

Before I close out this chapter, I should probably address the question people ask me most about Jim and Pam: WHAT WAS WRITTEN IN THE DANG TEAPOT LETTER??!! In our first Christmas episode from Season 2, Jim gets Pam's name in the Secret Santa gift exchange, and he is giddy with excitement, but per the rules he can only spend $20 on the gift. Knowing Pam loves tea, he gets her a teal teapot. He fills it with inside jokes from their friendship: a tiny pencil, a cassette tape, a Boggle timer, hot sauce packets, and a school yearbook photo of Jim (which was John Krasinski's actual yearbook photo). But most important of all, Jim includes a note. Because, he explains, "Christmas is the time to tell people how you feel." When Michael turns the Secret Santa gift exchange into a Yankee Swap, Pam loses the teapot to Dwight, who plans to use it to clear his nasal passages. Jim manages to get it back from Dwight and present it to Pam, but he steals the note before she can see it, tucking it in his pocket. We will have to wait until Season 9 of *The Office* for Pam to finally get the note.

What exactly is written on the note has been torturing fans of *The Office* for decades. Because even when Pam finally receives the note, we never reveal what was written on the card. Only John knows what was written on the first card, which was eventually lost. The replacement, which John wrote himself and was given to me while we were filming the final season, was an idea hatched by Greg Daniels. He suggested to John that he write me a personal note about what it meant to work together, bringing Jim and Pam to the screen for nine years. Greg knew I'd cry. And I did. I opened the letter and read John's message and burst into tears. I don't think they could even use the first take. I'll never reveal what exactly was in his note . . . but as Pam said herself, "Just know it was perfect."

I loved playing Pam on *The Office*, and I especially loved getting to be a part of a love story that resonated with so many people. But more than anything I loved Pam's journey from quiet receptionist unsure of how to direct her own life, to finding her voice and living her truth. I love meeting young women who tell me that Pam's story has inspired them. It inspires me too. Pam's dreams are not extraordinary. She wants to marry the man she loves, have a family, and feel creatively expressed in her work. In the end, she gets all three. It's not lost on me that the series ends when Pam's dreams come true. The documentary doesn't stop when Michael leaves. They keep filming. I like to think that's because they might have been following Pam all along.

10

big pregs, little pregs, fake pregs

We couldn't write a book about our best friendship without sharing about how we navigated our transitions into parenthood. As anyone with children can tell you, becoming a parent is life-altering. Schedules change, priorities change, and as a result, sometimes even friendships change. We definitely had some bumpy moments once we became moms. We're gonna give it to you straight, with all the details, because that's how we do it. Also, as you read the next chapter, be prepared to hear a lot about wedgies and bodily fluids. You've been warned.

Angela

While shooting Season 4 of *The Office* I was pregnant in real life, but my character of Angela was not. So we had to hide my belly behind all kinds of crazy things.

Jenna

In Season 6 of *The Office*, Pam was pregnant, but I was not pregnant in real life. I wore a prosthetic belly for the show that we affectionately called "fake pregs."

Angela

In Season 8, Angela Martin was pregnant, and I was the one who was "fake pregs."

Jenna

In Season 8, Pam gets pregnant again, but this time I was also pregnant in real life.

Angela

This back-and-forth of one of us being real pregnant and one of us being fake pregnant became a source of confusion for everyone. One day on set, our script supervisor Veda looked up from her notes and said, "Wait, who is fake pregnant and who is real pregnant???"

Jenna

The journey of our real and fake pregnancies and the way our friendship evolved during those times is the subject of this chapter: Big Pregs, Little Pregs, Fake Pregs.

Angela

I got pregnant first. It was the summer of 2007. I was so excited when I found out, and I couldn't wait to tell Jenna. It took everything I had not to call her the second I knew but I wanted to deliver the news in person, so I decided to tell her at our lunch.

Since we usually ate together in Jenna's trailer, I knew that was my best shot at getting her alone. As soon as I walked in, Jenna launched into a long story about her cat, Andy. (This was a common lunchtime subject. Her cat was always doing the craziest things.) "OMG! Lady! Listen to this. When I went into my kitchen this morning, all the bottom cabinets were OPEN. Like alllll of them, lady . . ." This story went on for five minutes, you guys. Jenna loved that cat. Long story short: Andy had learned how to open the cabinets.

I listened, laughed at her story, and waited. When she finished, I blurted out, "I'm pregnant." I vaguely remember a thud and shrieking, and then after an epic bear hug, Jenna yelled, "WHY DID YOU LET ME GO ON AND ON ABOUT MY CAT?!"

Jenna

This is accurate, but let me explain the thud. I had been sent to lunch early because we were shooting something that didn't involve front reception. By the time Angela got to my trailer, I was finished eating and had gotten up to do some exercise. I kept five-pound weights in my trailer and would do bicep curls or push-ups from time to time and call that a workout. (I was trying, okay?) So I was pumping iron and droning on about my cat as Angela listened patiently. Mid-curl, she told me she was pregnant. I dropped the weights to the ground, causing the loud thud, then screamed for joy and hugged my best friend. Our production assistant knocked on the door to ask if everything was okay. "YES!" we yelled through our tears of joy. I knew how very much Angela wanted a child. I knew she would make a wonderful mother. I was just so happy for her.

Angela

In the weeks ahead, I shared the news with the rest of the cast, crew, and writing staff. Everyone was so excited. The writers started discussing how they might

work the pregnancy into the show and what that might mean for Angela Martin. Then something crazy happened. The entire television and moviemaking industry shut down due to the writers strike, and our show went on a hiatus. No one knew how long the writers strike would last. We had already filmed the first part of Season 4, and I wasn't showing then. When we finally started production again four months later, I was seven months pregnant! I had a very obvious, very huge belly.

Jenna

The characters and story lines of the show were meant to pick up right where we'd left off. There was no way Angela's character could be pregnant out of the blue. We knew we'd have to hide it, and for that, we had to get creative. Angela did a lot of scenes standing behind the copier or the ficus plant in the bullpen. My personal favorite belly hide was during "Dinner Party." Andy Bernard and Angela Martin arrive at Jan and Michael's party together. The writers were puzzled as to how to disguise her pregnancy as they entered the condo. There was no copier in Michael's apartment. They came up with the idea of having Angela enter with a bouquet of flowers as a host gift. Pam brings wine; Angela brings flowers. Problem solved, right? Oh no. On the day of shooting, the prop team had to keep adding flowers to the bouquet until it was ENORMOUS. I mean, a truly ridiculous bouquet. But that's how we hid the belly!

Angela was the first regular cast member to be pregnant on set, so it was as if we were all having that baby with her. Everyone was so protective, making sure she got enough to eat, drank enough water, sat down often enough. The crew even threw her a surprise baby shower in the set parking lot. At that same time, I teamed up with Angela's sister-in-law Susanne Daniels and we threw a

friends-and-family shower. Angela's mom, sisters, and grandmother all flew to Los Angeles for the event. Celebrating Angela's pregnancy with this multigenerational group of women was moving to me. These women, who had raised children of their own, were bringing Angela into the fold. It was a beautiful thing. At the same time, seeing Angela at her baby shower really drove home the fact that I was very far away from joining that flock.

Angela

During the same month of the dual showers, Jenna was turning thirty-four. I wanted to be there for Jenna as her birthday approached—she was doing so much for me. But to illustrate the different directions our lives were taking, Jenna wanted to celebrate her birthday at a bar in West Hollywood called St. Nick's. It's no longer in business, but during its heyday, it was a great dive bar: dark interior, old pleather booths, a jukebox, the best greasy burgers, and a back room with a dartboard. Imagine being eight months pregnant and walking into *that* bar holding a sheet cake. Yes, I bought Jenna a sheet cake from the grocery store, and then I waddled to the back of the bar and ate half of it.

Jenna

Angela, I will never forget looking over at you as you happily ate sheet cake and sang at the top of your lungs to Lynyrd Skynyrd playing on the jukebox. You were super pregnant, in a dive bar, getting all kinds of side-eye from the other patrons. You did that for me, and I am forever grateful.

Angela

The day I had my little girl, Jenna drove my mom to the hospital. It was about a half hour through curved roads over the canyons of Los Angeles. My mom told me she held on to the passenger door handle with white knuckles as Jenna took those turns. She described Jenna as a "speedy driver," and picturing the two of them zipping through those winding roads still makes me laugh.

I love that my best friend was with me the day I became a mother. My daughter once said to me, "Mama, I've always known Jenna." And that is certainly true.

Jenna

I remember walking into Angela's hospital room. Isabel was so beautiful. A little pink peanut snuggled close to Angela's chest, a sunbeam casting a gentle glow from the window. It was one of those perfectly peaceful moments you see in movies. Then Angela asked if I'd help her to the restroom. Remember how Angela showed up for me when I broke my back in New York? Now it was my turn to lower Angela onto a toilet. Our friendship had come full circle.

But things definitely changed after Angela had Isabel. It was summertime. The show was on hiatus. I didn't see Angela every day at work, and she was busy caring for her newborn. To be honest, I felt a little lost. I didn't know how to best support her, as at that point I knew nothing about babies, so I had no helpful advice to offer. She mostly talked about her nipples being sore and how tired and hungry she was. Stories about my cat and my single life felt out of place. It felt insensitive to tell her that I was sleeping in, reading books, and watching movies during the break. I didn't know how to connect.

Angela

Jenna was still in what I called the "sexy life." The sexy life is that phase of your life where you decide to meet up with friends for margaritas at 10 P.M., see the midnight showing of a movie, then grab a hot dog from a late-night food truck and talk about music, art, and travel. You know that phase. It's amazing. All friendships go through challenges in some way, but nothing really challenges a friendship like one of you becoming a parent while the other is still in the sexy life.

Looking back, this was probably the most disconnected time in our friendship. We were in two different worlds. It probably didn't help when, on one of my first days home from the hospital, I sent her a text that went something like this:

> I just had the craziest five minutes of my life!!! I was breastfeeding Isabel but stopped abruptly because I could tell that she had pooped and was cranky about it. So, I took her to the changing table to quickly change her diaper and my boobs were still hanging out of my nursing gown when all of a sudden, I felt this warm sensation on my legs. I looked down and blood was running down my legs! I quickly picked up Isabel (who was naked) and rushed to the bathroom. I grabbed some towels and gently laid Isabel on top of them as I sat on the toilet and all of this blood came out. Isabel started to cry and when she did, milk started squirting out of my boobs across the bathroom and hit her in the face!!! She then cried more and then I cried and WHAT THE HELL?!

Jenna

I'm not going to lie; I'm still haunted by that text. Digesting that amount of information about poop and fluids and blood was more than I was ready for. I mean, after you become a mom, you text other moms about poops and bodily fluids all the time. But I didn't know that yet. This was quite a share. Also, I was hosting a poker game at my house when it came in. I was sipping whiskey and had just folded a pair of 5s when my phone dinged. I read the text and my face went gray, then green. I excused myself from the table. I stared at the screen not knowing how to respond. Is there an emoji for this? Was I supposed to text "OMG" or "LOL"? Or "OMG LOL"? Was I supposed to rush over? Did she need help? The dealer yelled from the other room, "Do you want us to skip you this round?" It truly hit me how different our lives were in that moment. (BTW, Angela later texted me that she was fine and that everything she was experiencing was totally normal.)

When work started up again, I felt more changes. Suddenly there was a baby on Angela's lap in the hair and makeup trailer. Our ladies' lunches were over because lunchtime belonged to Isabel. Sometimes Angela would bring Isabel to my trailer, where I kept a few baby toys, and we would talk a little. But for the most part, lunchtime was Isabel time.

I watched as Angela navigated the responsibilities of parenting with the demands of work, because the work demands were the same. She was expected to keep up with our twelve-hour days as if she wasn't breastfeeding, pumping, and barely sleeping.

Angela

Going back to work brought a mix of emotions. I was happy to see everyone and thankful for my job, but I really wanted to be home with my baby. Our producers went out of their way to make my transition as easy as they could. They found a trailer that had two sides connected by a small bathroom. Isabel had one side,

and I had the other. I set up a travel crib, some blankets, and a cozy chair where I could nurse her and eventually keep a high chair, toys, and tiny table. Of course, her little pink push car was parked right outside. I was incredibly thankful that she could spend time with me at work. I know what a gift that was.

Jenna

I learned that my best chance at serious BFF talk came while Angela was pumping. That's right, folks. We chatted while she pumped. The sound of that pump is stuck in my brain forever. *My-CA My-CA My-CA.* It was the soundtrack to many of our deepest conversations.

Angela

One day while I was pumping, Jenna stopped me midsentence. "Oh my goodness, your left boob makes waaaay more milk." And I said, "Oh, I know! It's the better boob! But my sister says if I don't make Isabel nurse on my right

234

boob, my left boob will get bigger and bigger, and I'll be lopsided for life." So as the weeks went on, Jenna policed me about my right boob. "Don't forget, fifteen minutes on that right boob. It's looking a little sad today."

I think the hardest part about returning to work was the fatigue. I was up through the night feeding a newborn, and then whenever I had a break at work, I was pumping. I felt a bit out of it. A perfect example of my loopiness happened while filming "Weight Loss" for Season 5. It was my first week back to work, and we were having an extremely long day. We were filming in the warehouse, and as we approached the thirteenth-hour mark, I went to get a water. Our script supervisor Veda offered me her Sharpie to write my name on my water bottle. As I chatted away with her, I wrote my name, and she said, "Oh, Angela, you wrote 'water.'" I wrote WATER on my water bottle! That's how tired I was!

Jenna

At this point, Angela was on fumes, and it felt like our friendship was too. I wanted to tell Angela I missed her, but I felt selfish feeling this way. I knew what she had on her plate. Instead, I gave her space, which I later realized made her feel like I was pulling away.

Angela

For a while, Jenna continued to reach out. She invited me to all sorts of fun things, but usually at the last minute. For example, she would text me at 9 P.M. to see if I wanted to meet her for dinner. 9 P.M. dinner?? I was already in bed! My life wasn't as flexible as it once was, and I had to say no. Then Jenna had an impromptu barbeque at her house, and I wasn't invited. I didn't blame her; I had turned down so many invitations. But it stung. I admit, I had definitely been hibernating with my little girl. I couldn't get enough of those little newborn moments, Isabel sleeping on my chest after a feeding, smelling her hair and listening to her tiny noises. Of course, I worried I was doing everything wrong as a new mom, but I also felt so at home with it all, at peace with giving my life over to this little baby. I didn't miss anything from my previous life. Still, I didn't want to lose my best friend. I decided we needed to talk. I invited Jenna over during Isabel's naptime, made us some iced tea, and we sat on my back porch. We had a huge heart-to-heart that day. I told her I was sorry if I had disappeared and that I loved her. She said she was sorry she hadn't invited me to her barbeque and explained she felt like she'd been bothering me with all her crazy invitations. Most of all, she told me she missed me too. We cried and hugged and pledged to keep talking and texting, no matter what. When Isabel woke up, Jenna stayed with us for the rest of the afternoon. She watched me nurse, burp, change Isabel's clothes, and be a mom. We talked about anything and everything, and I was just happy to be with my friend. At one point, I noticed Jenna staring at me. "What is it?" I asked. She told me I was such a natural mom, like I had always been one. She said I seemed so at ease and happy. I can't tell you how much that meant to me, because that was exactly how I felt.

Jenna

That one afternoon put our friendship back on course. Sometimes that's all it takes. We didn't need to be doing anything particularly exciting at all. We just needed to connect. It felt so good to have my friend back.

Next, it was my turn to be a trailblazer in our friendship. In Season 6, Pam was pregnant. I was nowhere near being pregnant in real life. This is when I became "fake pregs." What does fake pregnant on a TV show look like?

"PAM BEESLEY"
Pregnancy Costuming chart 10/5/09
A Raycraft, Costume Designer   SEASON 6

Episode		Air Date	Prosthetic Size and Information
6004/05	"Niagra"	10/08/09	Belly A, small/smallest 5ᵗʰ month
6006	"Mafia"	10/15/09	Belly A, small/smallest 5ᵗʰ month
6007	"The Lover"	10/22/09	Belly A, small/smallest 5ᵗʰ month
6008	"Double-Date"	11/05/09	Belly B, medium 6ᵗʰ month
6009	"Koi Pond"	10/29/09	Belly B, medium 6ᵗʰ month
6010	"Murder"	11/12/09	Belly B, medium 6ᵗʰ month
6011	"Shareholders Mtg" 11/19/09		Belly C, large 7ᵗʰ month
6012	"The Banker"	1/14/10	Belly C, large 7ᵗʰ month
6013	"Scott's Tots"	11/26/09	Belly C, large 7ᵗʰ month
6014	"Secret Santa"	12/10/09	Belly D, larger
6015	"Sabre"	2/04/09	Belly E, largest 9ᵗʰ month
6016	"Manger/Sales"	2/11/10	Belly E (possibly F)
6017	"Town Hall"	3/18/09	Belly A
6018	Birth	3/04/09	Belly F
6019	Post Birth	3/11/09	Belly A (possibly B)

The Fake Belly Tracker

236

Fake pregnant means wardrobe gives you a weird wetsuit/leotard and padded belly to wear under your clothes. Imagine a girdle with a pillow attached. The pillow size grows as your character journeys through her pregnancy. It's awful. The boy shorts of the leotard ride up into your butt and lady business. Constantly. After about thirty minutes of wearing this contraption, I'd develop a thin layer of sweat underneath the bodysuit. On top of it, I was still wearing pantyhose (*why?*), a microphone wire, and the battery pack that goes with it. And guess what happened if I needed to pee? I had to take it all off and then put it all back on again. That process takes about twenty minutes. Can you guess how annoyed people got when I said, "I need to pee"? Also, the bigger the fake belly, the more it pressed into my bladder when I sat down, so the more I felt like I had to pee. I hated being fake pregnant. I was grouchy and complained constantly. I couldn't help it. You would too.

Look at how miserable I am in these photos. We were trying to decide which sweater looked best with this outfit. I just wanted to tear the fake belly off.

Angela

For the episode when Pam and Jim get married, Jenna had to wear the fake belly contraption under a wedding dress. She kept complaining that she had a wedgie from the leotard. At least once an hour she would need to aggressively dig that wedgie out. Imagine Jenna looking radiant in a wedding dress and then digging at

her undies. I laughed a lot. I did not really take her complaining all that seriously.

She told me that as the pillow size got larger the wedgies got worse, so one day when she was complaining, again, I suggested she wear different underwear under the leotard as I thought this might help. I wish you could have seen Jenna's face as she rolled her eyes and told me I absolutely didn't get it. And you know what . . . I didn't, but I would soon enough.

Jenna

Finally, in Season 8, I became pregnant in real life. At first, I didn't want to share my news with anyone at work. For many reasons, I wanted to wait until after my twenty-week ultrasound to share publicly about my pregnancy. Of course, Angela knew, but no one else. It was easy enough to hide at first. I didn't experience any morning sickness. I was crazy-tired all the time, but no one seemed to notice. Then, at around fourteen weeks, I started to show. I needed to unzip my skirts and keep them fastened with a MacGyver-like contraption of hair ties and safety pins. Since Pam wears her blouses untucked with a baggy cardigan, I felt I could hide the bump. But around eighteen weeks, I really popped. Nothing fit me anymore. I couldn't explain to wardrobe that I needed bigger sizes, because they would ask for a fitting, which meant being measured with a measuring tape and trying on many different outfits. My cover would be blown. I had to take matters into my own

238

hands. That weekend I went to J.Crew at the mall, where I bought a pencil skirt, a button-down shirt, and a cardigan in the next size up. (I actually bought two of the same outfit since wardrobe always kept duplicates. I'm a genius!) I went into work on Monday with my new clothes, handed them to the costume crew, and told them emphatically, "I saw this outfit over the weekend, and it felt like Pam to me. I have to wear it." Our costume designer Alysia stared at me confused. I mean, I had *never* done anything like this. She must have thought I'd gone insane, but she didn't argue. And I wore it that week. I did the same thing the following weekend.

Angela

I was so excited when Jenna told me she was pregnant. We would soon be mom BFFs together! Jenna also told me she wanted to keep her pregnancy a secret for a bit. I think I got *way* too into the secret-keeping. I made up excuses about why I was getting extra snacks, ridiculous things like "I saw a baby squirrel, and I think it needs some nuts and granola," and then I'd bring them to Jenna. I covered for her when she was drowsy in the hair and makeup chairs. I tried to convince everyone it might be the moon or the tide or the rotation of the planets that made her overly sleepy. In my mind I was the ultimate wingman, super spy, BFF protector, and mastermind of hiding this pregnancy. She called me from the mall when she went to get new clothes. I told her it was a "brilliant plan! No one will suspect a thing!"

Jenna

When I hit the twenty-week mark, I was excited to finally share my news. I waited until the whole gang was gathered on set, stood up at my desk, and asked for everyone's attention. Then I took a deep breath and made my announcement! "I'm pregnant!" Everyone just looked at me blankly and replied, "We know." I was shocked. Our camera operator Matt Sohn said, "Jenna, my wife has been pregnant twice. I look at you all day through a lens. It was totally obvious. And then you did that crazy thing with the clothes. I mean . . . we all thought it was really sweet how careful you were being. Congratulations. It's the best thing." And then I cried. And felt silly. I was so grateful for how thoughtful everyone had been.

When she told everyone, I was just as surprised as Jenna that they knew already. Note to self: Never go into any kind of espionage work. It won't go well for me.

Jenna

A few days later Greg and Paul asked me if they could write the pregnancy into the show as Jim and Pam's second baby. They thought the timing was right. I hesitated at first. What if something happened and I lost my baby? Would I still have to pretend to be pregnant as Pam? Would they write the loss into the show? Both options seemed awful. I was nervous about blurring the line between fiction and reality. On the other hand, I had seen Angela hiding her belly behind flowers and stacks of papers. It seemed easier and more fun to just let it all hang out. Lee and I talked, and we agreed to let them write my pregnancy into the show.

Angela

Once everyone knew about Jenna's pregnancy, I could take on the job I truly loved and was better suited for—BFF party planner! The crew threw her a baby shower in the Dunder Mifflin warehouse, and I hosted her friends-and-family one. Jenna's mom, Anne, made the baby shower invites by hand, and they were adorable. Jenna's sister, Emily, helped me figure out what games to play. The big hit was Baby Shower *Price Is Right*. Guests held up baby items—a pack of diapers, a pacifier, rice cereal, etc.—and Jenna had to guess the price.

Jenna

Guys, my baby showers were amazing. I truly felt showered with love and support. I also LOVED being real pregnant on set. It was way, way, way better than being fake pregnant. Peter from craft services brought me snack trays, no one cared when I had to pee, there were no wedgies, and I was never grumpy.

Angela

When I think about Jenna being pregnant on set, the image I see is of her laughing and sitting at her desk sewing a Christmas stocking. She made both of her children Christmas stockings while she was pregnant. It was the sweetest thing. I would walk over to talk to her as she would be adding a little sparkly sequin to Santa's hat. We would talk about her food cravings and how she was sleeping, and I would give her pregnancy tips, like buy a triangle pillow to support your belly at night. I loved this new chapter of our friendship.

And as a bonus, we soon had a big story line together! The writers decided that my character would become pregnant too, so now Pam and Angela were pregnant together! Hence, Big Pregs, Little Pregs!

Oh my goodness, did we have fun with that. And I suddenly had newfound respect for all Jenna had endured with the fake belly. Toward the end of Angela Martin's pregnancy, it was so cumbersome to walk in the Spanx/fake belly/pillow/leotard contraption. It pushed down on my bladder and pinched in places I didn't even know I had. Jenna had talked so much about the wedgies that I was prepared for the "butt" wedgie, but the front wedgie was a bit of a shock. No one deserves a wedgie in their lady business.

Jenna

Talk about Big Pregs! My son was just shy of ten pounds when he was born, and my belly was HUGE! I loved getting to share this story line with Angela. This meant lots of scenes with my BFF. That was perfection. We had so much to talk about now. I could give her advice on how to keep the bodysuit from jamming into her crotch, and she showed me ways to reduce the swelling in my calves. I could understand the stories from her real pregnancy in a whole new way. And I was able to share my anxiety about becoming a new mom and having to juggle work and parenting.

My last day on set before giving birth.

My biggest worry about becoming a mother was postpartum depression. The women in my family have a long history of postpartum depression with several requiring medication and, in one case, hospitalization. I consulted my doctors and read everything I could on the subject. Most of the advice boiled down to three things: Build a network of support, get as much sleep as possible, and don't be afraid to ask for professional help. One piece I read suggested I have my placenta turned into pills that I could take every day to level out my postpartum hormones and increase milk supply. I was sold. (If I'd read that sprinkling crushed grasshoppers around my bedroom might ward off PPD, I would have done it.) Through my prenatal yoga class, I found a woman who could take my placenta, dry it in her oven, and put it into pills. (I understand that is a crazy sentence. I live in Los Angeles. Over half the moms I know have done this with their placentas. It's just not that strange here.) Anyway, the hardest part of the process is getting your placenta to the woman in time. Someone has to get it from the hospital and transport it in a little cooler to her house within twenty-four hours of giving birth. For me, that person was Angela. Let me tell you. When your friend has transported your placenta in a cooler, you've crossed the best-friendship finish line right there.

Angela and Placenta

243

Angela

The day Jenna gave birth to her son, I sat in the waiting room of the hospital, anxious and excited. I watched a nature show set in Australia about the eating habits of the duck-billed platypus. (Unbeknownst to me, they are carnivores. Also, why do I remember this detail from the day Jenna gave birth? Seriously, brains are weird.) I zoned out, and then I prayed. I prayed that God would go before her and that she and the baby would be healthy. Finally, Jenna's husband texted me that Weston was here and that I could visit them. My heart was racing. I could barely contain my joy as I walked quickly down the hallway to see my best friend and meet her son. I wiped tears from my eyes and had the biggest smile on my face. As I write this, I am tearing up. I was so happy for her. And he was perfect! I sat with Jenna for a bit, and we stared at his sweet little face. I even took their first family photo: Jenna and Lee and their adorable little baby boy. And then she handed me a bag with her placenta inside. I felt like we were now even for my text to her about poop, blood, and spewing breast milk.

Jenna

Unlike Angela, who conveniently gave birth right before our summer hiatus, I had a due date at the end of September. Our next scheduled hiatus wouldn't be until Thanksgiving. I wondered how this would work, but I was optimistic that the powers that be would find a way to schedule creatively since we'd done it before when other cast members needed time off to do movies. After much back-and-forth, I was eventually told there would be no break in filming, but I could take the legally allowed eight weeks of unpaid disability. I hated the idea of Pam being absent from such a big chunk of the season, and missing those episodes would mean losing a third of my salary that year. So I pushed myself to go back to work after five weeks of leave. It felt too soon. But I hadn't been left with much of a choice.

I confided in my sister, Emily, a lot during this time. She's a Catholic school teacher, and a mom, and her job also did not offer any paid maternity leave. She had to save her sick days for *six years* before getting pregnant. That way, when she had her daughter, my niece CeCe, she had logged twelve weeks of sick days. But she took only ten weeks. She wanted to leave herself extra days in case CeCe got sick or had a doctor's appointment. I think my sister assumed my acting job would be different. Turns out that was not the case. And the more women I talk to, the more I hear stories like this.

The whole experience broke my heart. Not just for me, but for our culture and for all women. Soapbox moment: It shouldn't be this hard. Other countries have figured this out. We can do better. We need to do better. Needless to say, this made my first months as a new parent very stressful.

Angela

It was difficult to watch Jenna come back to work so soon. I could tell she wasn't physically or emotionally ready. On set, I tried to help her in any way I could. From sharing the pump schedule that Kelly Cantley had created for me to making signs for Jenna's trailer door that said BABY SLEEPING—DO NOT KNOCK. I reached out to our grip department to see if they had any extra blackout curtains for her trailer windows to help Weston nap better. And I put a basket in her trailer full of those special postpartum underwear. You know the ones that hold in your stomach, and put less pressure on your healing incision, making it easier to walk around? They are huge and wonderful, and I wanted to make sure Jenna had a bunch. Sometimes I spoke up on her behalf about something in the script. For example, her first episode back, Pam was supposed to carry baby Phillip into the office in a car seat. Jenna was recovering from a C-section. She could not carry anything that heavy, so I told Phil Shea to get Pam a stroller. The truth is it felt like a double standard that other cast members had their schedules accommodated for films, but Jenna was not given the same consideration after having a baby. I wish Jenna had had more time at home, and it broke my heart to see her struggle.

Jenna

I honestly don't know what I would have done without Angela. Or that underwear. I've never loved underwear more. I should say, the entire cast and crew were wonderful when I returned. They rallied around and helped me make the best of a challenging situation. After becoming a mom, I reflected on those few years when Angela was a mother, and I wasn't. I remember calling her

and saying something to the effect of, "Thanks for hanging in there with me. I must have been so annoying during those years. I should have called you more. I should have come over more. I should have brought you food or held Isabel so you could take a bath. I had no idea how to support you, and I'm so sorry. I didn't know. Now I know." Angela just laughed and told me she'd had faith it would all work out. And it did.

Angela

Our friendship has grown so much deeper since we both became mothers. Luckily, we both "mom" the same way. I think that is due to our Midwestern and Southern upbringings. We are hands-on, roll-up-your-sleeves parents. We are kind but have rules and aren't afraid to be silly. But we also expect you to clean up your mess. Between the two of us, we now have five kids: Isabel, Jack, and Cade at my house, and Weston and Harper at Jenna's house. I am still moved by how graciously Jenna's family welcomed my stepsons into their lives. The weekend Josh and I and our kids set up our home together, Jenna sent us the biggest housewarming bouquet of cookies! Yes, cookies! The kids were thrilled!

Over the years, our families have trick-or-treated together, welcomed one another's new family pets, had Easter brunches and Christmas get-togethers, celebrated birthdays, enjoyed afternoons in the pool, and watched the Super Bowl together. I cherish the fact that Isabel was in Jenna's wedding. I am thrilled that our kids go to school together and I get to see Jenna at school assemblies. I love that Isabel gives Harper a hug as she runs by her at recess. We've celebrated family milestones and weathered many storms together. We've listened while the other cried or worried or brainstormed about how to juggle work and family life. I know we will all share many more moments together, and my heart is full of gratitude. And, Jenna, if by some insane act of God (because I just entered my fifties and have zero plans of having any more children) I ever become pregnant again, I promise not to text you about any of my bodily fluids.

11

dwangela forevah!

by Angela

Here are some phrases that have been used to describe Angela and Dwight's romance in the press and on fan sites:

Strange love.

Toxic.

Ewww.

Wildest, for better or worse.

Hot and awkward.

Relationship goals.

Weird.

Gross.

Sexy but kinda disgusting.

Like watching a train wreck.

The greatest love story on *The Office*.

I love them all.

I meet thousands of *The Office* fans every year who adore the odd, geeky couple that is Dwangela. This fandom is fiercely loyal. It is a mix of people that spans cultures, ages, and degrees of quirkiness. I have had strangers at airports, at baseball games, and in the dressing room at a shopping mall show me their Dwight and Angela tattoos. I am constantly surprised at their size and placement. Imagine seeing a version of yourself on someone's calf, shoulder, wrist, or most recently on their upper thigh. Walking, breathing tributes, forever a couple on someone's body. Then there are the couples that dress either themselves or their children as Dwight and Angela for Halloween. Thank you for tagging me every year when you post your costumes. You are my people and I love you all.

But of course, when Rainn and I first met, we had no idea that there would be a "Dwangela" or that we'd have nine wonderful years to develop these characters and their relationship.

Let me tell you about my first conversation with Rainn Wilson. It was during our pilot episode. I was seated with several cast members enjoying lunch when he approached us with his very pregnant wife, Holiday Reinhorn, who was visiting the set that day. When they got to the table, he gestured to her belly and said, "This is Holly. Bearer of my seed." It was in that moment I realized I might have a hard time telling the difference between Rainn and Dwight.

As you know, I am a big journal-keeper, and the first time I wrote about Rainn was on October 18, 2005. It was during the first Halloween episode on *The Office*, and I was dressed like a fluffy white cat. I wrote, "Today on set, Rainn said I looked like a chinchilla." It is so perfect that the first time I ever wrote about Rainn, he was likening me to a rodent.

As I sat down to write this chapter, I was curious about how Rainn described me in *his* book. (It is no surprise that his book, *The Bassoon King*, is wonderful. It is thoughtful, funny, and a delightful look into the man, the myth, the legend who is . . . Rainn-with-two-*ns* Wilson.) On page 263 of *The Bassoon King*, he describes me thusly:

". . . Angela Kinsey, who has no discernable body fat and is the size of a baby sandpiper . . ."

And then on page 264:

". . . truth be told, she bruises like a tiny, overly ripe, albino nectarine."

Never in my wildest imagination did I think I would be compared to an overly ripe, albino nectarine. He's not wrong though. I do bruise easily.

In preparation for writing this chapter, I also combed through countless emails and texts that he and I have shared over the years. In them, Rainn affectionately addresses me as: Tiny Dancer, Little One, Darling, Friend, and Lazy Fuck. I address him as Tall Guy, Tall Friend, Fella, and Old Fuck. These emails and texts usually involve us catching up, sharing pictures of our kids, inviting each other to hang out, or sending each other links to random things on the internet we find interesting.

October 18, 2005

Today we are filming scenes for the Halloween episode!

My character is dressed like a white fluffy cat. I have little cat ears, a white long sleeve shirt, white tights, white ballet flats and a huge puffy fancy fur skirt. The skirt has a tail made of wire and fur. It is so hard to sit down!! And the skirt keeps sliding down.

Today on set Rainn said I look like a Chinchilla!

Is he rough around the edges? Sure. Will he sometimes text you out of the blue just to say, "You suck"? Sure. But he also texts you that he loves and misses you even if you do have "feet the size of a cricket." Rainn is the type of person who reaches out to tell you he's thinking of you and his messages seem to come through just when you need them most. I have a video he texted me from New Zealand that I love. He was making a film there and so was going to miss my wedding. With a loud waterfall as a backdrop that caused him to yell to be heard, he created the funniest and sweetest message wishing me a wonderful wedding day. He is also my only friend who wanted me to send him a photo of a disgusting-looking cyst I had removed from my abdomen. So I did. His reply? "It's beautiful."

I think this level of oversharing came naturally to our friendship because of the way we first got to know each other. When I look back, it all started in Season 1, Episode 5, "Basketball." It was Dwight and Angela's first onscreen interaction, and most people might not remember this brief moment, but to me it was foreshadowing. Everyone is in the bullpen working away, but Angela is rummaging through the supply shelf looking for something and getting frustrated. She turns to the room and says:

ANGELA: Has anyone seen the first-aid kit?

Dwight holds the kit up.

ANGELA: How many times have I told you? *I'm* the safety officer, not you.

Dwight drove Angela crazy from the very beginning. His love of rules and her need to be in control made them a perfect match. Of course, we didn't know then what Dwangela would become. We were only five episodes into our first season. So many of the show's relationships were still developing, and that was true offscreen as well. Rainn and I barely knew each other. Aside from pleasantries and occasional small talk at the lunch buffet, we were basically strangers. But in Season 2 that would all change.

It was a normal week on set; we were filming Episode 8, "Performance Review," and things were going great. I was excited because my character had a talking head about her youth pageant days, and we had a fun scene in accounting. Maybe it's because I was so caught up in the fact that I had a talking head (which was always a big deal for the supporting cast) that I missed a clue about my character's future story arc. If you remember, Jan and Michael had hooked up outside of Chili's, and Kevin is gossiping about it. Angela sternly tells Kevin, "Don't talk about it. Office romances are nobody's business but the people involved." I didn't think much about that line until we sat down at lunch to read Episode 9, "E-Mail Surveillance." It was at that table read that I first learned Dwight and Angela were going to become a couple. There was a mixture of laughing and groaning in the room when the script read something like, "The camera pushes in on a playhouse in the backyard, there is something moving inside it. As we get closer, we see two sets of Birkenstocks, one very small pair and one very large pair, rubbing back and forth."

Up to this point in the show, Rainn and I hadn't done a single scene together alone. I wasn't sure what we would talk about between takes or if we would even have good chemistry. I was both nervous and excited about this new story line and what it meant for my character. One of my biggest fears was that I would somehow blow it. Rainn is such an amazing actor, and I wanted to be able to hold my own with him.

Our first scene took place at the copier. Dwight says to Angela, "If you have any sensitive emails, they need to be deleted immediately." Pam overhears this and tells Jim she suspects they are a couple.

For the next scene together, we have a secret conversation outside on the patio of Jim's apartment. Paul Feig told us to improvise a few lines. We were in the background of the shot, but this little moment places our characters together at the party. And importantly, there is an establishing shot of our Birkenstocks. This way, the audience recognizes whose feet belong to the Birkenstocks once those sandals start grinding. I improvised the line "Jesus drank wine," justifying the fact that Angela was enjoying an adult beverage at Jim's party. Scandalous.

Many fans have asked me what it was like in that tiny playhouse with Rainn. Well, we had to look like we were having a major make-out session when, in real life, we were only just getting to know each other. We did not kiss in this scene, but we did have to roll around on top of each other, so yeah . . . it was a little weird. Also, these scenes can get tricky because everything has to time out perfectly. Jim and Michael are harmonizing "Islands in the Stream" when the camera pans over their shoulders and slowly zooms in on Angela's and Dwight's feet. The biggest issue for Rainn and me was that we couldn't hear what was happening inside Jim's apartment. We kept missing our cue, so our assistant director gave us a walkie-talkie so we would know when to start our fake make-out session. In the first take, we were lying side by side, kind of flipping our feet back and forth. Paul Feig said we looked like we were swimming a sad breaststroke and that the camera couldn't really see my feet. Rainn Wilson is six foot three; I am five foot one. My feet did not protrude out of the little house the way his did, and so the shot wasn't working. We had to find a way to capture both sets of feet, despite the height difference. Paul bashfully walked up to us with this note, "So, umm, all right, how do I say this? This is a somewhat odd request, but, Angela, I think we need you to lay on your back and wrap your legs around Rainn. I'd love to see your feet rubbing his legs back and forth." All I could think was, *I'm not sure I am that flexible, but okay.* That didn't work either. After a few tries we finally figured out the right position. It was as uncomfortable as it was awkward. Still on my back, I had to scooch way down Rainn's torso, my face in the middle of his chest. I could barely breathe. And poor Rainn was doing a plank move so that he didn't crush me. And then I realized another problem. How would I wrap my feet around his calves? Shins don't bend that way. The best I could do was this odd rubbing of the sides of his calves with my feet. You know, the super-sexy side calf rub that you do while making out.

In between takes we would lie there in silence. I'm not sure either of us knew what to say. It was an odd way to spend time with someone you don't know that well. But as the night wore on, I began to relax and became my chatty self. I started peppering Rainn with questions about his life, and we launched into deep conversation. We talked about our childhoods, our spiritual beliefs, and what we hoped for in our lives. In between the big stuff we also covered the random things like places we had traveled to, that year's football season, and our crazy rescue pets, and then I taught him some phrases in Indonesian. In particular, "I'm cold." "Saya dingin." Because despite wearing a huge winter coat, I was still freezing, and the little playhouse had no heater. Rainn let me borrow his scarf, asked for hand warmers for me, and made sure the assistant director gave me bathroom breaks. I would learn that that is just the type of guy he is. He looks out for the people he cares about. It was such a strange juxtaposition, doing this silly scene, and having a heart-to-heart at the same time. When we heard "Action" on our walkie-talkie, I would quickly give him his scarf back and scooch down to his midriff, he would roll over on top of me and do his plank move, and then I'd awkwardly wrap my ankles around his legs and rub my Birkenstocks on his calves. We did this every take, and there were many.

Somewhere in this face-to-chest suffocating plank straddle foot-rubbing craziness, we became friends.

Rainn would show up for me many times over the course of the show, but one moment in particular stands out. It was Season 3, "A Benihana Christmas," and the writers created a story line that involved me needing to sing karaoke. Here's the thing: I hate singing in front of people. It is the only time I get stage fright. It doesn't really make sense, because I love performing in front of people. I can do the zaniest sketch comedy, prattle away on talk shows, perform improv, and speak to huge crowds—but singing in front of anyone besides my family gives me

major anxiety. Angela Martin was supposed to sing "The Little Drummer Boy" in front of the bullpen, and I panicked. I went to Harold Ramis, our director that week, and told him I didn't think I could sing. He smiled, patted me on the back, and simply said, "But you will." I started to spiral. I confided in Rainn. I think I said something really eloquent like, "Rainn, I'm gonna shit myself." He told me to sing the song as Angela Martin and *not* Angela Kinsey. This felt like good "actor" advice, and I gave it a go. We did the first take, and I actually got through it, but barely. My voice wavered and my hands shook. In the second take, I somehow lost the beat. How is that even possible? It's "The Little Drummer Boy," not "The Star-Spangled Banner." By the third take, I couldn't find the tune at all, and clutched my hands tight in front of my chest so no one could see how much I was trembling. It was then that my friend Rainn decided to step in to help. I started the song again, and much to my amazement and gratitude, my big, tall scene partner dropped to one knee and held out the microphone for me and came in with the "*Pa rum pum, rum pum pum pum, rum pum pum pum!*" Rainn helped me find the beat, plus I was no longer alone! If you watch that scene, you will see a *huge* smile comes across my face. That is *not* Angela Martin smiling at Dwight Schrute. That is Angela Kinsey smiling at Rainn Wilson for saving her butt. He saw me struggling and improvised that moment. To this day when I hear that song, I think of him and smile.

On the other extreme, there was the time he nearly made me vomit (and not fake cold-soup vomit). We were filming "Goodbye, Toby" in Season 4. Dwight and Angela are sneaking around behind Andy's back when Phyllis catches them in the act. It was described in the script something like this:

> SPY SHOT: *An exhausted Phyllis comes out of the elevator with a BOX OF PARTY SUPPLIES. As she gets closer to her desk, she hears RUSTLING. It's coming from behind the file cabinet—she looks and sees a tiny blond head peeking out. Phyllis and Angela see each other. Phyllis then sees Dwight. Phyllis GASPS!*

As we began to rehearse the scene, we realized we had a problem. I was eight months pregnant, and not fake pregs. How would we hide my very big pregnant belly? Once again, poor Paul Feig had to brainstorm awkward "make-out" positions for Rainn and me. We tried lying on the floor behind the copier, a "standing" pose by the file cabinets, crouching behind reception, and finally settled on me sitting on Angela's desk with Rainn standing in front of me blocking my belly with his body. We really wanted the image of Dwight and Angela in the throes of passion to be shocking to both Phyllis and the audience. Because of my belly, there couldn't be much of my body shown in the shot, so Paul had the idea for Angela to have her hair down, giving her that tousled look, and for Dwight to be shirtless. To sell this "sexy" moment and cover the belly, Rainn had to lean way over to kiss me. By this time, we were old friends, and the scene would not have been much of an issue except for the fact that right before the take, Rainn ate a tuna fish sandwich. Let me repeat that . . . TUNA FISH! Kissing someone who has just eaten tuna fish is not pleasant for anyone, but for a pregnant woman, it crosses into the vomit zone. At this point in my pregnancy, I could have smelled that tuna fish sandwich if he had been eating it in New York, let alone a few feet away. I literally started to gag. After the first take, I forced him to eat a handful of mints.

Some of the funniest and most moving moments of my life as an actor have happened with Rainn. I didn't think we were going to get through the moment in "Beach Games" when Dwight whispers "sabotage" and I respond, "Did you say sandwich?"

And we couldn't stop laughing as he lists Dwight's ridiculous directions to get to the beet farm in "The Surplus" (Season 5), or when I list off all the steps required to take care of Sprinkles. That scene was so

special to me that I asked the props department if I could keep the notepad of Sprinkles's medical treatments.

Once when Rainn and I were featured in *Entertainment Weekly* magazine, they asked if we could also do an online interview (you can still find it on YouTube). For this, Rainn made up a song calling me a "cousin fucker," as a nod to my Southern family. I then made fun of his constant demands for Diet Cokes and called him a "colossal asshole." You should have seen the reporter's face. Most of our interviews ended with either fits of laughter or me whacking Rainn as if I'd lost all patience.

I know part of me will always be emotionally tethered to Rainn. We journeyed through a decade of life together. So in Season 9, when Dwight and Angela finally reunite, I felt so happy. I deeply cared for them as a couple. I had been rooting for them for so long, and in the last act of the episode "A.A.R.M.," they finally get back together. Dwight realizes he cannot live without Angela, and he decides to pour his heart out to her. When we started to film the proposal scene, Dwight tells Angela he loves her, and Rainn as Dwight tears up. I also began to tear up. We could feel the weight of the moment for our characters. I looked over to our crew on the side of the road and they were tearing up. We were all so invested in this couple's happily-ever-after ending. And I know that everyone always talks about that epic Jim and Pam proposal scene, and it is truly beautiful, but did it start with a car chase?

Sprinkle's Medicine

· Diabetes shot
  roll the insulin in your
  hand prior to administering
  - DON'T shake it.

· ACE Inhibitors
  - give with a meal
  - place bowl directly in
  front of her or she
  cannot see it!

· Omega Fatty Acid.
  - mix one capsule into
  the kidney medicine
  - give to her 15 min.
  after her meal.

· Fungal Cream
  - rub in under her tail
  to treat for parasites

Did Pam yell, "What the fuck is wrong with you?" Did Jim start his speech with "Shut up, woman!"? Did he promise to love her and raise one hundred of her lovers' children? Was his love expressed loudly through a bullhorn? Did he buy the ring in a jewelry store, or was it taken out of a family member's butt? I mean, come on. *This* is an epic proposal.

Dwight and Angela had many amazing moments on *The Office*. They fell in love. They gave each other fantastic gifts of bobbleheads and house keys. They created pet names for each other—Monkey, Possum, Half Pint, and D. They secretly slow-danced outside of Phyllis and Bob Vance's wedding, and mastered talking in code with "no cookie." They probably messed around in the Dunder Mifflin office more than any other couple: in the warehouse, the break room, the kitchen, and at Angela's desk, to name just a few of the locations. They kissed with the force of a thousand waterfalls and bonded over their mutual hatred of jazz. And yes, they fought, made up, were involved in the mercy killing of a cat (RIP, Sprinkles), broke up, dated, got engaged to other people, cheated on those people with each other, got fake married in a barn but actually real married except only one of them knew, broke up again, decided to procreate and have a contract about said procreation, bathed an elderly aunt together, conspired to have a coworker killed/badly maimed, had a baby, and survived a scandalous divorce. But through it all, their love could not be denied. They were meant to be together.

PROCREATIVE RELATIONS
EXPIRES AT MIDNIGHT ON DECEMBER 31ST

259

It's a beautiful love story, really. A strange, toxic, awkward, weird, gross love story that will stand the test of time and live forever in people's hearts and on their upper thighs.

Since *The Office* ended, our lives have taken us in different directions. I don't get to see my tall friend as often as I would like. But I am thankful that we stay in touch. We text and talk regularly, meet for lunch dates and dinners, participate in events together, and Rainn has even been known to drop by my house. He is a huge hit with my children, who he calls "idiots," much to their delight. We continue to show up for each other, and thanks to *The Office*, I have a friend for life. And, Rainn, if you are reading this you probably have horrible coffee breath and need a mint.

Love,
Angela

12

death bus

Remember earlier in the book, when we told you there were two episodes of *The Office* that involved travel that nearly ended in disaster? The first one was on a boat for "Booze Cruise" in Season 2, and the other was on a bus in Season 9. Well, it's time for the other half of that story, folks. You might know this episode as "Work Bus," but the cast of *The Office* know it as "Death Bus." If you thought losing half the cast at sea in the middle of the night during "Booze Cruise" was crazy, wait until you hear about this one.

Jenna

Before we head out on the open road (see what I did there?), we need to bring you all up to speed (one more), so buckle in (last one, I promise), because a lot had happened at Dunder Mifflin before the bus ever left that parking lot (okay, done with driving puns).

At this point in the series, the show had gone through some noteworthy transitions. Around Season 5, the tone of *The Office* changed a bit. Gone were the days of twenty-seven seconds of silence and long, lingering shots of random office work. With Paul Lieberstein and Jen Celotta as showrunners, we seemed to take on a faster, more comedic pace. Our fifth was a fun season that resulted in some of my favorite episodes of the series, like "The Duel" and "Lecture Circuit." In our earlier seasons, we had resisted casting big-name guest stars on the show. Greg feared it would destroy the authenticity of our little paper company documentary to have, let's say, Debra Messing walk in as a new client. But as the show went on, and our cast members became household names themselves, we abandoned this rule and started casting folks like Idris Elba, Amy Ryan, and Timothy Olyphant in recurring roles. Then in Season 6 we added Kathy Bates to the cast as Jolene Bennett, CEO of Sabre, the company that acquired little Dunder Mifflin. Of all our marquee-name guests, I never got used to doing scenes with Kathy Bates. From the first moment I saw her I was in awe. I'd been a fan forever. At one point my hair colorist had told me he also once colored Kathy Bates's hair, and I about died thinking I was one degree of separation from an acting legend. And now, here I was, about to share the screen with her.

As she walked through the door for our first table read, the whole space took on a different vibe, one of importance and class, like in the *Harry Potter* movies when Dumbledore enters a room. Kathy Bates walked slowly to her chair, sat, took a sip of water, opened her script, and then . . . the best thing ever . . . she took out a delicate golden folded fan. Apparently, she was hot. As we read the script, she would occasionally fan herself with her golden fan, all the while delivering her lines with expert precision. I looked at her and thought, *I hope that one day I earn the right to fan myself with a golden fan at a table read.* This woman is my life goals.

Angela

I had two moments with Kathy Bates I'll never forget. I was always freezing on set, so I kept a small heater under my desk to keep me warm. (Phyllis, Kate, and Jenna also had little heaters. Our set was super cold.) The accounting department had a scene with Kathy, and as she walked up to my desk during the camera rehearsal, she said something to the effect of, "My God, it's hot over here. It's like the Sahara!" I distinctly remember her referring to *my* desk as the "Sahara." I was mortified, so I quickly slid my foot under my desk and kicked the off button on the heater. My other memory of Kathy Bates (and it's how I always want to think of her) was in hair and makeup. We were sitting side by side one morning and began talking about our love of road trips. Turns out, Kathy is a big road tripper! She owns an RV and told me about this wonderful road trip she took and places where she would park her RV. I felt like this was our bonding moment and hopefully made up for my Sahara desk. Kathy, if you ever read this book, Jenna and I would like to throw something out there: road trip, the three of us, all with golden fans?

Jenna

We also added Zach Woods in Season 6 as Jo Bennett's minion, Gabe Lewis. He was a wonderful addition to the cast and a brilliant improviser. He also became one of our most treasured guests at Angela's real-life Yankee Swap parties.

Things were clicking along. Pam got married and delivered her daughter. It was a fun year. Then, in Season 7, Steve Carell's contract was up, and he told us he was leaving the show. We were devastated to see him go but not surprised. We knew those years as our leader, combined with doing multiple movie roles, had meant missing out on many family events. By leaving the show, he would have much more time to do his favorite thing, be a dad.

To bridge his departure, we welcomed Will Ferrell as new Scranton branch manager Deangelo Vickers. Having Will on set was a treat. If anyone could

challenge Steve for nicest guy and best improviser, it was Will. And Amy Ryan returned, as Michael was reunited with his true love, Holly. As we did our final episodes with Steve, it was difficult to contain our sadness at losing our friend and our trusted number one. We cried a lot. The worst was the day we filmed his goodbye song. People often ask if Steve knew we were going to sing to him, because the emotion on his face is so genuine. We'd all been given the lyrics and practiced the song in secret. Steve told me that as he was being led into the conference room, he knew something was up. But he did not know we were going to sing, and the whole thing was very moving. The first time we tried to film the scene, no one could get through it. You can hear Ed Helms's voice breaking before the song even begins when he says, "We want to thank you for everything."

Angela

During Steve's last week on set, I was doing some filming for "Adventures with Angela" for NBC.com. I'd film behind-the-scenes moments and answer fan questions. A LOT of fans wrote in that week wanting me to interview Steve about his time on *The Office*. Steve agreed, and I walked over to his trailer one day during lunch to chat. Before we could get to the fan questions, I started to cry. I had to compose myself and start again. During the interview, Steve shared that leaving the show was also emotional for him. He said that when he'd spoken with his wife, Nancy, about how difficult it would be to say goodbye, she reminded him that while the role of Michael Scott had been such a big part of his career and was certainly hard to leave behind, it was the friendships on set that were always the most important to him. Those he would take with him. We might have been losing Michael Scott and his ridiculous antics, but we would never lose our friend Steve. (This interview is still on YouTube, and it made me cry to watch it even after all these years.)

Jenna

When Season 8 began, we enlisted James Spader as new CEO Robert California. Many critics argue that Season 8 was clunky, as it was clear we were trying to figure out the show without Steve. And I won't argue. But working with James Spader was a highlight of my career. As a child of the '80s, I had seen almost every single one of James Spader's movies, and of course I was a fan. When the producers told us he'd be coming on board to play our new boss, I was beyond excited to work with him. It took me several weeks before I had the courage to bring up his filmography in the hair and makeup trailer . . . we had all wanted to do this, and one day I finally worked up the courage. I'm so glad I did! He told us everything about every movie I'd ever watched growing up. *Pretty in Pink*; *Less Than Zero*; *Sex, Lies, and Videotape*; *Bad Influence* . . . I won't include any of our conversations here (as they are mostly R-rated). But, guys . . . it was like attending a master class in 1980s Hollywood gossip.

I think my favorite thing about James was his love of rehearsal. In the early seasons of *The Office*, we used to do multiple rehearsals before shooting a scene. We'd form huddles with the writers and producers and talk at great length about our characters' motivations. But by Season 8, we all knew our characters so well we felt like we didn't "need" those lengthy rehearsals and discussions anymore. Enter James Spader.

For his first scene, the director said, "Okay, James, you enter the bullpen here, and land about here, talk with the group, and we will end with you over by reception." James asked if we could do a rehearsal. We explained that *was*

267

the rehearsal. A quick rundown of our movements. Well, that's not what James Spader meant by rehearsal. Not at all. He tried different takes on his lines; he tried different blocking. The theater nerd in me was delighted. I wanted to jump up and hug him! I was struck by how this acting legend was still devoted to meticulously planning every scene. This guy DOES NOT phone it in, folks. This became the new normal for scenes with James. We made space in the schedule to rehearse. Most people tolerated it, but I loved it.

Angela

Like Jenna and every other person on our set who grew up in the '80s, we were all pinching ourselves when we heard that James Spader was joining *The Office*. One morning I walked into the hair and makeup trailer, and James freakin' Spader was seated next to me. I mean, *Pretty in Pink* played on repeat on my giant Betamax back in the day. You know what I'm talking about! Steff. Sitting. Right. There. OMG!!! I played it cool, you guys, but it was not easy. For weeks we were seated side by side in hair and makeup. We would say our hellos. James Spader was always friendly and professional. He usually reclined and closed his eyes as his makeup was applied. James Spader was so relaxed. James Spader is a pro. I, on the other hand, would chat away with my makeup artist, Kenneth Paul, about my life and everything else. I was newly single, and one morning I was telling K.P. how I let my daughter sleep with me in my bed. She was still little, and since it was just the two of us, I didn't see the harm. James Spader sprang forward as if awakened from a deep slumber. He turned to me with great force and said, "Angela! If you ever want a man in that bed, you must get your child to sleep on her own!" I was so stunned I think I squealed. From that day on, we would have amazing conversations in hair and makeup.

I remember the day his adorable young son visited. James shared with me that his in-laws were in town. I told him that my mom, dad, and sister were also about to visit, and I was worried about where everyone would sleep. He shared with me his strategy for having guests. He makes sure that the guest room is uncomfortable and placed in a location of the house difficult to get to and far away from the bathroom. This delighted him. His theory was if guests are uncomfortable . . . they won't wear out their welcome. I couldn't help but laugh.

Jenna

We also added Catherine Tate to the mix as special projects manager Nellie Bertram. Her sketch comedy television show on the BBC, *The Catherine Tate Show*, is incredible. If you haven't seen it, give it a watch. The writers had seen her show and asked her to relocate from London to Los Angeles to play the role of Nellie. My favorite story about working with Catherine is from shooting the episode "Andy's Ancestry" (Season 9), when Pam has to teach Nellie to drive. Because CATHERINE TATE COULDN'T DRIVE! When she came to America to join us on the show, they had to hire a driver to bring her to and from set. But when we shot the episode, they put her behind the wheel! So when you watch the scenes, just know that all the fear in my face is real. At one point, Catherine actually drove on the wrong side of the road while we were filming—and not on purpose. If memory serves, Catherine actually ran the car into some things. They made her eat a salad in the scene while trying to drive. I honestly think I might have peed my pants a little, from fear and from laughing.

Angela

That brings us to Season 9. Our farewell season. James Spader left the show. We added two more new cast members, Clark Duke and Jake Lacy (playing Clark Green and Pete Miller, respectively). Andy Bernard (Ed Helms) moved into the position of Scranton branch manager, and Greg Daniels returned as our showrunner. One of the first orders of business was to load fifteen actors onto a traveling work bus and embark on a journey of doom.

"Work Bus" was written by executive producer Brent Forrester and directed by Bryan Cranston. We want you to know that we see the irony that Bryan Cranston, aka Walter White Sr. or "Heisenberg" as he was known in crystal

methamphetamine circles, was an accessory to almost murdering the entire cast of *The Office*. I assure you this is pure coincidence.

It was also the source of great humor that when Bryan finally got a week off from filming *Breaking Bad*, a television show that takes place primarily in an old RV in the desert with the main characters constantly dodging death, he then spent his vacation directing an episode of a show that normally takes place in an office with the main characters trying to survive boring conference room meetings *but* for that week was set on a bus . . . in the middle of nowhere. He went from an RV to a bus. It was almost like he brought it on himself.

The plot went this way: In the hopes of getting some free vacation days, Jim tricks Dwight—who now owns the building that houses Dunder Mifflin—into thinking that the office is unsafe and in need of repairs. Dwight agrees, but instead of sending everyone home, he calls Jim's bluff and presents the employees with a "mobile office" to use while the repairs are being made. The majority of the episode occurs on the bus that Dwight has transformed into a mobile workplace. Of course, this is a very Dwight move.

Jenna

Imagine a small airport shuttle filled with desks, chairs, lamps, printers, a watercooler, a microwave, a giant-screen TV, a coffeemaker, fourteen actors, and four crew members. What could go wrong? Who could have predicted that Ellie Kemper would pee her pants, or that the entire cast would almost be killed—twice?

Things started off fine, because the first scenes on the bus were shot in the Dunder Mifflin parking lot, not moving and close to home. Sure, the bus was hot and crowded, but we could unload between takes, use the restroom, eat snacks, and stretch. The bus was a novelty, sort of fun. John Krasinski and Bryan Cranston were doing comedy bits. We were all laughing.

Angela

In the story, Jim convinces Andy that since they are stuck on this work bus, he should take everyone to get pie at the best place in town, Laverne's Pies Tires Fixed Also. Andy agrees, and so it was time to roll! The producers decided the best use of our time was to transport the actors from our home base to our rural pie stand location on the actual work bus. We had scenes that needed to happen on a moving bus, and the idea was that we could grab little bits of the script along the way. A shot of Dwight driving. A shot of people trying to work. This all sounded fairly easy, but it was a very hot day and whenever we started filming, the air-conditioning on the bus had to be turned off because it was too noisy. We were basically in a moving hot tin can with no air. I thought Brian and Creed were going to melt. Oscar looked dead inside. Plus, it was a very curvy road. Jenna was getting a little carsick even though she had a forward-facing chair. At that point, the heat and the nausea seemed like our worst obstacles.

Jenna

Once we made it to the country road, we were able to disembark and get some fresh air. Sweet air! We were all given little battery-operated fans and water. We loaded back onto the bus refreshed and started into the main action of our first scene. For this, John Krasinski's character, Jim, does a chant called "Shabooya Roll Call." It also appeared in Spike Lee's film *Get on the Bus* and later in the cheerleading movie *Bring It On: All or Nothing*.

Angela

For days this chant lived in my head. As I went to sleep at night all I could hear was, *"My name is Kevin. That is my name. They call me Kevin. 'Cause that's my name."*

Each cast member was so funny trying earnestly to sing their introduction—especially Phyllis—we would dissolve into laughter each time. I'm sure this was extremely frustrating to our crew who were trapped on a hot moving bus full of actors who couldn't get their takes because they kept breaking. (Only a portion of what we shot ended up in the actual episode, so go to the deleted scenes on the DVD for more fun moments. Trust me. It's good stuff.) It was during one of these laughing fits that Ellie peed her pants. That's right, folks—she laughed so hard, she peed her pants. Then, like only Ellie Kemper can, she adorably screamed, "Oh my God! You guys!! I just peed my pants!!!" Cue even more laughter!

Jenna

To be fair to Ellie, it wasn't a huge pee. More like a large tinkle. But it was enough that she needed a change of wardrobe. We put some prop work papers down on her chair to try to cover the wet spot for her, while she used some napkins from the prop coffee station to dry her skirt. That's all we had on the bus. Fake work papers and a few napkins. And we could not stop laughing. Our camera operators then radioed the producers in the follow van to explain what had happened. Poor Bryan Cranston. I bet he couldn't wait to go back to the New Mexico desert at that point. His actors were losing it and peeing themselves, and we'd just gotten started.

Angela

We should probably explain about the van that was following us that day. When you are filming in a moving vehicle, there is usually a van behind you with the director, producers, and hair, makeup, and wardrobe team. It's creatively called the "follow van." The folks in the follow van have a monitor with a live stream from the camera in the vehicle, and the actors, directors, and producers communicate on walkie-talkies. It's very handy in case of wardrobe malfunctions. And peeing.

Jenna

Eventually, our follow van directed us to a remote park with a walking trail and public restrooms. The bus pulled over, and out poured the cast of *The Office*. The wardrobe department appeared with a new set of clothes for Ellie.

We all laughed and laughed in the park as some very confused hikers passed by. We were joking this would go down as "the episode when Ellie peed her pants!"

Little did we know that would *not* be the most memorable part of the day. Not by a long shot.

We loaded back onto the bus.

The next scene involved Dwight driving like a maniac. For this, the bus was hooked up to a rig that pulled us along as Rainn pretended to drive. The idea was that as Rainn would pretend to swerve, the assistant director would yell "Right," and we'd fling ourselves to the right. Then Rainn would "swerve" the other way, the assistant director would yell "Left," and we'd all lunge left. We tried this. The bus stopped. There was a discussion. I guess our flailing looked fake, and it was clear the bus was not swerving at all. Rainn Wilson was told to get off the bus. The bus was then detached from the rig and a stunt driver climbed on board. There were no stunt actors, however. We stayed on and were told to keep doing what we'd been doing. And off we went.

Angela

We were all bouncing down the road, blissfully unaware of what was about to happen. We were saying our lines and everything was going smoothly when all of a sudden, we heard the assistant director yell, "Swerve!" The stunt driver swerved HARD. I mean he cranked that wheel like Cole Trickle in *Days of Thunder*. As a result, the entire cast and contents of the bus went flying into the side of the party bus! What no one had considered when they told this stunt driver to swerve as hard as he could without flipping the bus over was that none of our office furniture, props, or set decorations were securely tied down. Let me remind you what was on the bus: desks; lamps; laptops; printers; a five-gallon water dispenser (full of water); a coffee station complete with a microwave, coffeepot, coffee mugs; paper . . . lots of paper; pens; calculators; notepads; mini fans . . . oh, and our rolling desk chairs! One hard stunt-driver swerve to the right and everything and everyone went flying. Everything.

Plus, they had somehow gotten a portable air-conditioning unit! "We can pull it behind the bus with a hose that goes through the sunroof. It's totally quiet. So this afternoon, the bus won't be so hot." We were thrilled, and as we loaded back onto the cool, reorganized bus, everyone relaxed and decided to put the morning behind us.

Off we went. No more laughing fits. No more peeing. We were nailing our shots. That's when I noticed a funny smell. "Hey, guys, does anyone else smell that?" I asked. Nope. "No, seriously. Guys. It smells like gas." No one. "Jenna is being sensitive" was the consensus. I mean, I was known for having allergy attacks on set because of the tiniest bits of dust. But this was different! "No. Stop the bus. I'm serious, it smells wrong." Soon it wasn't just me. Others piped up. We began debating whether the bus smelled funny. Then our camera operator spoke up. She didn't feel well. She stumbled and set down her camera.

STOP THE BUS!!!

Guess what? The portable air-conditioning unit's INTAKE hose was right next to the EXHAUST pipe on the bus. So that hose was sucking in exhaust and blowing it straight into the sunroof of the bus. We were all being slowly poisoned. Or not so slowly, actually.

Angela

Now, you guys know my BFF, especially those of you who listen to our *Office Ladies* podcast. She was not at all happy about (1) being nearly poisoned by exhaust and (2) being ignored when she rightfully pointed out said poisoning. She was fired up, to put it mildly!!

Jenna

My exact words were "I am not EVER getting on that bus EVER again!" Leslie David Baker backed me up. His eyes were watering like crazy.

Angela

So it was off the bus again, for a third time. Our medic was waiting when we got off to make sure no one was going to keel over. Our camera operator Sarah had a terrible headache for hours. The rest of the crew was trying to air out the bus and reattach the air-conditioning tube somewhere besides right next to the exhaust pipe. Meanwhile, the producers were trying to figure out how we could finish shooting this episode. Poor Bryan Cranston. I gave him a big hug. He was so calm and kind even as the wheels were literally coming off the Dunder Mifflin bus. But there was hope! The producers remembered THE PIE SCENE! We hadn't shot the scene when everyone eats PIE! Pie makes everyone happy.

Jenna

That scene is not on the bus, and it involves PIE! Well, that's all I needed to hear. I very willingly walked to the setup for Laverne's Pies Tires Fixed Also. It felt so, so good to sit on a bench next to John Krasinski in the fresh nontoxic air and eat pie. I mean, after the day we'd had, it was the best. I wasn't allowed to pick my favorite pie, strawberry rhubarb, because Pam says rhubarb is her least favorite. So I had blueberry pie, and I was happy. I might have purposely flubbed my lines a few times just to extend the scene and get more pie.

Angela

I was only in the background of the pie scenes, but that didn't stop me from eating my heart out. I got my favorite, chocolate cream! (You can tell how vividly both Jenna and I remember getting pie.) The scene took place on the side of the road by an old pickup truck and a little shack. In between takes Catherine, Kate, and I leaned up against the truck and chatted. Pie mends all things, including near carbon monoxide poisoning.

277

Jenna

Just as I finished the last delicious bite of my third helping of pie, Bryan Cranston came over and gently asked, "Jenna, would you consider getting back on the bus? There is just one shot we don't have. I promise, no more accidents. It will be quick." John looked at me and said, "Come on, we got this." Then he did what only John could do. He started a funny chant about getting back on the bus. He got everyone energized, laughing, happy again. So we all got back on the bus.

I'm not going to lie. I was still on edge. I felt slightly traumatized at this point. I mean, who wouldn't? But guess what?! We got the scene! It was as simple and short as Bryan had promised it would be. Operation Death Bus, complete. Thank God.

As we pulled into the parking lot, John was again at the front of the bus, chanting as we clapped and smiled. The day was done. We'd filmed the episode. We'd survived. Then the bus went over a bump, we all stumbled, and John hit his head on the camera next to him. Of course.

Angela

So there you have it. The stories of how the cast and crew of *The Office* almost bit the dust. Twice. Once on a boat, once on a bus. Looking back, we learned a lot about one another in those moments. Our original cast had come a long way together, and no matter what was thrown at us, we would get through it. Brian will help you into a dinghy in the middle of the ocean; Jenna will detect poisonous fumes; Oscar will make sure you have a place to sit; Phyllis will smile even as you sweat to death; Leslie will put his arm around you; Ellie will remind you to pack extra underwear; Kate will get you a beverage; Rainn will be a smartass; Creed, Craig, and Ed will sing you a song as the ship sinks or the bus swerves; and John will make sure you are laughing through it all.

Jenna

Whether it was in a conference room, on a boat, or on a bus, there is no other group I would have wanted by my side. And it ended up being a pretty amazing episode and final season.

Jenna and Angela

P.S. We love you, Bryan Cranston. Thanks for getting us through such an insane day!

13

our epic
finale

On May 16, 2013, the final episode of *The Office* aired on NBC. It was the culmination of nine seasons and ten years of our lives, seen by 5.69 million viewers. What an amazing run. We assumed our show would go the way of most syndicated television comedies at that point, rerunning on cable and slowly slipping into obscurity. But so far, that's not what's happened. *The Office* has found a second life in the streaming world. (In 2018, 52 billion minutes of viewing on Netflix alone!) We never could have anticipated how much the show would continue to gain fans once it left the air. Who could have predicted that young people who originally watched the show on NBC would grow up and rewatch it with their kids on streaming? It's humbling, for sure. And we are so grateful.

OUR CURTAIN CALL

Angela

It was August 2012, and the whole cast was sitting on a bus in the Dunder Mifflin parking lot, trying to stay cool amidst a record-breaking heat wave in Los Angeles. We were gearing up for the "Work Bus" episode (soon to be known as Death Bus). What we didn't share with you before is that early that morning, as we prepared to begin shooting, Greg came on the bus and asked the crew to leave. This was unusual. Greg was very serious, and for a moment I felt like I was leaving my body. Once we were alone, he shared that NBC had offered to extend the show two more seasons, but that many of the cast's contracts were up, and he was afraid that we'd lose people to other projects. He expressed concern over what the show would become with only a handful of the original cast. The bus was silent. And then Greg looked at all of us and asked how we felt about saying goodbye on our own terms and making Season 9 the last season of *The Office*. It was a sobering moment, as we all contemplated the end of such an important era in our lives. But as sad as we were to say goodbye, we all decided that we'd rather go out together. How often in television do you get to decide that? Almost never.

Jenna

I knew Greg's talk was coming, but that didn't make it any easier to hear. Over the summer, before we began production on Season 9, Greg called John Krasinski and me to talk about the upcoming year. He explained that Rainn and Ed were only signed up to do half of the season. Ed had some film roles, and Rainn was being held by NBC for a possible spinoff series called *The Farm*. If *The Farm* didn't get picked up, Rainn would be with us the entire season, but for now, John and I would be the only lead cast members coming back for the full run of episodes that year. He also told us he wasn't sure the entire supporting cast would be back either. Many of our longtime writers, including Mindy Kaling, Jen Celotta, Gene Stupnitsky, Lee Eisenberg, and B. J. Novak, had left for new projects. It was clear that Season 9 could be our last. Greg also told us he would be coming back as showrunner, and he had a vision for a final Jim and Pam story line that involved their marriage being tested. He asked John and me to come on as producers. This meant we would be going into the writers' room on a regular basis with the intention of weighing in on the Jim and Pam story. As we sat with the news that this was probably our final year on the show, we were, once again, so grateful for Greg's trust in us as creatives. That summer, John and I met with the writers and brainstormed what might happen with Jim and Pam. But we weren't the only ones. After the bus chat, Greg invited every single cast member into the writers' room to pitch ideas for their character's final season.

Angela

The writers spent months crafting the final season, considering all we had shared. The toughest nut to crack was the finale. How do you wrap up a series like this? Greg thought it would be interesting to jump forward in time, for the documentary of Dunder Mifflin to have aired, for our characters to have seen themselves and reflect on their journey. The final episode would be an hour long, centered around two big events that would bring everyone together: a PBS interview panel with the staff of Dunder Mifflin, and Dwight and Angela's wedding. Greg also shared that he wanted to find ways to incorporate former guest actors, crew, writers, family, and friends into the finale. He wanted it to be a big reunion. And Dwight and Angela's wedding was the perfect way to bring everyone back.

THE LAST TABLE READ

Jenna

I don't think any of us expected just how emotional the experience of filming the last episode would be. The feelings started with the final table read. I was hoping our last table read could be held in the same building we'd used for years, but we were filming on location that week, so going back to our stages was not an option. As soon as I walked into the room, I realized there was no way to have used our regular space anyway. Normally our table reads were in one of the writers' trailers, because we were a small group. For our series finale, we needed a cafeteria-sized room. Almost a hundred people were there. There were so many actors in this final episode that long tables were placed in a giant U-shape configuration with Greg at the center. We all had microphones, there was a photographer, and everything was videotaped. The tables were facing rows and rows of chairs filled with network executives, crew members, agents, managers. As I sat down at my spot, I looked around the room. It seemed as if everyone who had ever worked on the show was there. I was overcome with emotion, the most prevalent being gratitude. I squeezed Angela's hand, and the tears started.

Angela

Jenna and I walked from set together to the big room they had reserved for the table read, holding hands as we walked into the crowd. I was shaking, I was so full of emotion. I was thankful that Jenna and I were seated next to each other. Greg started by telling us what the show meant to him. His whole speech is beautiful. (It is on YouTube if you want to check it out.) Greg had asked Ken Kwapis to direct the finale. Ken had directed our pilot episode, helping to create the look and feel of Dunder Mifflin, so it was only fitting that he would close out the show. Greg thanked everyone for coming, and when he got to Ken, he said, "I'm very happy and proud to have Ken Kwapis back to direct our finale. Ken was the country vet who birthed this puppy, and now he's gonna put it down." Greg then warned us that things were about to "get very sentimental." He asked us to open our scripts to the first page. There was the famous Allison Jones polaroid from the very first table read of *The Office*. Greg read the cast list for the final time, and as he said each actor and the character they played, I began to cry.

SO MANY LITTLE GOODBYES

As filming began, we realized we were going to have a million little goodbyes along with the big ones. For me, these started with my final wardrobe fitting. I was standing there looking at myself as Angela Martin in her wedding dress when I turned to our costume designer Alysia Raycraft and we had a big, tearful hug. Angela Martin was marrying the man of her dreams. I love that I got to say goodbye to this character on such a happy day in her life.

Literally, everything was emotional. Vartan's last batch of albondigas soup (it *was* legendary), the last time Sergio made his famous salsa, our last bullpen scene, and on and on. Every moment brought tears. I was trading emails with Steve during this time, and he asked me how it was "going into that last stretch." I told him we were a bit of a mess and that I was making a scrapbook for everyone and feeling very nostalgic. It had been two years since Steve was on our show, but there he was, still checking in on us. Little did I know that I would see Steve in just a few weeks at Dwight and Angela's wedding! At this point, we'd been told that he would not be returning for the finale. It must have been so hard for him to keep that a secret.

Jenna

As promised, Greg brought back a ton of characters, most notably Devon, the man who fought not to be fired by Michael on Halloween in Season 1. When Creed went in to talk with the writers about what he'd like to see in our final season, he asked for two things: to play one of his songs in the finale, and to bring back Devon. Creed and Devon had stayed in touch after Devon left for New York. Greg liked Creed's idea, and Devon came back for a cameo in the final episode.

Perhaps one of the most emotional days was when we shot the question-and-answer panel scenes. Greg had members of our writing staff asking the questions. He also cast Jennie Tan, the creator of the *Office* fan site officetally.com, as the woman who asks Pam why she didn't trust Jim's love. He cast his wife, Susanne Daniels, as the moderator. Greg also used this opportunity to wrap up a few of the characters' story lines. The scene where Erin finally meets her birth parents, played by Joan Cusack and Ed Begley Jr., gets me every time. It is so emotional. When we finished shooting, the entire auditorium of background actors stood up and applauded. The cast all cried and took a bow. It was incredibly moving.

Angela

Despite the tears, there was still a lot of laughing and levity, including pranks. We had one final conference room scene, for which Ken had to choose where we would sit depending on the reaction shots he needed. Our assistant director made little Post-it notes with our names on them and stuck them to the chairs, so we knew where to sit during rehearsals. At one point, Oscar put his arm around me as I sat down. I thought that was so sweet. I'm not sure how long I had the OSCAR sign on my back, but it was long enough for Jenna to take a photo. Well played, Oscar.

Jenna

I've shared before that some of my favorite moments from the series were when we had story lines with just the women in the office. I was happy to see the finale had an all-ladies scene, Angela's bachelorette party. We shot the bachelorette party late into the night on location in a funky little farmhouse. Between camera setups, we hung out on couches laughing and snacking like teenagers at a sleepover. It was the girl time I'd hoped for. It was during this shoot that Ellie and I discovered the deliciousness that is Raisin Rosemary Crisps from Trader Joe's. I think we ate four boxes. We couldn't stop. Catering ran out. Several years ago, I got a mysterious gift for my birthday—a GIANT jar filled with Raisin Rosemary Crisps. I knew immediately it was from Ellie.

Angela

My memories of the bachelorette scenes are a mixture of laughter and of pure embarrassment. I was very excited that my friend Rachael Harris had joined as Angela Martin's sister. Rachael and I met while studying at the Groundlings Theatre & School in our twenties, and we've been friends ever since. Then there were the stripper

scenes. OMG. The writers brought back Spencer Daniels, the actor who had played Meredith's son, Jake, in "Take Your Daughter to Work Day." He was all grown-up now. Jake and Meredith both gave Angela Martin awkward lap dances. If you rewatch, I put my hand over my face because I am beet red. Aw, look at that! I worked beets into this chapter! Dwight would be proud.

THE WEDDING

Jenna

The finale also has a few stunts, the most notable being when Dwight fires a bazooka during his bachelor party. But did you know that Phyllis and Angela had their own stunt? On her wedding day, Angela Martin has leg pain from the night before, when Mose kidnaps her and hides her in the trunk of his car. This is part of a Schrute wedding tradition called Brautentführung. Angela blames Phyllis for leaving the door open, thus giving Mose the opportunity to kidnap her. To make it up to Angela, Phyllis promises to get her down the aisle. This simple promise in the script resulted in a complicated stunt.

Angela

It wasn't safe for Phyllis to physically carry me down the aisle, so we had to fake it. First, a camera filmed us from behind, showing us walking down the aisle toward Dwight. A young stuntwoman who resembled Phyllis carried me on her back. You couldn't see her face, so we were able to sell her as Phyllis. Then the camera was moved to the front of the ceremony, where Dwight was waiting for me, so we had to walk directly toward the camera. You could definitely see our faces, which meant no more stuntwoman. For this shot, they built a long wooden plank with two poles on each end to hold me. I sat on the plank and two stuntmen lifted me up behind Phyllis. (Imagine a medieval queen being carried through the streets on a palanquin by her

subjects, but not that elaborate.) I wrapped my arms around Phyllis's neck, but my weight was supported by the two men. We had to practice the timing of our collective walk several times. Phyllis couldn't get too far ahead, or I would fall forward. The men behind her had to keep me at a specific height, or I would pull Phyllis backward. In one rehearsal, I started to slide off the wooden plank, and the men almost dropped me. After a few tries, we got it, but even as we started filming, I wasn't sure if we were going to pull it off. In postproduction, they used CGI to edit the two men and the plank out of the scene. There you have it. Phyllis carries Angela down the aisle to her grave to marry Dwight!

But perhaps the biggest stunt we pulled off was getting Steve Carell back for the shoot without anyone finding out. This involved a months-long campaign. Steve always said he would come back for the finale, provided the story line was not centered around Michael Scott. He didn't want to come in after two years away and steal everyone's thunder. When Greg told him the idea that Dwight and Angela would be getting married in the finale, Steve agreed that Michael would be there. Greg pulled me, John, and Rainn aside a few days prior to tell us the news, swearing us to secrecy. Then Rainn turned to me and said, "Jenna. Not even Angela." Oh man! Do you have any idea how hard that was for me?!

All the secrecy was because Greg wanted Steve's appearance to be a surprise for the audience. He didn't even tell NBC about his plan. In fact, he turned in a script that included a scene between Dwight and *Creed* before the wedding, not Michael. It had the same page count as the scene between Dwight and Michael. That way, the scene could be scheduled into the day and budgeted for shooting. On the day of the shoot, Creed's name was even on the call sheet for that scene, but it was all a huge ruse!

Angela

Early in the morning on our first day of "wedding" scenes, I was making my way to the hair and makeup trailer when our second AD whispered to me, "Steve's here!" I was shocked. It was a foggy day, and as I opened the door to the trailer, this burst of light spilled out, and in the middle was Steve. I screamed, "Steve!" He smiled so big and said, "Ange!" I immediately teared up and we hugged. I COULD NOT believe he had come back! There was such an electricity in the air that morning. I also could not believe my BFF didn't tell me! I mean, Jenna, I get it and I'm impressed, but still!

Jenna

I was so excited when Angela finally knew the secret—now ALL of us had to keep it. Greg made an announcement to everyone on set that day—the crew, cast, background performers—asking us all to stay quiet. I kind of can't believe we pulled it off. (The fact that Instagram didn't exist yet was likely a big factor.) Greg's biggest worry was that if NBC knew about Steve's return, they would turn it into a press opportunity to build excitement for the finale and it would ruin the surprise for the audience. When Greg turned in the episode to NBC, he had different scenes edited in as placeholders for the ones where Steve appeared. He didn't let NBC see the real footage until *the day before* it aired. We all had to do massive amounts of press in the weeks leading up to the finale, and everyone lied and said Steve hadn't come back. John Krasinski even lied to David Letterman.

Angela

Then came time for Dwight and Angela to exchange vows. Right as Angela climbs into her shallow grave, Michael gives her a hug—Steve improvised that in the first take, and I thought I was going to completely lose it—and then Angela turns to Dwight . . . I was already tearing up . . . then we turned and faced our wedding guests. These were not just the faces of Dunder Mifflin for me, they were the faces of my friends for nearly a decade. Nine years of memories washed over me. I cried several times throughout the ceremony, and you can see me wiping away tears.

The only thing that kept me from completely breaking down was how cold I was. The wind was really blowing, and I was freezing. Between takes, I took a photo of everyone looking at Rainn and me so I could remember that beautiful cold, windy moment forever. Look at Catherine Tate's face—it's completely covered by her hair!

Jenna

When I think of this scene, all I remember is the wind. I literally remember nothing else. Wind and cold. I kept trying to block the wind using John Krasinski's broad shoulders. It didn't work. But if you watch the episode, you can see me burying myself into his shoulder to stay warm.

THE RECEPTION

Angela

Well, the wind was just the beginning of our weather issues. As we got ready to film the wedding reception, a big storm appeared on the horizon. The lanterns the set dressers had hung began to sway, and there was worry our tent might come apart. It started to lightly rain, and we huddled together in the tent or sought refuge in the farmhouse.

Thankfully, the storm passed by quickly and the tent held steady, so we were able to get to the fun part—Angela and Dwight's first dance. In the script, Dwight and Angela dance to "Angela" by Mötley Crüe, celebrating Dwight's love of heavy metal. Rainn improvised picking me up and twirling me around. I purposely let my legs flail about. We were having the best time! I think about Dwight choosing that song and how perfect it was on that stormy day.

Angela & Dwight

Saturday, the fourteenth of June
Three o'clock in the afternoon
The Schrute Farmstead
Honesdale, Pennsylvania

The Wedding Ceremony

Processional
Treulich Geführt .... Wagner

Willkommen

Andacht

Exchanging of Vows

Exchanging of Rings

Announcement of Marriage

Recessional
Traditional Wedding March

Release of the Doves

Hochzeitspaar

The Bride	*The Groom*
Angela Noelle Martin	Dwight Kurt Schrute
Co-Maids of Honor	*Bestisch Mensch*
Pam Halpert	Jim Halpert
Meredith Palmer	*Groomsmen*
Phyllis Vance	Andy Bernard
Rachael Martin	Oscar Martinez
	Zeke Schrute
	Mose Schrute

Mother and Father of the Bride	*Mother and Father of the Groom*
Annemarie Martin	Hedda Mannheim Schrute
Sean T. Martin	Dwight Schrute Sr.

Flower Girl
Cece Halpert

Ring Bearer
Philip Halsted Lipton

Officiant
Rev. Gerhard Schultz

We thank all our friends and family for attending.

Reception to follow the ceremony.
(Please keep your hay bales or plan on standing.)

Jenna

My personal favorite moment from shooting the reception was sitting with Steve. It was my chance to be alone with him and catch up. He told me that life after *The Office* had been good. He was able to be home for more family dinners, more bedtimes, more school concerts. Despite being one of the industry's biggest movie stars, Steve's main topic of conversation was always his love of family. Ironically, in the scene, Michael is showing Pam photos of his children with Holly and telling her stories about them. And that is just what we were doing.

Angela

I was sitting with Rainn, Jenna, and John when Steve had his final talking head during the reception. Michael says, "I feel like all my kids grew up, and then they married each other. It's every parent's dream." And when the camera pushes past him, you can see the four of us laughing. Those laughs were real. You might also notice that I am incredibly animated for my character, and that is because in that moment I am not Angela Martin Schrute, I'm Angela Kinsey, and I am telling an insane story. I have NO idea how this conversation started, but Rainn was telling us he once had a tapeworm as a child when he lived in Nicaragua. One day while he was walking, his bottom itched, and he reached up and pulled a small tapeworm out of his butt! (I feel okay sharing this story because Rainn has told it many times and it is also in his book, *The Bassoon King*. Seriously, go to chapter 2, titled "The Worms of Nicaragua.") Not to be outdone, I then launched into my own story about my sister and a tapeworm incident while we were growing up in Indonesia. (It lived in her belly for years. She's fine now. No need to worry.) We were all grossed out but also laughing hysterically. I know this might ruin the moment for some fans, but we were laughing about tapeworms during that famous Michael talking head. For me it makes the moment even more special.

Jenna

Thinking back to the four of us laughing about tapeworms gives me the warm fuzzies. That's us in a nutshell.

After the wedding reception, the PBS crew throws a big wrap party for everyone in the Dunder Mifflin warehouse. This scene warms my heart, because this is when Pam's mural is finally revealed. She has painted everyone in the office and suggests they take a group photo in front of it. As the camera pans across the room, so many amazing people who made the show possible are featured, including Greg Daniels, who is right beside Pam, grinning. Our casting director Allison Jones, our script supervisor Veda Semarne, our executive producer Howard Klein, and our editors Claire Scanlon and Dave Rogers are all there too. Incidentally, when you finally hear the voice of the documentarian, it is Dave Rogers. We had talked about who it should be. Some people thought it should be Greg, or Ken Kwapis, or even Ricky Gervais. In the end, we chose Dave. He was the perfect choice. He worked on the show every day since the second episode and probably watched more footage than anyone.

Angela

Dwight and Angela decide to put their honeymoon on hold and join the rest of the Dunder Mifflin employees at a secret after-party in the office bullpen. As Creed sings "All the Faces," the camera pans around the office bullpen one last time. The end is near, and there is a weight to the room. We can all feel it.

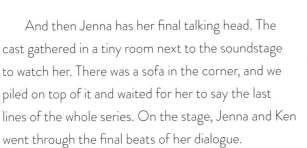

And then Jenna has her final talking head. The cast gathered in a tiny room next to the soundstage to watch her. There was a sofa in the corner, and we piled on top of it and waited for her to say the last lines of the whole series. On the stage, Jenna and Ken went through the final beats of her dialogue.

I filmed us watching Jenna say her final lines: "I thought it was weird when you picked us to make a documentary. But all in all . . . I think an ordinary paper company like Dunder Mifflin was a great subject for a documentary. There's a lot of beauty in ordinary things. Isn't that kind of the point?" It was an emotional moment for us in that little video room. I can't imagine how Jenna felt saying it. I have never shown her the video. Maybe now is the time. Jenna, grab your tissues.

When I first saw the shooting schedule, I noticed that Pam's talking head was scheduled last. That meant the entire cast would have been sent home and I'd have to end the series as the only actor on set. I went to Greg and Ken and asked if there was any way to change that because I didn't want to be alone. Greg and Ken told me that it would be poetic for the last scene we shot to be the final line

of the show, but they understood how I felt. They changed the schedule so that my talking head was the second-to-last shot, followed by a group shot of us all leaving as Pam takes her painting off the wall.

Angela

I can't express how special it was for us all to be together in that final scene, ending the series together. Even though it was a simple scene, just the group leaving the office, the entire cast felt the weight of the moment. On "action" we would walk out the front door and into the lobby. Then, out of view of the camera, we'd file into the narrow hallway by the elevators and wait to hear if Ken would say, "Cut . . . Going again!" Or "Cut . . . That's a wrap." With each take, we grew closer to "That's a wrap" and the show being over. The air was heavy with anticipation. I remember I was standing next to Phyllis in the hallway, and we held hands waiting to hear what Ken said each time. Greg kept making small adjustments. I don't think he wanted it to end either. After a few takes, Ken had the crew gather in the bullpen so they could be there when we finished. We knew it would be soon. On "action," we walked out of the office one last time and gathered in the hallway. There was a pause that felt like forever, and then it was Greg, not Ken, who yelled, "Cut—that's a wrap!" We disintegrated into tears and poured into the bullpen and into the arms of our crew. It was fitting that Greg, who had created this amazing world of Dunder Mifflin, was the one to say our collective goodbye.

PACKING UP

Angela

After lots of hugs and even more tears, you'd think we couldn't cry anymore, but we did; it was time to pack up our trailers and get to the wrap party across town. As I was loading my car, I looked over and saw John putting the DUNDER MIFFLIN sign into his trunk. I couldn't help but laugh. We all took little mementos from the show. The props department gave me the giant portrait of Angela Martin that hung in her home with Robert Lipton, the state senator. I took Angela's cat paper clip holder. I kept the ring that Dwight gave me when he proposed. You know, when he ran me off the road and shouted his love for me through a megaphone and then gave me the ring that had been in his grandmother's butt, put there by the gangster patriarch of the Coors dynasty, melted in a foundry by the Mennonites . . . that ring. I still have it.

Jenna

I took Pam's candy dish, purse, and wonky giraffe pen (which never worked but was on her desk for all nine seasons). Earlier in the week, I had gone into the wardrobe trailer and swiped one of Pam's old cardigans and a skirt. When I was supposed to turn in Pam's wedding rings, I couldn't. I kept them. (They are fake, just sterling silver and cubic zirconia.) I also kept her watch. But what I wanted most of all was Pam's watercolor of the Dunder Mifflin office. I had asked for it and been told that it had to be cataloged and returned to storage in case we ever revived the show. I was heartbroken. But that night as I was leaving, our prop master Phil Shea met me at my car. "You should have that watercolor." "What about the cataloging?" I asked. "Shhh . . . I'll make a color copy. They'll never know the difference." The day after our finale aired, our line producer Steve Burgess emailed me to see how I was feeling and to say Phil had made good on his promise. The original is hanging in my foyer today.

THE FINALE AIRS

Angela

It was a few months before the finale aired. We had all gone our separate ways, but for the most part it felt like a typical hiatus. I filmed a new television pilot for Fox, visited my family in Texas, and started to tackle all the home projects I'd been putting off. At first, I began with simple chores like organizing my pantry, and then as the weeks went on, I decided to knock out a wall or two. Three months into the show being over, I had completely gutted my kitchen. I remember Jenna calling and asking if I was okay. I told her that it was finally hitting me that the show was over. I was clearly trying to self-soothe the only way I knew how, with complete chaos.

Jenna

The week after we wrapped, I flew to New York with my family to star in an off-Broadway play at MCC Theater. I'd always wanted to do professional theater, but more than anything I needed the distraction. I knew the reality of the show ending would hit me hard. The crazy part was that the night of our first audience preview was the same night as the finale. Just as I was walking onstage in my first big theater role, the finale of *The Office*, the thing that launched my career, was airing. Insane, right?

Angela

The day of the finale also happened to be my sister's birthday. I started the day by making her a video of my plants (she loves to garden as much as I do). Then I sent her a video from my daughter and me, wishing her a happy birthday. My phone began dinging with messages. My first thought was it was my sister replying to my plant photos and birthday videos, but it was my friends and coworkers from *The Office* with messages about the final episode set to air that night. Then I had a realization. The show wasn't truly over until that last episode aired. After that night, there would be no more episodes. Dwight would never walk up behind Angela and ask for "cookie," Meredith would never flash us again, and we would never know what happened to Jim and Pam in Austin. I was so attached to these characters. I felt a loss that I can't put into words.

Greg graciously offered to host a final viewing at his agency, WME, where there was a very fancy screening room. He invited anyone who was in town to come. It was a bittersweet night because not all the cast was able to attend. My BFF was in New York City. How was I going to get through it without her? I sat with one of our producers, Steve Burgess, and Craig Robinson. The whole evening was very emotional. I was trying to keep it together because I didn't want to ugly-cry on their shoulders. And when the final scene played and I began to sob, Steve Burgess put his arm around me. I couldn't process any of it until I spoke to Jenna, and she was onstage in New York!

Jenna

As I stood backstage in New York waiting for curtain, my mind was on my castmates back in Los Angeles. Viewing parties had been such a staple of our experience together, and here I was missing the very last one. Coincidentally, B. J. Novak was also in New York that night. He came to see my show and we toasted the finale. I had big feelings about *The Office* ending. On the one hand, I was ready. After the play ended, I knew I wanted to have another baby. The stress of juggling a full-time television role and a newborn had been rough. On the other hand, I also knew I was going to miss everyone. It wasn't just that I would miss seeing Rainn or Brian or Kate. I was going to miss seeing Dwight, Kevin, and Meredith. Rainn I could grab lunch with. But Dwight was now gone forever. When I got back to where we were staying, I watched the episode with my husband, Lee, and called Angela.

Angela

I think we talked for almost two hours that night. We talked about the finale, and then Jenna told me all about her play, and I told her about my bold choice to order blue kitchen cabinets. I remember being so thankful. Thankful for this beautiful show. Thankful for how it blessed my life. Thankful for the friendships it brought me. And so very thankful that it gave me my "Lady!" . . . my life anchor . . . my BFF.

Jenna

As I was crying with my best friend and reminiscing about our time on the show, I also remember feeling so grateful for everything *The Office* had given me, but the greatest thing was exactly what Steve had told us it would be: our friendship. *The Office* changed my career. It gave me financial security. It gave me access to experiences I'd never have had otherwise. But most of all, it gave me a best friend.

14

boss ladies

This part of a book is often referred to as the "wrap up" chapter. It's where we ride off into the sunset, nostalgic and grateful for our nine years of working at Dunder Mifflin, filled with magical memories and wondering what comes next. Well, we can tell you exactly what comes next: *Office Ladies*. Because these two gals are not ready to wrap things up. In fact, we are just getting started.

Angela

As soon as *The Office* ended, our lives and jobs took us in different directions. Literally. Jenna moved to New York for a play, then London for a TV show, then San Diego for another play, while I did film and TV projects in Canada, Louisiana, Georgia, and Florida. Gone were our daily BFF lunches and journaling out loud. Gone was even being in the same city at the same time! But even though we were both all over the place, often in different time zones, we had an unspoken commitment to staying in touch. At first, we were mostly texting and emailing, but eventually we discovered we could best communicate by sending each other voice memos. This was perfect for us because we were staying in touch the best way we knew how, by talking! We would trade multiple long voice memos every day. The messages might contain anything—venting about the broken knob on our washing machine, a story of our kids doing something adorable, asking advice about a big meeting coming up, or basically just rambling on and on. We soon took to calling them "Ramblies" and they seriously got us through many ups and downs over those early post-*Office* years.

Jenna

When I got near the end of the run of the play in New York, I started getting very anxious about the future. *The Office* was over, the play was in its final weeks, and I wasn't sure what I was supposed to do next. And although I had my family with me, I really missed my home in California. I left Angela a long Rambly, telling her how the nonstop energy of New York was wearing on me. I distinctly remember that while I was leaving the message, I spilled hot coffee all over my arm trying to navigate my son's stroller through the park. The next day I woke up to a video from Angela. She had gone to my house (of course she has a key) and made a little movie, filming the knickknacks on my shelves, the sunset from my porch, my favorite coffee mug, and our backyard. She left me a Rambly reminding me that my home would always be my home, and that although I was in a time of

transition, it would sit peacefully waiting for me to return. It was exactly what I needed. Then an hour later, she sent another Rambly, this one from the hospital. She told me that after she sent the video, she tripped on the bottom step of my staircase and broke her toe. She was getting fitted for a boot that she would have to wear for weeks. But she said it was worth it, because she knew her best friend needed her help. A few days later she surprised me by flying to New York (wearing the boot) to see my play!

In an odd twist of fate, years later I would break my pinky toe at *her* house. We have both broken toes at each other's houses! Over the next several years, it was rare for us to both be home in Los Angeles at the same time. But because of Ramblies, I always knew what she was doing and what she was feeling. And she me.

Angela

We could be on either side of the world and still stay in touch. When she was in London, I remember the sound her feet made when she walked on the rocky path in Hampstead Heath. She left me daily Ramblies from those walks. Sometimes she would be pushing her daughter in a stroller, and sometimes she would be on her own. I began to look forward to the sound of the rocks crunching beneath her feet. It was soothing to me. Then there was the time I was working in Canada and I couldn't sleep. I was at a crossroads in my life and struggling to know if I was on the right path. I went on

an early morning bike ride around English Bay, leaving Ramblies for Jenna along the way. She responded right away, and even though we were thousands of miles apart, she helped me process all that I was feeling. I texted her a picture in the moment, and she did the same back to me. It was like she was there with me in Canada, and I was there with her in London.

Jenna

Eventually my kids started school, and I didn't want to keep pulling them out of their routine as we traveled the world for work. So I accepted a regular role on a Los Angeles–based series called *Splitting Up Together*. Almost everything about this job was perfect. The cast and crew were amazing, the studio was close to our house, the role was fun. I was even reunited with some of the *Office* crew, and Angela popped in as a guest star!

The only downside was the hours. With 5 A.M. call times and late evening wraps, I was "home," but I was missing school concerts, costume parades, and parent/teacher conferences. I loved acting, but the job was pulling me away from too many of the parenting moments that I cherished and that I knew would too soon disappear forever. I started craving a job that I could do while my kids were at school, and that I could put away when they got home.

Angela

After years of traveling for work, I felt the same way. We started trading Ramblies about how we might be able to better shape our lives. We daydreamed about what our lives would be if we were in charge, if we were the bosses. It was a conversation I had many times with my own sisters, about the struggle of providing for your family but not sacrificing precious milestones with your children because of work. Trying to find that balance is not easy no matter what your profession, but in the entertainment industry there is the added element of odd, erratic hours. I was craving a set schedule that I could count on and plan around. Jenna and I both never wanted to miss another soccer game or dance recital and we needed jobs that gave us that kind of structure. We sat down and made a wish list of what we wanted. In addition to having control over her own schedule, Jenna laughed and said she'd like to earn a living while being in sweatpants. That lady loves a drawstring pant. I know that one of the main reasons she took that job in London was because she was playing a woman who spent every episode in a jumpsuit. She gleefully told me it was like wearing pajamas to work.

Jenna

I was sharing all of these feelings with my costar at the time, Oliver Hudson, and he said, "Jenna, what you and Angela should do is a podcast. I'm telling you, that job is going to tick all the boxes for you. You should really look into it." The following week, June Diane Raphael was a guest star on the show. I knew her from her role on *Grace and Frankie* but she also has a podcast called *How Did This Get Made?* I asked lots of questions. She had lots of answers. Oliver was right. Podcasting would tick all the boxes. As soon as we wrapped for the day, I called Angela.

Angela

The minute I answered the phone, Jenna yelled in my ear, "Podcast! We should do a podcast! You don't even have to wash your hair!" Of course, Jenna and I knew NOTHING about podcasting. If you asked me to write and pitch a television show, I'd know exactly who to call and what to do. I've sold five TV shows and had a development deal, but podcasting was completely foreign to me. But just the idea that we could be our own bosses and set our own schedules and produce and create our own content was so enticing we knew we had to follow this thread.

We started by listening to many, many podcasts in a variety of genres. We noticed there was a subgenre called "rewatch" podcasts. A lightbulb went off. Who better to host a rewatch podcast than the people who were on the show? Joshua Malina, who had been on *The West Wing*, was cohosting a popular rewatch, and it got us thinking. We decided to do a test run. Jenna came over to my house, and we set my iPhone between us and hit record. She had a fully outlined document (of course). I had a stack of colorful notecards. We rambled for about forty-five minutes. My husband, Josh, is a great editor, and he cut together a demo for us to listen to. Later that evening, he asked me if we had listened. We hadn't, as the day had gotten away from both of us. He said, "I think you guys are pretty good. I really liked it." Now, if my husband says he likes something, you better take note. He is not from overly verbose stock. We both listened and then immediately called each other. I said, "I think we can do this! I loved it!" And Jenna said, "Lady, Lee loved it! I loved it! Let's do it!" It gave us the boost we needed to give podcasting a try.

Jenna

While we didn't know much about podcasting, we both had experience building an acting career from scratch. We'd practiced perseverance. We knew how to be scrappy. Then, during *The Office*, we learned together how to navigate the world of marketing and publicity, how to pitch, produce, and write our own projects, and how to build our own brand. When it came to starting our new business of podcasting, we weren't totally starting from scratch. We had the benefit of our experience, our name recognition, and a few relevant connections. My husband, Lee, recommended we call his friend Jeff, "who used to work in podcasting," and ask him some advice. Jeff agreed to meet with us. So we got together and started asking questions. "How do we produce a podcast? Do we need to buy microphones? Rent a studio? How do you upload a podcast? How much does an editor cost?" He patiently answered our questions, then started talking about potential download numbers, ad sales, reach. He had charts and graphs. He suggested we start an LLC. He said we needed a lawyer, we needed to trademark our name. We were stuck on "But where do we buy the microphones?" It was around this time that I realized who we were talking with. Lee's friend Jeff was Jeff Ullrich, one of the FOUNDERS of the podcasting giant Earwolf.

Angela

Jeff listened to our demo and told us we had a hit on our hands. His actual words were "You have the special sauce." He told us we should absolutely run with our idea. Can you get a better vote of confidence than that?! Over the next few months, we talked to probably a dozen more people. We spoke with podcast producers and hosts and engineers. I am so grateful to each and every one of them for speaking with us. I can't tell you how many stupid questions we asked along the way. I mean, we asked the cofounder of Earwolf where to buy microphones. We probably would have asked him where to plug them in. I cringe thinking back to that time, but that's what it takes when you are plowing a new path for yourself. You have to ask dumb questions, to not know things, to feel silly and vulnerable. Putting yourself out there is part of the journey when you start a new chapter in life, and asking questions is all part of the process. After all those conversations we basically had to decide whether we wanted to produce our podcast independently or partner with an existing podcast company.

Jenna

We took meetings with several podcasting companies. We played them our demo and pitched them our ideas. I was also googling "how to publish a podcast" and "best microphones for podcasts" just in case we still wanted to do it on our own. (Microphones became a minor obsession for a while. But they are important for podcasting! Almost as important as the sweatpants!) After all our research and meetings, I told Angela I didn't think we could do this on our own and achieve our goal of working only while the kids were at school. There was still so much we didn't understand about this world, and even though it meant sharing the profits, we needed a partner. The company we'd loved most from our many meetings was, ironically, Earwolf. They understood our vision, and we liked their slate of other shows. The one thing we weren't sure of was *when* we

could do this. I was still working on *Splitting Up Together* and Angela was in New Orleans shooting the movie *Tall Girl* for Netflix. When could we be in the same room, in the same city, to actually build this podcast? Then a crazy thing happened. My television show got canceled. Angela wrapped her movie. Earwolf offered us a deal. Welp . . . the moment had finally come.

Angela and I had a big heart-to-heart. To get this off the ground, we would have to turn down other jobs and focus 100 percent on the

podcast for a while. It was scary. But this was our chance to be our own bosses. To call the shots for ourselves. We'd never had that before. We decided to bet on us—and *Office Ladies* was born! We started a media company. We named it Ramble in honor of the many rambling messages we have left each other over the years. It seemed fitting that our company name reflect how we kept our friendship going through hours and hours of rambling and sharing and journaling out loud. *Office Ladies* would be our first production, and Earwolf was our partner.

Angela

When we stepped into the Earwolf studios for the first time we were, as my daughter says, "nervous-cited." Starting with the pilot seemed too daunting, so we decided to begin by recording "Basketball" from Season 1 since that is the one that solidified our best friendship. We hadn't really discussed how we would prepare or what we would say. We just agreed to both watch the episode and come in with notes on what we wanted to share. We thought it was important that we surprise each other so that our reactions were genuine. When we sat down, Jenna got out her twelve-page document outlining the episode with notes, facts, and trivia. I set out my 140 brightly colored notecards with time codes, background observations, and my own research. This seemed like a good sign since that was exactly what we'd done for our demo. Sam Keiffer, our sound engineer, told us he was ready when we were. We sat there and blankly stared at each other. We didn't know how to start. How ironic that after years and years of nonstop talking, now that it was literally our job to speak, we didn't know how to begin a conversation. We eventually found a way in and stumbled our way through our first official studio recording of *Office Ladies*.

The next week we tackled "Health Care," which included our first interview,

with none other than Rainn Wilson. We knew he would be kind to us as we were new to podcasting. When we got those first recording sessions back, we loved Rainn, but hated the part where we broke down the episode.

Jenna

They were a mess. We were all over the place. I remember standing in the kitchen at Earwolf talking with Angela about what we should do. We wanted a polished, entertaining, informative show. We knew we could do better. So we did it again. And again. And again. We recorded and rerecorded three different versions of "Basketball" and "Health Care." We would save some things, cut others, and rerecord. We affectionately call these the Frankenstein episodes.

It was during this time that we discovered how we would both contribute to the structure of the show. I came up with the idea of Fast Facts, while Angela dove into deleted scenes and DVD commentaries. We would both reach out to cast, crew, writers, directors, and producers for different behind-the-scenes details. We found our three-act structure and the show was solidified. The podcast became two things: an informational *The Office* rewatch, and two best friends sharing about their lives. And it worked! Now we just had to announce it to the world.

Angela

We flew to New York for a press tour. We had done this many times over the years for *The Office*, but this time it was different because we were traveling to announce a project we had created ourselves. At each press event we were listed as the "cocreators" of *Office Ladies*. I have been in this business a long time—and seeing my name listed like that was a dream come true.

Jenna

For me, the highlight of our press tour was when the *New York Times* called and asked to do a piece on us. I've been getting the *New York Times* delivered to my house for years. This was an honor. *The Office* had been covered in the *Times*, of course, but this was about something I had created with Angela. We were in New York when the paper came out, and I'll never forget running to the newsstand to get copies. OMG. There we were. We jumped up and down squealing. It wasn't so different from "Booze Cruise," when Angela found out she'd become a series regular on the show. It's too bad Oscar wasn't there to snap a photo. Angela and I both framed the article and put it in our home offices.

Angela

The podcast premiered on Wednesday, October 16, 2019. We grabbed breakfast that morning and told each other that no matter what happened, we were proud of what we had done. We hoped people would listen so that we could continue to work together. Earwolf had told us that a successful podcast gets about 50,000 downloads in 30 days. They were hoping our podcast would get 300,000 in our first month. Guys, we got 2 million downloads in a matter of weeks! We were a hit! Jenna and I were thrilled, but we also felt a huge responsibility to the legacy of *The Office* to keep on delivering quality episodes. So that's what we've been doing.

Jenna

People are always asking me, "What is it like to work with your best friend?" Their tone suggests our working together must be affecting our friendship in some negative way. I get why they ask. It's one thing to become friends with a coworker. It's another thing to maintain a friendship with someone who is your business partner. But the thing is, working together has strengthened our bond. I don't know how to explain it exactly, but I knew from the very beginning that working with Angela was right. As you've surely learned while reading this book, we've navigated a lot of life together. I know how this woman shows up to a challenge, how she handles stress. I know her creative mind and her work ethic. I shared a JAM brain with John Krasinski; I share an *Office Ladies* brain with Angela. Sometimes in life, you find a creative partner you just can't deny is a perfect fit. That's us.

Angela

That doesn't mean it's all been smooth sailing. We've gotten on each other's nerves several times. But one of the things I'm most grateful for is our ability to have honest, compassionate conversations that come from a

318

place of wanting to build the other up. We know, without a shadow of a doubt, we have each other's backs. It's not scary to have one of us say "I'm not happy" about something. We face criticism as an opportunity for growth. We've both learned so much about the depth of our friendship since starting our podcast. Being in the driver's seat, being the boss, and watching the podcast become a success is a testament to our friendship. We get to put family first, and we get to do it our way. It's not lost on me that Jenna and I both have daughters who are watching us build this business. They are watching us model a strong female friendship and badass boss ladery. (Let's make "boss ladery" a term—T-shirts? Coffee mugs? Okay. Thanks.) Our sons are seeing it too. I couldn't be prouder of what we've built together.

Jenna

It's been a wild few years. We kept our podcast going from our closets during a pandemic, added an *Office Ladies* animated series to our slate, and published the book you are holding (or listening to) right now. So far, we've recorded over

100 episodes of *Office Ladies* and logged over 200 million downloads. Thanks to the folks at Pandora music, our achievement was commemorated on a billboard in Times Square! *OFFICE LADIES* WAS ON A BILLBOARD IN TIMES SQUARE!

I think it can be hard to imagine what we do all day. I know my family back home in St. Louis is mystified. Our social media often makes us look like two gals who shop at Target and laugh on a podcast together. And, yes, that is true. But don't be fooled. We are calculating, hardworking, goal-centered boss ladies. We are constantly thinking, dreaming, doing, and raising the bar for ourselves. We sometimes work seven days a week, but now it's on our terms. As I reflect on what we've built I want to say this: After working for someone else for over twenty years, I couldn't be prouder of what Angela and I have created together. Most of my career was spent feeling as if I had to speak louder to get my voice heard, worrying that I'd be labeled "difficult" because I'm direct and ambitious. Even after being the lead of several projects after *The Office*, I never quite felt like I had the agency I wanted. I knew Angela felt the same. So rather than fight for another seat at their table, Angela and I created our own table. When women band together, we can do great things.

Angela

That's right! We created our own damn table, and you are all sitting here with us! I still can't believe the range of people who stop me to say that they listen to our podcast and how much it means to them. College girls from Miami, a tough-as-nails middle-aged construction worker in Battery Park, a mother and daughter from North Carolina, two guys from London, a whole entire family from Brazil, and a dance group in Central Park. Honestly, the list goes on and on. After meeting the folks from Brazil, I called Jenna from a busy street and yelled, "OMG, we are global! Woo-hoo! We are badass boss ladies all over the world!" A bus was driving by, and she couldn't hear a word I said, but she knew I was happy. Jenna and I work so well together because we believe in each other. It's incredibly empowering. I can walk into any room with Jenna and feel like we can conquer it together. Folks reading this, invest in the people in your lives. Find that friend who makes you feel ten feet tall and bulletproof. Build them up and encourage them. Show up for each other no matter how big or small the occasion. Link arms, and walk into any crowd fake-laughing like you own the world, and you will.

2004

2022

acknowledgments

We always end our podcast by thanking the people who contributed to the episodes. We'd like to do that here too.

First of all, thank YOU for buying this book. Yes, you. We wouldn't have jobs without you, and we are humbled by your support.

In our research for the book, we reached out to so many of the cast and crew of The Office. We must thank them for continuing to show up for us in our pursuit of documenting this time in our lives. Especially Greg Daniels, Ken Kwapis, Randy Cordray, Carey Bennett, Kent Zbornak, Steve Burgess, Alysia Raycraft, Michael Gallenberg, Kim Ferry, Paul Lieberstein, and Jen Celotta, who provided us with interviews and answered our countless fact-checking emails.

Thank you to our representatives, Erin Malone, Adam Griffin, and Naomi Odenkirk—who, like Angela, is a digital hoarder and uncovered many treasures in her old emails. Thanks as well to our technical expert, Bryan DeGuire.

Thank you to our editor, Carrie Thornton, who never imagined this book would take three years to write and encompass a pandemic along the way. Your guidance, wisdom, and compassion got us through many tough spots.

Renata, our designer, we could not love you more. We hope you meet Billie Eilish one day.

We need to thank our husbands, Lee Kirk and Josh Snyder. They solo-parented our kids many weekends so that we could write this book. Josh was also our photo recovery master and technology tutor. Lee, thank you for reading and rereading and, in many cases, polishing our writing. Their support—both practical and emotional—was truly unwavering.

We would like to thank our children, because they were often the bright spots in our long days of writing.

And thank you to our families back home, who cheered us on and helped us find old pictures from set visits and other events.

Finally, we need to thank best friendship. There were many times in this three-year process that one of us wanted to quit writing. The events of the world seemed very overwhelming and scary, and it was hard to find value in writing. Whenever this happened, one of us would give the other a pep talk and we'd keep going. Thank goodness neither of us wanted to give up at the same time. It's not lost on us that while we were writing a book that centered around our friendship, our friendship is what got us through it.

PHOTO CREDITS